DESIGN ISSUES

How
Graphic
Design
Informs
Society

Edited by
DK Holland

ALLWORTH PRESS
NEW YORK
Communication Arts

05   04   03   02   01   5   4   3   2   1

Published by Allworth Press
An imprint of Allworth Communications
10 East 23rd Street, New York, NY 10010

Cover design by Doris Palmeros/DK Holland, Pushpin

Cover photography by Roger Whitehouse

Interior design by Doris Palmeros

Page composition/typography by C A Brandes

Printed in Canada

Library of Congress Cataloging-in-Publication Data:

Design issues: how graphic design informs society / edited by DK Holland
Includes bibliographical references and index.
ISBN 1-58115-202-7
1. Graphic Arts. 2. Visual communication. I. Holland, DK.
NC997. D448 2001
741.6—dc21

CONTENTS

Contributors

Carolyn McCarron

Véronique Vienne

Ellen Lupton

Hugh Dubberly

Philip Marshall Durbrow

William Drenttel

Tucker Viemeister

Peter Good

Justin Vood Good

J. Phillips Williams

Cecelia Holland

David Sterling

Maggie Macnab

Michael Bierut

Sean Kernan

John Bielenberg

David Lance Goines

Mark Fox

Larry Keeley

Michael Cronan

Peter Laundy

Brad Holland

Back in 1992, when Patrick Coyne, publisher of *Communi–
cation Arts*, asked me to write a column for *CA*, he said that he wanted to call the column Design Issues, "because then it could be about anything." How wise, I thought.
Because ubiquitous graphic design is just that—about everything. And anything and
everything have been the subjects of this column ever since.

But I told Patrick that I would not write such a column. I would only be annoyed
if I had to write about subjects I didn't care passionately about. And to be asked to
write "on command" would set up the dilemma: With what do I fill the pages? I didn't
want to become a journalist, but I was very curious about exploring the world as it
related to design through the written word. No, I said, I would prefer to find those in
our profession who were passionate about a subject that I also cared about and then
encourage them to write. I would then only assign myself the articles I was right for.

As time went on I got used to listening to people speak and, even if they had
never been published, being able to tell if they could write, if they had the requisite
curiosity, intelligence, and passion. (I've never had a dud.)

And that's the way it has worked ever since: I get into conversations with people
on the street, in the subway, at a party or conference, and end up assigning them
an article.

Under the artful and watchful eye of my editor, Anne Telford, the column was
developed into one that gets read, quoted, downloaded, and reprinted in college texts
fairly often. And it has attracted some good writers and some aspiring writers: It's
quite rewarding to know that Design Issues has created a platform through which
some really insightful design professionals have found their voices.

Several of the writers who have contributed to Design Issues have gone on to
become regular or repeat contributors and, when appropriate, I have grouped their
chapters together. Read together you get a greater sense of the writer's point of view.

It wasn't until my colleague Tad Crawford, publisher of Allworth Press, asked me
if I would consider making a book of *Design Issues*, that I thought of the column as a
body of work. Since the writers were from all over the map, what held it together?

I was quickly answered (with much relief) that *I* held it together. I found great reassurance of that fact when I gathered all the articles for a look at them together for the first time: ethics, context, critical thinking were threads of continuity that wove their way through most of the articles. I realized that these were my interests; that I had been succeeding in selectively assigning articles based on my own priorities all this time.

So as you read through this book you might consider if there is a writer inside you. If so, let it out! And if you develop an idea relevant to Design Issues (which, of course, is just about anything) please send it my way.

—DK Holland, *Editor*

Graphic design, a discipline that has often defied descrip-
tion, was given its name sometime in the middle of the twentieth century. Called
commercial art or advertising art until then, graphic design was starting to become
recognized as a legitimate area of design. So in an effort to provide structure for the
design industry, graphic design took its place alongside its sister disciplines—interior,
industrial, fashion, architectural, and textile, — in design school curriculums. The
term "graphic design", unlike the other disciplines, is a bit contrived and confusing
since it is difficult to define. Because graphic design is meant to cover such a broad
range of applications, the term is also a bit meaningless (in fact, more specific areas
of graphic design have since split off—information and environmental for instance).

Plus, the term "graphic arts" refers specifically to
printing, which, especially in this century, is not the
sole focus of graphic design.

**"Everyone is trying to commu-
nicate a message to some
kind of audience somewhere.
And no one is asking to see a
diploma first."**

Publishing, packaging, way-finding, corporate
identity, promotion, and advertising all needed design
professionals to help develop new approaches to their
visual communications. They needed professionals
with a depth of knowledge, talent, and commitment.
In the mid 1950s, Thomas Watson, Jr., the man who
built IBM, coined the phrase "good design is good business" and hired visionary
designer Paul Rand to create and guide the graphic identity of IBM. A handful of well-
educated, well-connected commercial artists, mostly in New York and mostly male,
were starting to have sway in the minds of corporate America. Those designers (along
with the European designers of the Bauhaus) were to become the model for a generation of designers who emerged in the sixties. Also, fairly rapidly, graphic design
departments were evolving in the better art schools—mostly trade schools—in the
United States. Many of them offered only associates degrees—providing no liberal
arts education and usually only offering a two or three year program.

By the new millennium, many universities had B.F.A. and M.F.A. programs in

Anne Telford/Street Seens
Garage Door in San Francisco

graphic design. (There is also one Ph.D. program, at Illinois Institute of Technology, and several in the development phrase.) The numbers of designers entering the work force each year is estimated at 5,000.

Along with the maturity of our profession came the need for design criticism. It took several decades before there would be enough critical mass of writing to form a book of any power, and the *Looking Closer* series, of which I was an editor, was first published by Allworth Press in 1994. It represented the best writings on graphic design from the best design magazines. In the first volume, we selected from a decade of writing. In the second volume, we covered only four years. In that time, many new writers had emerged, and by absorbing hundreds of individualistic points of view on design, I started to grasp the ultimate democratization of design.

By the nineties, graphic design had spread to all corners of the United States, and at least 50 percent of the designers were women. Graphic design had become accepted, assimilated into American culture and business in the forty-year span beginning when graphic design got its name. And graphic design was metamorphosing because of it.

Yet even today, compared to the other design disciplines, graphic design has relatively little writing in its archives, which are otherwise bursting with images. The age-old rationalizations are "Design is a visual expression," "You shouldn't have to explain a design," "It defies explanation!" "Designers aren't verbal, they're visual," and my absolute favorite, the self-fulfilling prophecy, "Designers don't read."[*] And, of course, any one of these rationalizations explains why most graphic design annuals don't include captions that would shed light on the work by putting it into context. It also explains why it's okay to reproduce graphic design in magazines and books at such reduced sizes that you cannot possibly understand what you're looking at (rationalization: "It looks so great, who cares what the purpose is?"). Witness: The 2001 AIGA

---

[*] Note: Proof of all these rationalizations lies in the fact that the AIGA once included John Bielenberg's stunning annual report design for the bogus corporation, Virtual Telemetrix, in the annual report section of the AIGA Annual—uncaptioned, unexplained, and out of context, of course.

annual is a travesty—vast amounts of white space, microscopic type, and over-cropped images. And this also explains why most design competitions do not require judges to actually understand what they are looking at before they give it an award (rationalization: "it's really a beauty pageant, isn't it?")!

In fact, Design Issues doesn't try to explain graphic design either. Because for the most part, it's true: You can't explain design. And even if you could, it may just be really boring to read about. But you can talk about everything that surrounds design, and in doing so, understand it as we understand the sun through the shadows and light it creates.

Graphic design, when done well, illuminates and guides. And graphic design, if you'll pardon a bit of prideful hyperbole, is, like the sun, essential to our daily lives. It's incorporated into so many areas of our existence (from the absurdly insignificant to the totally essential) that it does nearly defy definition. It's needed by practically every institution and business, plus many individuals, to communicate visual messages to an audience. As you'll read in J.P. Williams's essay on "The State of Our Ballot," it may have determined the presidency of the United States. And yet in "You Eat the Soup," you will read Cecelia Holland's ambivalent considerations of the value of the design of the most oft-tossed soup can.

And, let's face it, schooled or unschooled, we're all graphic designers, for better or worse. Some of the most inspiring design has been created by amateurs (from Latin, *amator* or lover) with an innate understanding of form, color, and image. No one who has ever traveled though rural America could deny this. Everyone is trying to communicate a message to some kind of audience somewhere. And no one is asking to see a diploma first.

But it's easy for designers to be elitist about design and pretend that the layperson could not possibly really understand what it is he is looking at (notwithstanding the lack of captions). And to reinforce this inscrutability, design, as a profession, tends to be self-referential, which makes many design messages seem cultish or cryptic. Ask a nondesigner to explain a graphic design that to you is a crystal clear, dead-on design statement, and you may have a rude awakening—because nondesigners have very valid design opinions, like it or not!

My hope is that the Design Issues column and now, this volume, help to make design more accessible. The articles are both introspective, examining the inner life of the designer, and "extrospective," exploring the role design has in society.

Most of the authors, while understanding that *Communication Arts* magazine has a large graphic design audience, were asked to write their articles for an audience of designers and nondesigners alike. We strive to shed some light on the objectives of design and related disciplines in order to demystify this very important form of expression. In doing so, we can contribute in some small way to creating the positive change that will further increase understanding, respect, and enthusiasm for our profession and its process and products.

–DK Holland, *Editor*

Designers: Branding The World

Branding, having replaced corporate identity in the United States, has forced many businesses to place a higher value on a well-designed, well-managed graphic identity. This part of the book looks at the many facets of brands—positive and negative—(and the requisite role that designers play) in the global marketplaces.

Those timeless double-breasted Brooks Brothers converse in **3** hushed tones, their lean torsos recline gracefully on the crisp white linen banquette. Every detail of their elegant appearance is meticulous, and absolutely nothing is remarkable. The Brothers give a subtle acknowledgment in your direction, but your attention has already been diverted by the more demonstrative and sexy Benetton who, with elbow precariously balanced on a mantle, is feverishly debating the flamboyant and totally pc Body Shop, her waist-length blonde Rasta hair tied by a thick hair knot at the back of her head. She stands arms akimbo, quite a stunning sight in African tribal robes and bejeweled, bare feet.

Body Shop struts back and forth in front of Benetton, thrusting her head back confidently, very arrogant. Their two voices spiral up, dominating the room: Body Shop's booming yet proper British accent jousts rhythmically with Benetton's passionate, streetwise Italian, since neither waits for the other to complete a thought. This tires you as you eavesdrop. Nike, their mutual pal, bobs up and down shouting impatiently to both of them to "Just do it!" You quickly realize that not one of this trio makes much sense, and, somewhat bored, you turn just in time to see that the casual, cool, khaki-clad Tiger Woods[1] has sauntered into the party arm-in-arm with none other than Barbie (recent breast reduction duly noted), all dolled up in Ralph Lauren haute couture, amidst a swarm of paparazzi. Now this is a photo op that's sure to sell truckloads of papers!

Whether you're conscious of it or not, you're perpetually in attendance at this fantasy party—we all are. We're exposed to hundreds of brands every day in packaging, advertising, and on products, and we feel our lives become just a little more exciting when the brands' glamour rubs off on us. It's totally Hollywood, a complete manipulation. We know it, and we just love it: Brands R Us.

How Could We Let This Happen?

Clubs, families, and religions have provided identity and a sense of acceptance for the human race since the beginning of history. We've simply traded in the old brands for newer, flashier, more convenient ones. We've quit the country club and joined Polo by Ralph Lauren. The disenchantment in the nuclear family as well as many religions in the America of the 1960s (along with fraternities, sororities, cults, secret societies, clubs) allowed the new phenomena of brands to fill a void, to take root and flourish. This sounds simply appalling, and yet, in a way, it's a very positive evolutionary step. Many cultures, democracies in particular, have encouraged individuality in the twentieth century. And so, individuals have incorporated into their lifestyles many different means of self-expression in the form of hairstyles, handwriting, jewelry, clothing, etc. Brands are responding to this by supplying products that, when adopted by the individual "say" to friends, family, and passersby, "This is who I am. This is what I stand for." In contrast, the cultures of the Orthodox Moslems or Hasidim, for example, dictate a lifestyle code in order to honor God's will and overtly subjugate free will.

Brands provide, through their products, a lopsided and fallacious sense of belonging (e.g., Members Only, Club Med, Izod), with no dues, no initiation rites, no rules and no obligations (except the literal "buy in"). You're automatically accepted, and you can drop out anytime you like with no repercussions! Can you beat that? And the brand relates to your lifestyle; ergo, the brand has relevance to you. The brand identity provides you with identity. That's the promise the brand makes, and it's a promise it must keep, or lose your business. It's a very one-sided deal, not at all the same agreement you make with your club, family, cult, or religion, all of which require a certain degree of effort, commitment, and closeness in exchange for the rewards of belonging. In Judaism and Catholicism, for instance, you must perform certain rituals, study certain writings, and embrace certain beliefs. In turn, you receive salvation, a benefit that is only realized in your afterlife. There's a hefty penalty for dropping out: e.g., if you leave Judaism, as far as other Jews are concerned, you "die," figuratively speaking. If you leave Catholicism, your punishment is that you are sent to hell, but only after you die, literally speaking.

In a fast-paced society, it's hard to find the time or energy for serious study (all that reading—and no pictures!). In an age where your lifestyle concerns are increasingly global, brands may allow you a way to take back some control of your future (read on).

Freedom of Choice

At the beginning of the century, industrialization started to change the economy of our western democracy. Before mass production, there was less choice because manufacturing methods were very limited. Consequently, packaging and identity had not been big issues for products and services. Freedom of choice created competition. Choice created the need for brand differentiation. Choice created jobs. Choice stimulated the economy. Choice improved the standard of living in our democratic society. Choice encouraged greed and over consumption. Choice is helping to destroy the planet.

1.1 Million Personal Bankruptcies in the U.S. in 1996 and Climbing

Many consumers have stood at the brink of destruction since the concept of instant credit became a way of life. Up from 874,642 in 1995 to 1.1 million in 1996, bankruptcy is all the vogue, especially in the youth culture. Imagine how many more people are maxed out financially, victims of the very "shop-'til-you-drop" sickness on which consumerism relies. Remember when there used to be peer pressure to maintain a solid financial profile as a citizen? You were scorned if you skipped out on student loans or had bad debts. The increasing acceptance of bankruptcy as a solution for indebtedness is a clear sign of the moral breakdown of society and coincides with the increase in the popular fixation on brand identities.

Tibor Kalman, principal of the newly resurrected New York design firm M&Co, says, "The power of brands has increased geometrically in the past two decades, in the past two years. Brands are out of control, creating cathedral—like Niketown, for example, where people go to worship the swoosh and renew their branding vows."

It's one thing to create a store environment where the goal is clearly to sell branded product, like Gap or Old Navy. Brands go too far when the unspoken strategy is to lure the consumer into an environment created at such a scale as to reinforce our human insignificance. When the objective is to appeal to the irrational (in a way similar to subliminal messages that were flashed on movie-theater screens in the 1950s) to elicit greater brand commitment, then the brand has gone too far. When the brand is overtly creating a climate that urges consumers to purchase overpriced goods that they can't afford and don't really need, the brand has gone too far.

Kalman's worst fear is that, because of their subconscious, emotional impact, the brands' abuses of power will increase dramatically as brands attempt to increase their control of people through the brand-loyalty programs that they are establishing. The primary goal of a loyalty program is to establish the profile and purchasing patterns of the consumer and to use that knowledge to manipulate customers to purchase more of their product (and purchase their product more often).

As with most branding, there is good and there is bad. Airlines have frequent-flyer programs and credit cards have other member-loyalty benefits, and many of us benefit from these programs and are glad they exist. It's the possibility of evil in brand-loyalty programs that you have to be concerned about. If you have an American Express card, for instance, think about what that means; i.e., what American Express knows about you: the restaurants you frequent, the clothes you buy, and where you travel. That is knowledge that AMEX has of you because you're a loyal card user. AMEX doesn't appear to abuse its knowledge and authority. But knowledge is power; it's very tempting to abuse it.

Kalman has had his own share of consumer corporations as clients and has his own product line, a brand called M&Co Labs. Kalman took a "sabbatical" from America in Rome where he published *Colors*, the magazine he started in New York in 1990 for Benetton. A very aggressive international brand, Benetton allowed Kalman to develop *Colors's* extraordinary global, edgy editorial/design attitude. Reopening his office has caused him to rethink the way he runs his business. "I'm avoiding being part of the churn. Most of our work is on communication projects, not consumer products. I want to use graphics to change people's minds, not feed consumerism."

Kalman has put any plans to expand his own brand, M&Co Labs, on hold because he has not resolved his quandaries about overfeeding the craven consumer animal. Kalman says, "Just think about the language that's used in branding—the target audience, tracking consumers—it's like they're out for the kill."

In January 1997, Kalman wrote the following piece for the Op-Ed page of the *New*

York Times[2] attacking the tobacco industry:

> Smoking is cool. Air Jordans are cool. Anything with the Nike swoosh on it is cool. Smashing Pumpkins are cool. Absolut ads are cool. Marlboros are cool. Kools are cool (and mentholated).
>
> Young people have anointed scores of brands, objects, and media as the accessories that will construct their unique and cool identities. Smoking is an important aspect of cool, and the cigarette pack is a critical fashion accessory.
>
> I'm a designer. I've worked all my life to make different products (including cigarettes) cool. Now I'm thinking about how to make smoking uncool.
>
> The brand is a mark of a group you belong to. Microsoft and Apple are actually competing clubs (gangs?) to which people, especially young people, pledge identities.
>
> You're either a Coke person or a Pepsi person. You wear either Nike or Reebok. You smoke Marlboro (mythic America), Camels (gutsy America), or American Spirit (natural America).
>
> The products are essentially identical; brand identity is the only distinction. The competitive advantage is brand name, not product attributes (this is because of overdeveloped product testing, but that's another story).
>
> So one way to reduce a product's desirability might be to reduce the coolness of the brand. With cigarettes, the brand's identity is most crucial in the pack design. The pack signals which club you belong to. It's a personal accessory, the thing you always take with you. It's your badge.
>
> There is a lot of talk of limiting or even banning cigarette advertising. But the allure is mostly in the package. Short of banning cigarettes, we'd certainly want to make them less alluring to the young.
>
> It might work to allow the cigarettes but remove the brand romance—the club insignia—and make the purchase of cigarettes as exciting as the purchase of (generic) aspirin. Any dorky cool that these plain packs have would quickly wear off.
>
> I volunteer to do the design.

When a brand manipulates a visual image to give a false or misleading impression, a designer is usually one of the key players. In that sense, that designers are accomplices in the crimes of branding (i.e., the overt creation of false images) is abundantly clear since it is the designer who makes the image. But, of course, it's easy to recognize the culpability in a situation as blatant as the tobacco industry where subjects like lung cancer, emphysema, and heart disease are now commonly spoken in the same breath as the word cigarette. Other product areas like liquor, gambling, and sex also encourage disease.

In a recent interview with me, Kalman said, "Brands are especially dangerous to those who are creating an identity for themselves (i.e., young people). Wieden & Kennedy make terrific Nike commercials that create intense desire (verging on identity crisis) among their young audience. Branded products aimed at the young are habit-forming (not unlike cigarettes and drugs), and the kid's first $150 pair of Air Whoever's can be the start of an expensive and insidious habit. Plus, the products these poor kids crave are often made by even poorer kids in a factory in some third-world country." To test the validity of what Kalman said, I walked into Sports Authority in Fort Greene, Brooklyn on a Sunday afternoon. It's a huge new sports superstore in my (80 percent African-American) neighborhood on the edge of downtown Brooklyn. I asked the athletic-shoe-department manager, an African-American male of about thirty-five, "So, do you have a big problem with shrinkage?" He said, "Oh yeah." I asked, "Is Nike worse than any other shoe in terms of theft?" He answered in a frustrated tone, "Let me just say that last week about eight pairs of the new Air Jordans almost walked out of the store. It was hard—those kids came in one large group, after school." I asked, "So were they African-American males?" He said, "Yeah. You know I don't know why Nike has to make those shoes so expensive. These kids, they want the products that come from their sports heroes, so they want the really expensive shoes—we have pairs for $189! None of the other brands' top shoes go above $100."

As I was leaving the store, I overheard a short conversation between an older white male and a younger white male who had run into each other in the checkout line. The younger guy was holding a pair of Nikes he was buying. The older guy said, "So you're buying Nikes even though they were probably made in some Indonesian factory by underpaid workers?" The younger guy, obviously not wanting to have to think about putting them back and making a new selection said, "If I had to hold myself to that kind of standard, I'd never be able to buy anything."

The Feel-Good Brands

Studies show that, all things being equal, you are more apt to buy into a brand that brings something positive into your life. For instance, Ben & Jerry's Ice Cream (*www.benjerry.com*) champions the preservation of the rain forest. Buy Ben &Jerry's, and you'll feel like you've done some good for the environment, however vague or minuscule that good might be, and even though what you've in fact bought is comfort food—a whole lot of great tasting calories with little nutritional value.

That's the strategy. Your favorite brands give you the products you crave, and they will go one better—they'll help make the world a better place. Isn't this a clear sign of how badly we collectively think things are going in the world? Potential brand identities Princess Diana and Mother Theresa touched the untouchables and that touched you. You wish you could be a better person. If only you had the time, resources and/or intestinal fortitude of those two much-worshipped women. If only you, as they had, found meaning in religion or the family or the club or cult of your choosing. No one can deny (but no one would dare to actually produce it) that a Mother Theresa–brand foot bath or a Princess Diana feminine hygiene deodorant spray could sweep the market simply because of the strong positive emotional connection we made with these idealized personalities when they were alive.

People may find comfort in brands (however false and inadequate) because of the failure of religion to get them to buy into the belief that God shall provide materially. God (who, as we know, works in mysterious ways) is a big letdown for those who want instant, rational results. And God is dismissed by those who bought into the view that religion was a crutch for the weak-willed and/or simpleminded. It's the relevance thing again: Even though, according to the *New York Times*, 97 percent of all Americans believe in God or the possibility of a God, organized religions have been seen as out-of-touch with the times. In a very tangible way, brands are the false idols that the Bible warns against. But, unlike God, brands provide in a predictable manner, and that's one of the ways they reaffirm their relevance.

A Religion for Control Freaks

If a brand isn't providing, maybe it's because that's not a requirement of its prime audience. Why not use your leverage? If you're not happy with the product you're buying, write to the manufacturer. If you have an idea of what it should be doing—whether it's the Gap (*www.gap.com*), Guinness (*www.guinness.ie*), Godiva (*www.godiva.com*), Gant (*http://pw2.netcom/˜dergan/gant.htm*), or Guess? (*www.guess.com*)—tell the company what you want it to do. For instance, do you know if the company is fair to its workers? Is the company manufacturing in the United States? Is the company creating any environmental hazards? Is the company giving back to the community in a way that relates to its profits? Is the company creating and promoting a better world?

The company will respond (and, in a way, this is the evolutionary advantage brands have over religions, cults, clubs, etc., which are steeped in tradition and may expect to control—not respond to—the will of the masses). Does the Pope have a Web site?[3] Is there a hot link where the Pope says, "Talk to me"? Nike (*www.nike.com*) does.[4] Unlike the Vatican, Nike says it wants to know your innermost thoughts and desires. Nike is flexible and responds to your desires as they evolve and change. Religions with integrity don't change at the whim of the marketplace.

Remember the reaction that animal activists had to manufacturers that exploited helpless furry creatures? The public outcry (and some outlandish guerrilla tactics like spray painting fur coats worn in public places) changed an industry and raised the consciousness and thus the ethics of society, at least temporarily. Note: In a fight-fire-with-fire strategy, *Baywatch* sex kitten Pamela Lee's nudity (complete with breast implants) is being [s]exploited on a billboard in Grand Central Station so that PETA (People for the Ethical Treatment of Animals, *www.peta-online.org*) could advertise the torturing and killing of animals for their pelts, because fur is starting to creep back in as a fashion trend. Public female nudity is reemerging as well, thanks to the likes of Pamela Lee, and few seem to be complaining this time (the billboards went up in London, Paris, and Berlin with no problem) except in the new Times Square (a brand?), which has cut down on sleeze in an effort to clean up its image. There, the billboard was declared indecent and Pamela Lee's bare breast had to be cropped.

Remember that what you think as a designer and as a human being makes an enormous difference. Your opinion is our secret weapon to affect change. Remember *War of the Worlds?* The alien creatures threatened to annihilate the entire world, and humans discovered the tiniest bacteria (which would have little or no effect on us) that could bring them to their knees. Don't underestimate your own power.

Clash of the Titans

The Walt Disney Company, a brand that stands for family values, has managed to tick off the religious right, which has declared a boycott against all Disney products. Here are several objections from the muscle-flexing Southern Baptist Convention: Disney condones homosexual behavior, which the Bible condemns (*Ellen* is a Disney-owned ABC network show and recently started showing women kissing on camera); the Native American Pocahontas was a Christian in real life, and Disney did not choose to make this point in its recent feature animation; and in a frame-by-frame examination of *The Little Mermaid*, they discovered a bulging penis on one of the

male animated characters.

Many of the believers are not buying into the protest, and so the boycott is having little impact on Disney sales. A recent poll shows that 55 percent of all Southern Baptists disagree with the boycott. Some cited that the Bible says nothing of boycotts and that Jesus would not have boycotted Disney. The boycott did, however, force Michael Eisner to appear on CBS's *60 Minutes* to defend Disney's position: *Ellen* is a fine show, and Disney doesn't dictate to ABC, anyhow; and Pocahontas became a Christian after the period in her life that the Disney film relates to; . . . as anyone can see, the erect penis was actually the male animated character's knee.

This power play put the media spotlight on two very controlling and powerful "religions." The only difference is that one of the religions worships a rodent. When I asked Kalman what concerned him most in the exploitation of brands, he replied, "If a religious fanatic became the head of Disney. Now that would be scary."

Each client we work with is a reflection of our integrity, so we must take precautions before agreeing to take on a new client relationship. It's amazingly easy to get hold of a company's annual report in the United States, for instance. In fact, a call to the company may land one on your desk the very next day because you will probably be seen as a potential investor. The annual report sets the tone for the company, and, although carefully and quite strategically crafted, it can give you an idea of the culture of the company, what the company stands for, and certainly the areas of business with which the company is most actively involved. What is it they produce? How is it doing financially? What issues does the president's letter speak to?

Reviewing the makeup of a company's board of directors is also illuminating: Where is it drawing its leaders from? Other industries, universities, banking? And what is the background of the chairman? Reading several major news reports a day keeps you abreast of breaking news about companies you might decide to work with. A barometer of your feelings about the ethics of the company or client you are considering working with is to say to yourself, once you have enough information, "Would I be proud to see news of me and my work for this company in print in my local newspaper?" When you pose that question, you can circumvent rationalizations that block your true feelings. Above all, choose your ethics—what you can live with and what you can't. This is a big, important factor: Ethical thinking requires discipline and a raised consciousness. The trick is to not get blindly sucked into the churn, dazzled by the allure of fame and fortune. Awareness of the issues allows you to be somewhat more objective and able to steer your course.

Beware: Blind Tolerance

I stopped dead in my tracks in a busy train station in Osaka last year when I saw a Bitch Skateboards woolen scarf for sale. Bitch is a very popular brand of outerwear products marked to Japanese youth. The year before I had photographed a uniformed school girl with a Bitch backpack in a Buddhist temple in Nara. Now I found, next to the Bitch logotype, an international design symbol of a man pointing a gun at the head of a woman. Later that night, I purposefully wore the scarf to a reception at which I knew there would be many Japanese designers. The odd, twisted use of English in advertising and packaging is an amusement to all Americans visiting Japan, and when I asked one of the designers how they could allow such a product to be sold in Japan, he answered patly, "We can't read English." Amazed, I pointed to the symbol, and through an interpreter said, "Yes, but can't you see he's holding a gun to her head?"

Penis-faced Joe Camel was tolerated for too many years by Americans and only recently has Camel started to phase out the image. Loaded, negative images had to originate with graphic designers when little black Sambos, Indian chiefs, and illustrations of women in compromising positions were applied to promotion, product, and packaging. The designer, as the creator of the graphic image, has an ethical responsibility to understand, with a higher level of consciousness, the impact the image that is going to be exploited will have. This responsibility is rarely acknowledged. There is too often a sloughing off of moral ownership to the client.

In fact, designers who are leaders will often inform their clients if an image is going to have negative backlash and advise against its exploitation. That's part of being professional. But graphic designers have a responsibility to familiarize themselves with many subtle stereotypes. Are designers doing their homework enough to know the difference? For example, many ads show very young girls in makeup and fashions designed to make them appear much older than their years. Reality: Every two minutes a woman and child will be raped, and of the forcibly 1.3 raped per minute, 61 percent are under the age of eighteen, with 29 percent under the age of eleven.[5] Younger and younger girls (one of the recent Guess? models is only fourteen) are being used as models for sexy, sophisticated clothing. Statutory rape can be the worst-case result of our fetish with youth. (Isn't that why Roman Polanski can't come back to the United States anymore?)

Relativity

When marketers develop product for the market, they get inside the heads of their target audience. They commission studies, conduct focus groups, and do research, research, research.

Take the youth market: The disintegration of the family has resulted in some pretty startling statistics. Generation Y (six to thirteen year olds), as MTV researchers call their newest market, is made up primarily of latchkey kids (33 percent) and single-parent kids (33 percent, up from 23 percent just two years ago). More preteens shop, do dishes, and cook their own meals; and, 16 percent of boys, as well as 21 percent of girls, help make dinner for their entire family. Tom Freston, CEO of MTV Networks says, "91 percent of these kids think it's very important to be part of a loving family. Generation Y kids are more worried about their future than Gen-Xers were. They're wary of trusting people beyond their moms and dads."

The brands design for the current lifestyle and culture. We see youths, often black males, wearing Tommy Hilfiger, DKNY (*www.donnakaran.com*), Ralph Lauren, and

CK on the subways of New York; they wear these brands pridefully. They become animated billboards for these brands. These brands have done a great job of listening and responding to their research, to their audiences.

These streetwise kids are fashion trend-starters, and fashion brands watch them anxiously to see what they'll pick up on next. White kids in the suburbs are emulating these street kids (i.e., sporting super wide-legged hip-hugging blue jeans and underwear that hangs out, with all the coolest brand identities in place), looking at the brands to provide a sense of belonging, of identity. Ironically, soon you can't tell the rich white kids from the burbs from the poor kids from the ghetto. But guess what? Both kids may be addicted to brands, but the ghetto kid can't afford an expensive brand habit. And these brands, as Kalman pointed out, are pricey! So where do these kids get the money to support the habit?

There is blacklash—New York kids wear Tommy Hilnigger shirts, for instance, and they're so well done and subtle you have to do a double-take to get the parody (and the tragedy).

Notes:

1. Tiger Woods fits the broadest definition of a "strong brand"—he's uniquely exciting, relevant, and held in high esteem by a wide audience. Plus he delivers reliably what his audience needs from him.

2. Tibor Kalman, "Losing Their Cool," *New York Times* (January 15, 1997): Op-Ed page. ©1998 by the New York Times Co. Reprinted by Permission.

3. The Web site for the Vatican is *www.vatican.va*.

4. For a listing of articles and information relating to Nike's hiring practices, etc., check out MoCHI's Anti-Nike resource page, at *http://home.inreach.com/mochi/nike/index.html*.

5. See "Rape in America" report, *www.about-face.org*, Spring 1992. Facts based on a three-year study.

First published in *Communication Arts*, March/April 1998

Branding presents a relatively new way of working for
designers, since the focus is on the needs and desires of the consumer, whose point
of view drives the language, the voice, and ultimately, the design. Marc Gobé, president and executive director of the international brand consultancy Desgrippes Gobé
Associates, observes, "A focus on customers and their evolving needs is a switch for
many graphic designers who have traditionally perceived their role as dictating to the
client about aesthetics rather than as partners for building successful brands.
Designers need the self-discipline to submerge their voice beneath that of the brand."

Language, of all types, is the most serious issue we face today, especially in the
communications business, especially in branding. The problem starts as internal confusion—in meetings and memos—spirals out to create conflicting goals among the
entire team, and ends up in a pool of chaotic brand images in the marketplace. Philip
Durbrow, Vice Chairman of the international design firm Frankfurt Balkind Partners,
recalls, "When I first started working in branding, it became obvious that there were
no clear universal definitions of key words like marketing, strategy, identity, image,
and brand. I've developed specific definitions so that we are clear on what we are talking about. Fuzzy words yield fuzzy thinking and fuzzy brands."

Some Definitions

There is very little consistency in people's understanding, or usage, of brand ter-
minology. To try to assure clarity, we have outlined, as follows, what Frankfurt Balkind
means when it uses certain branding terms.

A "product" is something that is produced to function and exists in reality.

A "brand" has meaning beyond functionality and exists in people's minds.

"Product quality" has major influence on "brand qualities."

"Brand qualities" are the thoughts, feelings, associations, and expectations created
by a "brand identity."

"Brand identity" is the way in which a brand is expressed visually and verbally.

"Branding" is viewing every customer-related activity as part of the branding process and managing it accordingly. Everything a company does that affects its customer, affects the value of its brand.

"Marketing" means making it easy for people to buy your product and motivating people to do so—through product design, pricing, packaging, distribution, advertising, etc.

"Brand marketing" is pushing beyond product benefits to fulfill a strategic core promise. It means looking past the tangible to the intangible, accommodating buyers' practical needs while resonating with their deeper feelings.

"Brand strategy" means deciding which brands are going to be used to deliver which products and services to which customers. (This may involve usage of global brands, umbrella brands, megabrands, subbrands, flanker brands, brand extensions, and brand families.)

"Brand equity" is the present value of the future combined purchases that are a result of the preference created, or the premium paid, for a brand's products.

Improve Your Brand Potential

The design of the label on the bottle of Amstel beer (*www.amstel.nl*) is not the point of branding, it's the concept of a devil-may-care Dutch youth culture. It's letting go and having fun. It's sports. The point is a highly cultivated Amstel brand image and the very positive emotional attachment Amstel elicits that captivates and holds the attention of a substantial audience. Brands these days have much more to do with lifestyle than product lines and are much more about image than graphic design.

Olympic skater Tara Lipinski, tennis star Venus Williams, and golf professional Tiger Woods (*www.tigerwoods.com*) are all brands-in-waiting for product lines directed toward the active youth market, whereas Diesel (*www.diesel.com*), Joe Boxer (*www.joeboxer.com*), and Phat Farm (*www.vibe.com/promo/docs/phatfarm*) are three brands that are currently out there on product lines, developed for the active youth culture. There is no shortage of new brand identities to stir into the consumer churn.

The strength of the brand can be calculated by analysis of the four major factors:

- Differentiation (Is the brand unique from others of its kind?)
- Relevance (Is the brand current with the times?)
- Esteem (Does the brand deliver consistently?)
- Reputation (How well do consumers know the braFnd?)[1]

All brands start by speaking to the needs and aspirations of an audience. The aspiration is the brand identity—that's a projection of how the brand wishes to be perceived by its target audience (as opposed to the brand image, which is the way the brand is, in fact, currently perceived).

Knowledge and appreciation of this core concept allows the steward of the brand to develop the mission, build and nurture the market, and maintain the brand philosophy, strategy, overall look and feel of the brand, and, of course, the logo. What is the audience going to be satisfied with/disappointed by coming from the brand? What is going to help build a strong brand identity, and what would weaken it? How can the aspirations for the brand identity be reached?

Reread the previous paragraphs, substituting the word "brand" with your own name or the name of a well-known product (or practically any proper noun), and you'll see just how versatile branding can be. And, in fact, you too will be able to not only identify the next strong brands but also improve your own brand potential.

Who's Minding the Store?

The brand steward, usually the senior executive from the parent company, must protect and cultivate the immutable core of the brand (about 50 percent) in order to ensure that the brand remains strong. The steward manages the part of the brand that must remain fluid (the remaining 50 percent) in order to keep the brand relevant and exciting. Typically we see a freshness and evolution in the brand's advertising and packaging; that's the part of the brand that is constantly evolving. The steward is responsible for overseeing the advertising agency's efforts to promote the brand, to develop brand segmentation internally (i.e., the subbrands), and to direct the packaging of branded products. The overall responsibility of the brand steward is to keep the brand on course and profitable.

The constant process of observing and probing is an essential part of Philip Durbrow's methodology in developing brands. He says, "We take pains to develop teams with diverse orientations to avoid arriving at branding strategies that are boringly predictable. For instance, I can see there's trouble when I walk down the hall and see a group of M.B.A.s in a huddle, discussing how they're going to develop the brand. Their strategy will be dominated by linear, logical thinking without emotional appeal or uniqueness. When building a brand it's important to remember that strong bonds and loyalty to a brand are not always rational. Often these ties are emotional ones. Mix up linear and nonlinear thinkers on the same team. Bring in a physicist, for instance, if you want to really crack the subject wide open."

Durbrow tells the story of Adobe's efforts to name a product that allowed programs to be read from different platforms. The engineers and producers of the software struggled with names, finally settling on "Rosetta," a historical reference to the Rosetta stone, which enabled the deciphering of Egyptian hieroglyphics—not a bad choice. But then Durbrow took a crack at naming the product. His first instinct was that the name should start with an A to alliterate with "Adobe" to tie the parent company and product together. He arrived at the name "Acrobat" because, as Durbrow says, "the software performs amazing feats between platforms."

Although "Rosetta" had a feeling of academia and antiquity, it was not legally available. "Acrobat" suggests strong visual images, is easy for a large audience to relate to, and has a strong entertainment connotation. Durbrow brought in the marketing perspective that the engineers lacked: He knew virtually nothing about the technology, and perhaps the engineers knew too much.

Virgin for Life

Companies that have broad, strong brand recognition can diversify through their subbrands more than narrowly focused companies. For instance, Brit Richard Branson, a courageous baby-boomer, started his first business in 1968 at the age of sixteen and has cultivated companies in the entertainment area ever since under the umbrella Virgin Group (*www.virgin.com*). First came Virgin Records. Ten years later Branson branched out to form Virgin Atlantic Airways, then a year later added Virgin

Holidays. Two years after that, Virgin expanded to include Virgin Airship & Balloon Company, Virgin Publishing, and Virgin Hotels, among others. Branson, a highly visible and consistently strong leader, is the very essence of pioneer spirit and innovation. Consumers "get" Virgin's abstract brand identity because Virgin's broad target audience identifies with Branson and all he stands for: unencumbered global vision and maverick style. He is a self-proclaimed virgin for life.

Apple Computers (*www.apple.com*), started by another baby-boomer, Steve Jobs, was also thought of as innovative and pioneering when it first came on the scene in the seventies. But in marked contrast with Virgin, Apple is still known as a manufacturer of computer hardware, creating a shallow universe to travel in. It's not hard to imagine that Apple could become so much more, especially in the areas of education and technology, but Apple seems to lack an expansive strategy. And its shaky leadership and financial history have kept the company from expanding.

Durbrow offers this wisdom: "There is no long-term advantage to having a brand image that is greater or lesser than the brand really is. If the image is greater than the reality, people will be disappointed whenever they encounter the brand. If the image is less than the reality, the company will never benefit from all its hard work, i.e., the brand won't command a premium or create a preference for the company's branded products."

The Brand as Asset

When included on the balance sheet, the brand's equity is an intangible asset like goodwill, and its value brightens the parent company's fiscal picture. This is one big reason why companies are eager to develop strong brands. An enhanced financial picture allows the parent company to generate revenue, grow, and expand. The brand, structured to be easily separated from the parent company, may be sold. The brand may be segmented to increase the market by creating subbrands that appeal to more specific consumer needs, further increasing the value of the brand.

It Takes a Big Effort to Walk the Walk

Marc Gobé is a designer and branding specialist. He started developing the branding of fragrances in 1980, an illusive and challenging task. Clients would come to Desgrippes Gobé with no name, no scent, but with a will and bankroll to launch a fragrance. Since branding is all about the consumer, designers, including Gobé, had to go through a big switch in their process in order to become professional branders. He says, "You have to speak the language of the target group. You have to immerse yourself in its lifestyle. The challenge is to make a real connection; otherwise it's false, and the consumer is too savvy to tolerate a fake."

Gobé adds, "Successful brands woo the heart. Consumers then respond to their wallet." In response to this need, Gobé developed a concept called SENSE that provided a philosophy for the development of fragrance brands. SENSE stands for Sensory Exploration + Need States Evaluation and helps identify a product's equities, profiles the customer, analyzes the competition, and develops an emotionally charged visual vocabulary that serves as the foundation for the design process. He calls emotion the fifth dimension, the essence of branding. "Corporations are making a conscious move toward branding," Gobé says. "When they ask what you do, the reply 'I'm a graphic

Name Your Brands

Write down the brands you are wearing today. Write the promise the brand makes to you (e.g., Nike is athletic, cool, young; Victoria's Secret is daring and sexy).

Write down what you think your personal image is (e.g., reliable, nice smart guy; wild, smart, sexy gal).

Now, read the brand promises only. What

do they say, objectively, about your image? Would your friends recognize you from this list? Ask a friend what your brand image is. Does it differ from what you wrote down? Do you have a point of differentiation from others? Are you relevant to your times? Are you held in high esteem? Do you have a broad reputation?

Are your brand names visible to the casual observer? Do you mind wearing a brand logo? (If no, why?) Should you develop your own brand logo and wear it?

If the brands you are wearing are your "packaging" and your image is your "

product," are they a good fit? How could you improve your packaging to match your product? Are you a strong or weak brand?

Brand of Socks:

Promise:

Brand of Shoes:

Promise:

Brand of Underwear:

Promise:

Brand of Pants, Skirt or Dress:

Promise:

Brand of Shirt or Top:

designer' does not have the same impact or speak as directly to your ability to use design as a strategic tool in solving real business problems as if you reply, 'I'm a brand expert.' Of course, the first question you need to ask back to the client is, 'Have you a real understanding of the commitment required to create and sustain a brand?'"

Buying Loyalty

When reliable statistics are developed about the purchasing power of consumers who are loyal to a specific brand, programs can be designed that will help to further secure the consumers' loyalty. For instance, if an individual were to purchase ten to fifteen Cadillacs in a lifetime, hypothetically, that could be a total expense of more than $800,000. Based on that information, Cadillac may decide how to ensure that

$800,000 makes it onto its balance sheets. For instance, Cadillac owners can be made to feel they are part of the family of Cadillac through premiums and special treatment. That locks in loyalty and repeat business.

The Vatican issues Papal blessings to individual Catholics in exchange for a substantial donation to the Church. Such an anointment is tangible reassurance of salvation. Mafia dons flaunt their generosity to their loyal compatriots to reinforce the notion that they "take care of their own" and, in turn, to reinforce an obligation, a dependency, and a greater love and fear of "the family." Both the Vatican and Mafia are, by definition, potential brands.

Now consider Ted Turner's decision to donate a billion dollars to aid the United Nations's causes, a strong public-relations move for a man of mixed reputation. Turner's dollars (one-third of his total net worth) will provide handsomely to rid war-torn countries of land mines. This doesn't make you love or fear the fabulously wealthy Turner, but it does increase your respect for him (and, by association, his movie-star wife, Jane Fonda). Turner and Fonda are brands, and this public act of generosity protects their brand names.

Since all American corporations have a clear mandate to maximize their shareholders' dividends, the act of giving can become a calculated corporate move. Philip Morris donates money to the arts because it's an important strategic move. The arts are a righteous cause to support, and donations are a way to persuade artists and arts' lovers to continue to support the tobacco giant despite Philip Morris's despicable core business, supplying nicotine fixes to tobacco addicts. Pressure from companies like Philip Morris forces artists to choose between their funding and their ethics. How does that make you feel about Philip Morris? Or about artists who take the support?

Denny's Restaurant chain is now a sponsor of Black College Football. Denny's has attempted to improve its much-tarnished brand image after losing a 1994 class-action suit. The lawsuit listed dozens of African-Americans who claimed that they were discriminated against by either being refused service or being forced to pay in advance at various Denny's restaurants. But more recently, Denny's waitresses have sued for sexual harassment by other employees. And Asians and Filipinos have come forward to make claims of discrimination. All of these situations occurred in different cities. No amount of goodwill gestures can right these wrongs, since Denny's is failing to keep its core brand promise—"All-American food for all Americans."

Unceasing multileveled chess games are being played by many large American corporations in attempts to protect or increase their brand's value. The more egregious the behavior of the company, the higher the stakes. Cigarettes, alcohol, fossil fuels, cosmetics, fur, gambling, and weaponry obviously head the list of product categories with big image problems.

Defending the Niche

Since America's publicly held corporations have a mandate to remain profitable and grow to the benefit of the shareholders, companies are always looking to increase their market share. With all things being equal in the quality of the product, it's the brand image that encroaches into the competition's territory.

Look at the cola race: Two pretty average-tasting beverages—Coca-Cola and Pepsi-Cola—have been going neck and neck for decades, and the race is all about image.

Recently, when Pepsi changed its trade dress color from red to blue because it was felt that Coke owned the color red, the *New York Times* actually covered the change, noting that this was a rather brazen move since red is "the" cola color.

If you check out the balance sheets, you'll see that Coca-Cola is a $14 billion company, while PepsiCo is only a $6 billion dollar company; yet they're vying for the same market. Image comes down to how many times you see an ad on television, how big the gondola is that displays the product in the store where you shop, and how much of a buzz is out there about the product.

Coca-Cola is clearly an American branding phenomenon . Todd Waterbury, a creative director of Wieden & Kennedy who works mainly on the agency's Coca-Cola account, gets involved in the methodology of research conducted on behalf of Coke. Waterbury, who comes from a design perspective, has developed a respect for well-conducted, focused research, research designed to educate. He says, "Good research results in focused work—but only if the same objectives, the function of the product, is understood by both the researchers and the creatives before the work begins. For example, if the research is a room in a house and the creative is the furniture for that room, it makes sense for the people thinking about the furniture to talk to the people building the room. Is it a bedroom or a kitchen? Who's going to live here?" In the end, research translates into strategy statements that allow the creative process to move forward. Waterbury says, "What is the core thought? What are we trying to say? To ask people to do? When the core thought is expressed in a single, declarative sentence, it's actually manageable to create a commercial or a billboard that really does leave the viewer with the message you want them to be left with. After all, thirty seconds is only thirty seconds. A single strategy statement makes it clear to the client and agency what's being presented. There's no room for someone to say that they interpreted that passage or that third sentence to mean something different. Brevity is bravery!"

In the long term, it's the brand's core message that must be honored. "The branding statement has to be honest, relevant. For example, the Coke brand is the value of constancy. The contour bottle and Spencerian script are promises that the Coke you'll have in Thailand is the same as the Coke you'll have in Oakland. The challenge for us is always to find ways to make something change and stay the same." People have a strong emotional attachment to Coca-Cola, it's something they grew up with. And Coke is a part of the history of America. Waterbury adds, "The Coca-Cola headquarters and museum in Atlanta are a testament to excellent management of a global brand: a brand that makes a personal connection for almost everyone."

All the strong brands—Coca-Cola, Nike, and Calvin Klein, to name a few—give the impression of unswerving confidence, through their billion-dollar advertising campaigns. And this is exactly the kind of motivational leadership our emotionally charged culture craves. Nike's brilliant "Just Do It" campaign from Wieden & Kennedy was a series of intensely motivational, calculated thirty-to-sixty-second spots that speak to the condition of America's sports-minded youth. Since Wieden & Kennedy's strategy is to say little and speak volumes, you can and will interpret these ads in a very personal way. Dan Wieden, president of Wieden & Kennedy, cites Vietnamese Buddhist monk Thich Nhat Hanh as saying, "Thinking by itself has no creative value. It is only when lit by understanding that thinking takes on real substance. Sometimes understanding can be translated into thought, but often thoughts are too rigid and limiting to carry much understanding. Sometimes a look or a laugh expresses understanding much better than words or thoughts." This idea is key to the strategy behind the advertising created for "Just Do It," which is often powerful and pedagogical in tone, containing a strong ethical subtext.

Wieden sees the limitations of time in the thirty-second spot in advertising as an obstacle to expressing thought. He says, "If I can't use thought to educate, maybe I can use thought to stir up trouble. . . .maybe I can take an issue and make it so over-heated, so emotional, make this thought so confrontational that you have to deal with it. You have to put aside your preconceptions and look again at this issue." Nationally broadcast thirty-second windows are excellent opportunities to effect change in that way. Wieden says, "Real learning is always subversive. Real learning attacks what it is you think you believe and makes you think about it in a different way. That's when learning takes place."

However, the billions of dollars available to agencies like Wieden & Kennedy versus the zero-dollar budget of our school system creates a real imbalance. It means we are "learning" much more from Dan Wieden than we are from educators. We are bombarded by advertising images that are teaching by subversion, and we are starved for the same kind of attention from real educators.

Why Here? Why Now?

Nineteenth-century New York City was a place of commerce where eighteen languages were spoken by immigrants who arrived here with little but a dream, ingenuity, and drive to invent a new fortune for themselvesThe environment in this newly democratic country provided, in general, an incubator for business in which a new visual language could grow and flourish. Because of the great mix of cultures, America became the land of innovation and ephemera. Brands from those early days (i.e., Levi Strauss, Ivory, Nabisco, Hershey, Ford Motors) are rich with emotionally packed inspirational stories—of immigrant struggles against the odds, of perseverance in the face of disaster, and, finally, of hard-won and much-deserved success. Many of the early Hollywood movies were based on this American Dream.

New York was then, and is now, the business capital of America, and even though a corporation's headquarters might have been in Grand Rapids, Kansas City or in Cincinnati, when it came to corporate identity (CI), all corporate heads turned to New York. Brand identity and CI both became key business tools in the middle of this century, and, ultimately, New York became America's center for CI and brand exploitation.

Since the early part of the century, tourists have gawked with utter amazement at the garish display of consumer culture in Times Square—a virtual cathedral to capitalism. And today, more than ever, the titans in the consumer-products industries line up proudly, their billboards like gigantic graphic gargoyles, reigning above Broadway's hustle and bustle. Mixed into this assemblage is an electronic billboard that ticks off the increase in the compounded federal deficit on a second-by-second basis. And the famous Zipper, an electronic band that surrounds the trunk of a triangular-shaped building, One Times Square, like a tightly cinched belt, brings another blast of cold reality into this fantasy land by printing out in ticker-tape fashion the hottest up-to-the-second news headlines.

In the early 1990s, the Times Square Business Improvement District was struggling to revitalize the area, and top brands were ultimately a big part of the revitalization. Roger Whitehouse, an environmental designer who designed the new flagship subway-station graphics at 42nd and Broadway, remarks, "We decided the subway station entrance should express a brand identity for the New York City Subway, one of New York's great hidden treasures, in just the same way as Nike or Calvin Klein would do, and as is appropriate for Times Square." Even the city of New York is compelled to compete for attention with brand images.

The World is the Width of a Fiber Optic

As brands reach sales saturation stateside, they expand into foreign markets to continue to grow. The media has made us all aware, minute-by-minute, of situations as they arise in Beijing, Barcelona, Bosnia, or Buenos Aires. And so as we get up close and personal with a whole array of cultures, we often see our own American brands staring us in the face from halfway round the world.

Writer Véronique Vienne says, "The Cambodian priest who sips from a can of Pepsi, the Chinese toddler wearing a Joe Camel sweatshirt, and the Iranian youth with Converse sneakers are deliberately trying to break away from their traditions. The right logo embossed, silk-screened, or stitched on a piece of goods becomes the official stamp on a new passport that gives you permission to put your identity as consumers before your national pride."[2] It's a reminder that freedom of choice has become a universal aspiration.

Why Make War When You Can Shop?

"Jesus wouldn't have had a logo. He wasn't interested in establishing a brand," observes Paula Scher, partner in Pentagram, "Paul was the marketing guy. The cross is a pretty powerful trademark, but it was introduced piecemeal and took a long time to permeate public consciousness. The redesigned swastika for the Nazi party made greater headway through a massive marketing campaign that involved enforcing armies.

"If we took all our favorite logos—Nike, Sony, the Jewish star, the swastika, McDonald's, Gap, IBM, Samsung, Disney, CK, DKNY, Coke, Pepsi, and the peace symbol—and hung them together in Times Square, they would all cancel each other out."

The Vatican's just one step away from that billboard in Times Square. The Vatican Library, according to the *Wall Street Journal*, has given its blessing to the development of lines of luggage, bed linens, costume jewelry, watches, greeting cards, and T-shirts, all bearing the Vatican's official seal. What is the core brand identity and strategy of the Catholic Church? Does the church have a brand steward?

Scher adds, "Branding is neutral, it's the products that are good or bad." She also observes, "I like going to Europe and seeing DKNY or Calvin Klein being sold in Paris. It means employment, tax revenues, and a healthy economy for the U.S."

Scher concludes, "War used to be our biggest export, now it's all our brands. Why make war when you can shop?"

Little Girls Just Love Barbie

The concept of Barbie (*www.barbie.com*) originated when Ruth Handler, a founder of Mattel (with her husband), observed their daughter Barbara playing with paper dolls she had made to look like grown women. She was acting out what it would be like to be an adult. After that, Handler spent years convincing her designers to develop the aspirational adult female doll we now call Barbie.

Even after Barbie was manufactured in 1959, the sales representatives were not convinced that the doll would sell. So Mattel put together a series of television advertisements to get to the consumer, and Barbie became an instant hit. In 1998, some mention of Barbie, this nearly $2 billion international brand, appears in magazines and newspapers daily. Controversy about Barbie (the size of her breasts, her affect on the development of little girls, her endless wardrobe) never ceases. Women obsess about Barbie's unrealistic measurements. Little girls obsess too, but not at all in the same way. Barbie is their special friend, and she's free to go anywhere, be anyone she wants to be. Barbie provides a Rorschach of infinite meanings for a little girl to interpret, reinterpret. The girl can dress and undress Barbie, act out with her, use her as a mirror through which to pass into a fantasy grown-up world.

Mattel, like any manufacturer of brand products, holds focus groups regularly. Recent studies showed that little girls (and their mothers) wanted Barbie to evolve. The last big change had been in 1988 when Barbie took on a glittery, white-blonde glamour look. Now little girls and their mothers clearly want her to be updated again. The new Barbie has straighter, blended hair, smaller breasts, and a wider waist and wears less make-up. The updated look will be integrated into the new line of dolls (around 100 new dolls come out a year). The changes are subtle, and Barbie still looks very much like Barbie to the casual observer, but to a Barbie fan, these changes are monumental. It's Mattel's respectful response to the consumer's needs that allows the Barbie brand to remain relevant.

Pushpin develops the Barbie licensing-program design strategy for Mattel, and I am in the role of design director. As part of that plan, our Pushpin and Mattel all-girl team creates seasonal style guides to be distributed to licensees for use in producing hard goods, accessories, and apparel for girls age three to seven. The intuition we inherently have as women about what little girls will respond to almost requires the team to be all female.

Recently we wrote a story for a style guide that described Barbie walking down a beach picking up starfish to take home. Mattel's legal department, which is, of course, female, informed us we had to change the starfish to a shell in the story "because Barbie would never do anything to disrupt the ecosystem." This kind of statement is always said with great affection and respect for Barbie.

Tarnishing the Brand

Roy Rogers became a chain of restaurants (you knew and trusted Roy, so you'd eat in his restaurants). Pee Wee Herman became a line of dolls, a series of movies, and a television program. Pee Wee (a.k.a. Paul Rubin) was arrested for masturbating in a porno theater. This appalling behavior didn't fit his brand image, so you no longer trusted him. You no longer wished to know him, and his empire collapsed. No more Pee Wee, just Paul Rubin, the man who created Pee Wee.

Elvis Presley's manager realized Presley's marketing potential in the 1950s, and Presley became one of the first and biggest brands ever merchandised (and his fans have remained faithful despite tales of his drug use and womanizing).

Such are the ebbs and flows of Hollywood. The stars, often not the movies they star in, are the brands. *Braveheart* is a brand because it had emotional appeal and sequels. Harrison Ford is a brand. He consistently represents the principled, sexy, American male. Lassie is a brand; however, when the current Lassie dies, another collie will do just as well.

Mel Gibson's *Braveheart* had no value as a brand: It had no sequels. We know what Mel Gibson stands for: To men he's attractive, a good role model. To women, he's attractive, sexy, charming, and daring. And we know about his real life (he's a family man, religious) because we read about him constantly in *People* magazine and other weeklies and he's on radio and TV magazine-format shows. Gibson provides both a strong fantasy and reality image, which is very attractive to the public.

Durbrow's firm, Frankfurt Balkind, is a leading force in the marketing and branding of movies. He says, "The flood of movies exported to other countries has branded America in a rich and deep way that has created American brand appeal, and other countries are clamoring for American products, culture, and lifestyle. Who aspires to 'Russian' or 'Chinese' lifestyles? Who pirates Korean- or Bosnian-branded products? Entertainment has provided us with great communicators." In fact, this is no longer exclusively an American phenomena. Russia recently changed the value of the ruble and, to avoid hysteria, orchestrated a campaign to educate its citizens by employing the most popular Russian actors to explain the switch to the Russian population via the boob tube.

We are all fixated on glamorous public figures. We probably know more intimate details about Elizabeth Taylor, Michael Jackson, and Lady Diana Spencer than perhaps we know about our own personal friends. It's easy to know about Elizabeth Taylor's tragedies: She's never going to call you on the phone and beg for your help in a crisis. And you can weep for joy in private when Michael Jackson has his second baby if he is someone to whom you have a secret emotional attachment. Unlike the communication you have with your friends and intimates, this is voyeuristic knowledge, and you're not responsible for taking any action to intercede, whatsoever.

I was vacationing on Ibiza, an island off the coast of Spain, in 1982, when I was introduced to a ninety-year-old native woman, a virgin, who had never been off the island and spoke only Ibizanco. She wore the traditional brown headdress and floor-length dress of an Ibizanco matron and rarely spoke to foreigners. But she watched television, and *Dallas* was her favorite show. This she told me through my friend who translated for her. She asked me excitedly what I thought of some of the characters on the show. Europe was two or three years behind in television, and I told her that J.R. had been shot and that Pam Ewing had been taken to a mental hospital. The bad news about Pam was very upsetting to her, and she cried because Pam was very real and dear to her. It stunned me, not only because she was so captivated by this Hollywood-ized soap opera but because she empathized so strongly with Pam—a "good" person, but someone who was, in every other way, her exact opposite.

Because brand loyalty is largely emotional, it's also inscrutable and fickle, and easily bored. But it's universal that, by and large, loyalists want their heroes to be (while allowing for some minor human failings) consistently decent human beings. There will never be a Hitler Airlines, Manson Baby Food, nor a line of Nichols & McVey Fertilizer.

But then again, there is the Belgian-made Black Death Vodka, a product first imported by a distributing company in California in 1991. The following year the Bureau of Alcohol, Tobacco, and Firearms, which asserted that the liquor's name and logo created the "misleading impression of bubonic plague and poison," sought to ban Black Death's sales in the United States. On appeal, the government lost. Perhaps it was just too absurd to argue that consumers were confused and thought they were buying the black plague in a bottle. Let us never lose our sense of humor, including black humor.

Branding Dead Artists

Over a quarter of a million people attended "Monet in the Mediterranean" recently at the Brooklyn Museum (*www.brooklynart.org/monet*). Admittance to the exhibition was an additional charge and often required reservations. With all these barriers, the show still raised a huge amount of revenue for the museum. To capitalize on Monet, the Brooklyn Museum also created a restaurant called Café Monet, which, by itself, brought in over a million dollars in revenue, as well as a gift shop with licensed products carrying Monet's images.

Whereas the café was appropriately tasteful and didn't exploit Monet's image beyond the use of his signature, the gift shop was a travesty. Since the essence of Monet's work is abstract light and color, you would have anticipated seeing products using great textures, airiness, and amazing pastels applied to product. The products were very poorly conceived. They were dreary in color: The image of the Doge's Palace in Venice was reduced to a gray blob on a 2" x 2" refrigerator magnet. That a museum would allow this to happen for the sake of increasing revenue struck me as endemic of a problem of branding. There is no brand steward protecting the differentiation, relevance, esteem, and reputation of Claude Monet. He has, in a sense, fallen victim to the public domain. And so it goes for Renoir, Degas, van Gogh, and many other artists whose work now indiscriminately adorn umbrellas, bags, and scarves for sale.

Intervention

Paul MacCready (*www.aerovironment.com*), chairman of AeroVironment and the genius behind human, solar-powered aircraft and the electric car, is emphatic in his message: "The point is the fight is over. We have dominated. We have won a battle we did not realize we were fighting (and in winning a battle have lost a grander war). Ten thousand years ago, before agriculture and civilization, the human portion (humans and their livestock and pets) was less than 0.1 percent of the total integrated mass (of flesh and bones). Now the 0.1 percent has grown to 97 percent, and the wild animal portion that was over 99.9 percent has fallen to 3 percent."

One example of how wildlife is dwindling is the bison slaughter on the Great Plains in Montana (*www.buffalo@wildrockies.org*), where the Department of Livestock is killing bison and bison calves. The ulterior motive may well be to make space on the plains for more cattle (*www.mcdonalds.com*; *www.burgerking.com*), since cattle and bison can't share the same land. Does the Department of Livestock understand the environmental impact of killing all the bison? Or do they view the situation with blinders on?

MacCready, whose company motto is "Doing More With Less," has become focused on the need to change the educational system in order to alter our environmental/technological trajectory. He thinks that the ability to think about the big picture gives people a basis on which to build reality. He says, "My goal is a desirable, sustainable world when my children reach my present age, not a habitable world. Environment is just one aspect. Bioengineering, the redesign of humans, is another. An additional aspect is information technology with benefits through linking the world's inhabitants . . . My interest in education is that, since human minds are now the most powerful force on earth, their thinking (or nonthinking) underlies all the challenges for the future of life on earth. . . Schools mostly reward students for learning, not thinking (with some exciting exceptions). We need revolutionaries creating a future, not sheep preserving past habits." When we support brands that contribute to the destruction of the environment, we are stoking the furnace instead of putting on the brakes.

Ben Cohen (ben@benjerry.com) of Ben & Jerry's understands the urgent need for activism. And he sees a huge potential reservoir of capital in the government's defense budget. Understanding that business (e.g., brands) are more powerful than government, Cohen has mobilized 400 top executives from different companies and formed an organization called Business for Social Responsibility to use collective pressure on Congress to redistribute wasted defense funds for use in underfunded social services and programs.

Powerful volunteer efforts like these need the support of designers, writers, photographers, digital artists, illustrators. People with talent—like you. Buckminster Fuller's words of thirty years ago were never more apt: "There are no passengers on spaceship earth, only crew."

Keeping Your Own Promise: Making Some Hard Choices

We have to believe that good wins out over evil; it's an integral part of human nature. Without that belief, we are hopeless. We want brands to reflect a high level of ethics.

But we also want brands to reflect the state of the world in a realistically positive way. And our awareness of the brand's ethics, true or not, can motivate us to buy.

Rufus Jones, an eminent Quaker and founder of the American Friends Service Committee, once observed, "There is an underived ethical core in us, or at least, in some of us, which gives us a fixity of soul for that which ought to be." We, each in our own way, have a need to reconcile our existence with the meaning of the universe, to work toward what "ought to be."

In the same vein, Jones says that conscience "is that basic foundation of the soul and which the mystics called 'synteresis,' or junction of the soul with God. It is what Kant calls the categorical imperative, or the soul's fundamental assertion of a distinction between right and wrong." The development of conscience is an affirmation that we Homo sapiens are truly an evolved species.

In fact, we are starting to take personal responsibility, to demand that brands respond to the state of our environment, protect our natural resources, and respond to our increasing world population. We now know that we can't leave it to the next generation to fix.

This new focus of what "ought to be" is going to require us to make different decisions in our lives, like what products and packaging are acceptable, like letting brands know under what conditions you will continue to support them, like who we'll work for, and like who gets the use of our money. The brands need to hear this from you, from all of us. Because they are us.

Notes

1. David A. Aake, *Building Strong Brands* (New York: Free Press, a division of Simon and Schuster, 1996).

2. Véronique Vienne, "Branding: A Uniquely American Phenomenon," *Communication Arts*, (August *Photography* Annual, 1997).

First published in *Communication Arts*, May 1998.

Your Education Is Brought
to You by Our Sponsors:

Advertising, Marketing, and
Corporate Sponsorship in
America's Public Schools

Carolyn McCarron

Solve this problem: The best-selling packaged cookie in the
world is the Oreo cookie. The diameter of an Oreo cookie is 1.75 inches. Express the
diameter of an Oreo cookie as a fraction in simplest form.

This is one example of a word problem that Joe Stein, a U.S. government lawyer
based in California, came across when helping his eleven-year-old son with his math
homework. Going through the rest of McGraw-Hill's sixth-grade textbook
Mathematics: Applications and Connections, Stein came across a number of other references to brand names, including Nike, McDonald's, and Kellogg's. The issue of
brand references in the textbook raised enough controversy to warrant an article on
the front page of the Sunday edition of the New York Times on March 21, 1999. Many
people like Stein consider the brand references to be blatant product placements
(even though the companies mentioned did not pay McGraw-Hill to have their brands
used as examples), and they are outraged that product placement, a common type of
advertising, has found its way into American public schools.

Brand placement in textbooks is only one marketing and advertising tactic being
used in American public schools today. Companies are also buying physical spaces in
schools to advertise for the year—on the walls of classrooms, hallways, cafeterias,
locker rooms, bathrooms, and on the outside walls and rooftops of school buildings.
They are advertising on the sides and tops of yellow school buses, handing out promotional book covers and product samples and buying spots over the public-
announcement system. Company representatives are even setting up promotional
tables during lunch or hosting assemblies during class time.

In addition to these forms of direct advertising, many companies market in a
more subtle way, through educational materials written and distributed by the company that promote brands in classrooms through subjects such as math and social studies. Corporations are also sponsoring literacy contests where children read a book and
win a free or cost-reduced product, thus associating academic achievement with a particular brand.

For the last decade, many adult community members have looked the other way for the sake of gaining extra income for their children's schools via advertising revenue. Parents like Stein are finding brand placement in their children's textbooks, however, to be the final straw in marketing to their children. Stein filed complaints about the brands in his son's math book with state education officials, prompting the chairperson of the California State Assembly Education Committee to introduce a bill to ban all corporate sponsorships and advertising programs in schools.

A Lack of Funding

While the United States government continues to increase funds for American public schools to buy textbooks and hire new teachers, many public schools in our nation still face decreasing operating and discretionary funds. Some communities continue to resist yearly increases in property taxes, which are often a school district's main source of revenue. As a result, many school administrators across the country are searching for new ways to close the funding gap, such as renting school space to companies for advertising, signing exclusive contracts with food and soft-drink vendors, and seeking corporate sponsors to pay for some of the school's educational and extracurricular programs. Schools use the advertising revenue to give teachers salary increases and pay for computers, sports equipment, art supplies, and other items they could not pay for with traditional funding. In return, companies get the opportunity to promote their brands while developing a positive corporate image within the community by supporting education.

A $160 Billion Market

What makes a school audience an appealing target is the large amount of money school children have to spend today, as well as the potential amount of money they will spend as they grow up. Dr. James McNeal, a professor of marketing at Texas A&M University who has studied the consumer behavior of children, states that by the age of five, many children begin to make purchases on their own, thereby becoming consumers at a very early age. By the time they are ten, they make more than 250 purchase visits to stores each year.[1] Changes in the American family have forced children into the marketplace sooner.

Working parents rely on their children to do more household chores, including shopping. McNeal states, "Today's kids really pack a punch—an economic punch—and they're not just one-punch sluggers either. They pack a one-two-three punch as primary, influence, and future markets."[2]

As a primary market, children have money of their own, and the authority and willingness to spend money to satisfy their needs and wants. American children have well over $8 billion of their own to spend, and they spend around $6 billion of it on toys, sweets, clothing, and other items. The remaining $2 billion goes to savings, creating a primary market for the financial industry. As a market of influence, children may very well directly request over $130 billion in household purchases from their parents or guardians, and they may indirectly influence that much again. As a future market, children have the potential to become consumers of a vast array of products and services as they grow older. Of the three dimensions of the children's market, this has by far the greatest potential for corporate profits.[3]

In the past, national marketers mainly reached children in the home through comic books and television. Today, however, children are spending less time at home. They are in school up to 7 hours a day, 5 days a week, more than 180 days a year, and they are pursuing more after-school activities than ever before. Even Saturday morning children's television-program ratings are beginning to drop. Finding alternative marketing channels, therefore, has become increasingly important for marketers trying to get a message to children. More and more companies see school-based advertising as the most effective and memorable way to reach children.

With so much present and future purchase power at stake, marketers know it is important to understand just who these children are—how they think, what they are drawn to, and what they don't like—especially when targeting them in an advertising campaign. In the past decade, an increasing number of experts on children's psychology have entered the marketing field with the intent to educate corporate America about the latest youth trends. Furthermore, an increasing number of periodicals and books are offering advice on how to develop new products, programs, and advertising by using children's psychology to tap into their changing needs and wants.

One reason some consumer-advocacy groups and the general public object to youth marketing is that companies are consciously tapping into children's natural vulnerability in order to influence them to select a given brand. Adding to the controversy is the fact that these messages are broadcast in school, where children can be more attentive to and accepting of messages due to the authority of teachers, principals, and other school staff members. In other words, students believe that if it's okay with the school, the product must be okay for them.

Opposition to Advertising in Schools

While many people in the education community appreciate the funds, equipment, and materials they get from corporations, others argue that advertising and corporate sponsorships clutter a school's environment, distort children's education, distract students from their studies, and, perhaps worst of all, target, at the earliest possible age, a captive audience largely ignorant of the persuasive effects of advertising and marketing—for the sake of winning brand loyalty potentially worth billions of dollars.

Some people are so alarmed by the sudden proliferation of advertising in America's public schools that they have formed or joined existing advocacy and consumer-awareness groups in an effort to protest against and bring an end to commercialism in schools. The Center for the Analysis of Commercialism in Education (CACE) is one such advocate for commercial-free schools. CACE is based at the School of Education at the University of Wisconsin-Milwaukee and is funded by Consumers Union, the nonprofit publisher of *Consumer Reports* and *Zillions*, a consumer-education magazine for children. CACE provides studies that support the argument against commercializing schools, should anyone want to use such supporting data in a plea to their local school-board members. Other organizations that provide similar support for this side of the argument include the Center for Media Education, the Center for Science in the Public Interest, and the Center for Commercial Free Public Education.

A Call for Businesses to Help Education

While there are leaders in education that oppose corporate involvement in public schools, there are also business and public policy leaders who are encouraging America's businesses to get involved in our nation's educational system. With the 1983 release of "A Nation at Risk," a federal government report that linked declining schools with the country's economic future, CEOs became concerned about the future of their companies and the education of future employees. In the decade after the report was published, corporate America dramatically increased its involvement in education. Businesses have been donating money and materials, helping to wire schools for the Internet and mobilizing employees to volunteer as tutors.

In 1997, Colin Powell launched the campaign Promise to America at the President's Summit in Philadelphia. Powell called on businesses, organizations, and individuals to get involved in their community and help America's children—especially disadvantaged children.

Richard W. Riley, the U.S. Secretary of Education, initiated two campaigns calling on businesses to help improve America's educational system. The Partnership for Family Involvement in Education asks companies to give employees the time and resources they need to participate actively in their children's education, or to get involved as mentors in the educational community. The second campaign, America Goes Back to School, encourages businesses to become "partners" with a local school, among other forms of community involvement. The slogan for both campaigns is "Better Education is Everybody's Business."[4]

Due to this encouragement, hundreds of companies, large and small, international, national, and regional, have gotten involved in their local public schools. Some have made positive contributions, while other efforts have been blatantly commercial.

The Beginning of Controversy: Channel One

One of the first controversies over advertising in the classroom came with the release of Channel One in 1989 by Whittle Communications, owned today by Primedia, Inc. Channel One is a ten-minute news program that features two minutes of commercials for products such as Nike and Pepsi. The show is designed specifically for middle and high school students and features music, bright graphics, fast visual pacing, and anchors between eighteen and twenty-eight years of age.

To subscribe to Channel One, a school district agrees to broadcast the show in 80 percent of its classrooms during 90 percent of the school term. In exchange, Primedia gives at least $50,000 worth of installed electronic hardware to each school, such as a color television set for each classroom, VCRs, and a satellite dish.

Advertising in schools by Channel One has generated serious questions in communities across the nation. Is it legal, not to mention ethical, to require students to watch advertisements on television in school?

One of the most convincing arguments against Channel One comes from Alex Molnar and Max Sawicky of CACE, who published a paper arguing that Channel One is not "free" in exchange for an audience but rather costs taxpayers money. They placed a monetary value on the time devoted to Channel One during the school day, and calculated that in the course of a year, Channel One takes up six or seven days of instruction and costs American taxpayers $1.8 billion annually.

Despite the negative publicity Channel One has received over the past ten years, the news program has spread successfully and is now aired in 40 percent of the nation's classrooms in forty-eight states. Approximately eight million students—more than one-third of America's teens—are now watching Channel One,[5] more than any other television program except the Super Bowl.[6]

While some question the educational content and financial motives of Channel One, others have placed positive values on the idea of students watching a brief news program every morning. In an article in *Time* titled "Hot News in Class," the introduction reads, "Channel One has drawn fire for bringing commercials into school. The surprise is that it has brought journalism as well . . . Perhaps most impressive is its coverage of world affairs. Channel One has sent its squad of nine correspondents, ranging in age from eighteen to twenty-eight, to Haiti, Rwanda, Bosnia, and other global hot spots . . . and [the stories] have an immediacy that a young audience can relate to." The author goes on to state that the eight million students watching Channel One is roughly five times the number of teens who watch newscasts on ABC, CBS, NBC, and CNN combined.[7]

Companies That Advertise in Schools

The following companies are merely a handful out of many that market or advertise in schools. They were chosen due to either the high level of controversy surrounding their marketing tactics, or the popularity of their marketing materials among teachers.

Nike

Nike is one company that advertises frequently on Channel One. The company uses athletic role models popular among teenagers to help establish its brand. It is no coincidence that Michael Jordan is not only the leading role model among children and teens but also the official spokesperson for Nike. *Fortune* recently estimated that Michael Jordan has been worth a total of $5.2 billion to Nike just by wearing and advertising those shoes with the swoosh. Nike has even developed an icon for Michael Jordan to be placed on the shoes next to the swoosh and used on packaging and advertising.

Roy Fox, a professor at the University of Missouri-Columbia and a specialist in media literacy, interviewed 200 ninth-grade students from a low-income area who watch Channel One every day. One conclusion that Fox made was that teenagers, whether they are athletes or not, are highly influenced to buy Nike sneakers by both peer pressure and commercials that feature Michael Jordan. He describes an interview he had with a student named Evan, who does not play basketball but wears Nike basketball shoes. Evan stated that he liked the commercial on Channel One that featured Jordan, and he enlisted his grandmother's help to raise $114 to buy the shoes featured in the commercial. When asked if he looked at other brands before buying his shoes, he said, "No."

When asked why not, he answered, "Because, it's kind of like, uh, most of the kids wear Nike, and so you should."

Fox notes that some students teased Evan about being short. He adds, "Evan did not respond to these comments. But the girls' taunting—along with his attraction to the Nike ads and his need for peer acceptance—helped me understand why he paid so much for basketball shoes when he never played basketball. . . . Never mind that Evan's family can't afford them. Never mind that Evan doesn't play basketball. Never mind that some kids are beaten and even murdered for such shoes today in urban schools."[8]

As DK Holland, a partner at the Pushpin Group, states, "When the objective is to appeal to the irrational to elicit greater brand commitment, then the brand has gone too far. When the brand is overtly creating a climate that urges consumers to purchase overpriced goods that they can't afford and don't really need, the brand has gone too far."[9]

Pepsi-Cola

Pepsi is another company that advertises on Channel One, and its most popular advertising campaign among high school students has been an antiviolence campaign titled "It's Like This." The ads feature close-up shots of red, white, and blue Pepsi cans between black-and-white and muted color shots of kids talking directly into the camera about experiences they have had with school and racial violence. Many students in urban schools especially like this campaign because they feel they are able to relate to the students featured in the commercials. There is some confusion among students, however, as to whether this campaign is a public-service announcement or a brand campaign. Many students said that they believe Pepsi understands them and the issues they deal with at school, and as a result, are willing to buy Pepsi.

Coca-Cola

Pepsi and Coke are fighting each other for exclusive advertising and marketing rights in schools all across the country. The situation has turned into a bidding war; the company with the highest offer wins the school district. While these contracts generate enormous income that a school can use to make curriculum or school improvements, some community members argue that it is "un-American" to coerce schools into exclusive contracts, thereby eliminating competition.

In one case, Seattle School District officials negotiated a ten-year contract with Coca-Cola for $6 million. The deal allows the district to spend $40 per student per year, as opposed to the $2 per student per year that the traditional funding provides. Pepsi previously had most of the business at the district's schools but lost the contract when Coca-Cola outbid them by millions of dollars.

Last year when a high school student in Georgia was suspended for wearing a Pepsi shirt to school on Coke Day to celebrate the signing of a contract (students were asked to wear red and white clothing), the amount of negative publicity forced the principal to apologize to the student and allow him to return to school. Marc Gobé, a creative director and partner of Desgrippes Gobé who has worked on designing and developing the Coca-Cola brand, considers Coke Day at a school—and asking students to wear red and white—to be an "oversaturation of a brand," which can be "dangerous" to both the brand and the company.

General Mills, Kellogg's, and Kraft Foods, Inc.

It's no coincidence that food-product and service companies target schools.

According to Gene Del Vecchio from Ogilvy & Mather, research shows that 74 percent of children aged six to twelve have strong influence on their parents' choice of cereals and fast-food restaurants. Sixty-eight percent influence parents' choice of snack foods. In addition, the amount of influence increases as children grow older. Cereal makers and schools, especially elementary schools, are a perfect fit. General Mills sponsors a fund-raising campaign in elementary schools called "Box Tops for Education." Parents are encouraged to buy General Mills products and send in the box top to the company in exchange for a check made out to their child's school. Each box top earns the school ten cents. Kellogg's writes and distributes numerous branded educational materials to be used in the classroom—featuring Tony the Tiger, Toucan Sam, and Snap, Crackle, and Pop—all with the same message: A nutritious breakfast is important. Post Cereals, a division of Kraft Foods, Inc. partnered with the American School Food Service Association this year to promote National School Breakfast Week. They donated three million servings of cereal to various schools throughout the country.

McDonald's

Along with incorporating its menu items into high school cafeterias, McDonald's distributes a number of educational materials about nutrition, the environment, and safety that are popular among teachers. McDonald's is criticized for excessive commercialism, however, when it sends Ronald McDonald to visit schools to teach nutrition. Ronald McDonald is the company's most powerful marketing tool for reaching children. Geoffrey Guiliano, an actor who played Ronald McDonald, confirms in an interview that because children love Ronald so much, no expense is spared in training Ronald McDonald how to respond to children.[10] In Utah, there was an outcry in one community when a junior high school had a crowded flagpole featuring the American flag, state flag, and McDonald's golden arches. The school, which was sponsored by McDonald's, was forced to take the flag down. McDonald's aggressive tactics in targeting children to visit and eat at their restaurants often overshadows the goodwill generated by its understated promotion of substantial charities. To date, Ronald Mc–Donald's House Charities has contributed nearly $200 million in grants to children's programs worldwide.

Procter & Gamble

Procter & Gamble's first-grade Crest dental program has been in demand by teachers for thirty-five years and is used in 90 percent of the nation's first-grade classrooms. Each year, P&G sends out to enrolled teachers an educational program on dental hygiene that contains toothbrushes, samples of kids' sparkle toothpaste, brochures designed for children about how to brush their teeth, and red tablets for children to chew after they brush their teeth to see where they missed. There is also a take-home package of samples to give to parents. Many more elementary teachers would like to receive the program, but because P&G makes the most profit from the parents and teachers of first graders, the program is sent only to first-grade classrooms, and the company refuses all other requests.

Sheila Vey Becker, manager of educational programs at P&G, states in an interview that the Crest dental program is acceptable to teachers because the materials designed to be used in the classroom are nonbranded. The products that are handed out to children and the materials that they take home to their parents are branded, and "this is where the brand gets something out of it. This is where the business has to make its hit." She adds that it is imperative for programs like Crest's to have a "dual objective. If your primary and only objective is to sell a product, you won't make it through to the school. If your objective is strictly to be altruistic and do educational stuff, the company will go out of business. The reality is, if we can't sell more toothpaste, then we can't afford to do the program. At the same time, if it's not educational or beneficial to students, you're not going to get access to the kids."[11]

R.J. Reynolds

R.J. Reynolds, the tobacco company that is currently fighting litigation in fifty states, distributes an antismoking educational program titled "The Right Decisions, Right Now." Many doubt the intentions of R.J. Reynolds, the creator of the controversial Joe Camel. Like Ronald McDonald, children loved "Cool Joe." The proof is found in the statistics. According to the Centers for Disease Control, the number of children and teenagers smoking today is now at an all-time high, and R.J. Reynolds is catching the blame—justly or not—for these dramatic numbers. In 1997, the Federal Trade Commission charged that R.J. Reynolds violated federal laws by using Joe to peddle cigarettes to children. The decision was based on internal Reynolds documents suggesting that the brand Camel relied on Joe to boost its share of the under-eighteen market, which leaped from 2 percent in 1987, when Joe Camel was first introduced in the United States, to 13 percent.[12]

Many believe that R.J. Reynolds published and distributed the educational program only to counteract the political heat of its Joe Camel campaign, not to prevent children from smoking. Designed specifically for grades six through nine, the program focuses on how and why kids make the decisions they do when deciding to smoke.

Provided that Reynolds's motives are genuine and not political, the classroom activity suggestions do have merit. The illustrations commissioned for the program, however, need to be compared to the slick series of high-drama photography used in the R.J. Reynolds current advertising campaign for Camel, with the headline "Mighty Tasty." In this campaign, R.J. Reynolds capitalizes on antiauthority themes and sardonic humor that are so appealing to teenagers. By creating a parody of the label, the ads undercut the seriousness of warning labels that are required on all cigarette ads.

Because more teenagers are smoking than ever before, designers and advertising art directors need to work harder to change teenagers' image of smoking—not promote it—especially through the imagery created for advertising campaigns and packaging. DK Holland urges graphic designers and art directors to take care to consider the images that will be used to appeal to children and teenagers: "When a brand manipulates a visual image to give a false or misleading impression, a designer is usually one of the key players. . . . Joe Camel was tolerated for too many years by Americans and only recently has Camel started to phase out the image. . . . The designer, as the creator of the graphic image, has an ethical responsibility to understand, with a higher level of consciousness, the impact the image that is going to be exploited will have. This responsibility is rarely acknowledged. There is too often a sloughing off of moral ownership onto the client."[13]

The Backlash

During the last decade, the commercialized efforts of companies to reach children while they are in school have unfortunately overshadowed the positive and much-needed contributions of corporations who have supported their local schools. The lack of responsibility on the part of some corporations has resulted in a backlash against all corporate sponsorships in education.

Dr. Howard Gardner, professor of cognition and education at the Harvard Graduate School of Education and one of the country's leading researchers on child development, wrote, "I find it deeply offensive that businesses are advertising, explicitly or implicitly, in American schools and lamentable that so many school systems feel pressured to use these materials. Of course, as you note, businesses can make positive contributions to education; I much prefer if that is done through separate nonprofit divisions of firms."[14]

Jonathan Polansky, the creative director for the Public Media Center in San Francisco, stated in an interview that any form of advertising and marketing does not belong in our schools: "Respecting the learning work of children means that we should clear away the clutter of commercial messages and let them focus on information that is to their benefit. Sorting and discarding commercial messages is work of another kind, work that benefits the sponsor, not the child. Schools, like libraries, should be a marketplace for ideas, not a clearinghouse for products."

Ben Cohen, cofounder of Ben & Jerry's, lobbies in his campaign "Business Leaders for Sensible Priorities" for the federal government to allocate more money for public education so that schools do not have to resort to selling school property to corporate advertisers or even holding fund-raisers. In fact, Cohen believes advertising and marketing in schools should be illegal. In an interview, Cohen states, "I was amazed that it was even legal, just amazed, and I was amazed that schools would go along with it, because as a marketer I think it is such a powerful marketing medium and methodology. When teachers push a product, it is a powerful endorsement."[16]

Finding the Benefits

Many acknowledge the hardship that underfunding causes and accept that businesses can become important partners to schools. Rebecca Mulzer, a director of marketing in the School Division at Houghton Mifflin Company and formerly an elementary teacher, stated that "unless we are replacing that needed revenue, I don't believe we have the right to criticize schools for accepting advertising."[17]

Dr. Jim Thompson, superintendent for the Grapevine-Colleyville School District in Texas, states, "I never thought that one day I'd actively seek advertising, but it's a different world now. School districts can't rely on traditional funding. Property taxes are at a point where people are saying they can't take any more. We had to start searching for supplemental revenue."[18]

According to John Leavitt, a public relations officer for the Colorado Springs School District, the advertising program helps to improve student achievement. "The program gives us the financial resources to enhance schools or add to curriculums. We've purchased furniture, computers, software, and copy machines and paid for extracurricular programs and field trips—a whole variety of things we wouldn't have been able to do if these resources had not been available. And they do help to enhance the learning environment and curriculum, which in turn helps us to help our students achieve their goals. The other thing the advertising program does is it connects companies with the schools and gets them more involved."[19]

Taking the Next Steps

Balancing the negative aspects of corporate marketing in schools against the desire to keep corporations involved for the sake of financial and educational assistance has led many schools to establish guidelines, although a national set of guidelines does not yet exist. Perhaps this would be a good next step, before some states pass laws that prohibit useful corporate sponsorships altogether.

Corporations can make positive contributions to our nation's educational system. There are benefits to be gained from the educational materials, equipment, time and, most of all, the funding that corporations can afford to give to America's schools. It is not always possible for schools to provide these benefits to their students on federal funding alone. In return, the corporations deserve to be given public recognition for their generous contributions to America's public education system. It becomes imperative, however, that corporations not abuse or manipulate the financial vulnerability of public schools or of low-income communities for the financial gain of the corporation. The psychological influence of advertising on children and the parameters of corporate sponsorships in public education must be respected.

There has to be some form of quid pro quo for commercial companies to invest in our youth and their educational process. Overall guidelines would be mutually beneficial to both companies and schools. The guidelines could be developed by a joint council of representatives from education, business, marketing, advertising, and design. The formation of a School Support Advertising Council, which would detail the "do's and don'ts" of promoting brands in schools, could be addressed through professional organizations that represent the advertising and design industry, such as the Association of National Advertisers (ANA), the American Association of Advertising Agencies (AAAA), and the American Institute of Graphic Arts (AIGA). The Council could work closely with companies trying to reach children to ensure that the established guidelines promoting ethical practices are adhered to and that children's consumer rights remain intact. Overall, the council and established guidelines would provide a mechanism that would ensure maximum company support of educational goals while staying within the boundaries of responsible branding and advertising.

It is to the benefit of American companies to support education and help today's students achieve academic success. Today's students will be tomorrow's workers and business leaders. Companies will be much better served in the long run by taking the high road and providing support, recognition, funding, and incentives that will help to increase competency at all student levels. Such a noncommercial strategic direction will return greater dividends in terms of worker skills and preparedness versus a strategy that is designed to sell more burgers, soft drinks, or basketball shoes.

Notes:

1. James U. McNeal, *Children as Consumers: Insights and Implications* (Lexington, Massachusetts: Lexington Books, 1987).

2. James U. McNeal, *Kids As Customers, A Handbook of Marketing to Children* (Lexington Massachusetts: Lexington Books, 1992): 17–18.

3. Ibid.

4. *www.ed.gov*

5. Jolie Solomon, "Mr. Vision, Meet Mr. Reality," *Newsweek* (August 16, 1993): 62–64.

6. Ellen Goodman, "Turn on 'Channel One,' Turn Off Values," *Los Angeles Times* (March 8, 1989): II–7.

8. Roy Fox, *Harvesting Minds: How Commercials Control Kids*, (Westport: Praeger Publishers, 1996): 33. Praeger Publishers is an imprint of Greenword Publishing Group.

9. DK Holland, "Keeping Promises: The Impact of Brands on Society," *Communication Arts* (March/April 1998): 25.

10. Gene Del Vecchio, *Creating Ever-Cool: A Marketer's Guide to a Kid's Heart* (Gretna: Pelican Publishing Company, 1998).

10. McLibel: *Two Worlds Collide*, One-Off Productions, 1998. Film.

11. Interview with Sheila Vey Becker, April 1999.

12. Jill Smolowe, "Sorry, Pardner," *Time* (June 30, 1997).

13. DK Holland, "Keeping Promises: The Impact of Brands on Society," *Communication Arts* (March/April 1998): 25.

14. Howard Gardner, letter to the author, November 30, 1998.

15. Interview with Jonathan Polansky, November 1998.

16. Interview with Ben Cohen, December 1998.

17. Interview with Rebecca Mulzer, October 1998.

18. Brian Boney, *The Dallas Business Journal* (July 11, 1997).

19. Interview with John Leavitt, March, 1999.

First published in *Communication Arts*, December 1998.

Branding: A Uniquely
American Phenomenon

Véronique Vienne

These days, most Europeans view American culture with a
mixture of awe and anguish. The increasing ubiquity of American brand names in
their lives makes them leery. My twenty-something French niece, for instance, works
on a Power Macintosh, subscribes to America Online, watches CNN, uses a VISA
card, buys Calvin Klein fragrances, wears Gap jeans, and thinks it's cool to meet
friends for ice cream at the Häagen-Dazs café on the Champs Elysées. She gets
annoyed when I point out to her that these brands, which help define her self-image,
are, in fact, American creations. For her, U.S. brands are the medium, not the message.

I've noticed that it's usually the European kids with their Levi's jeans, Ralph
Lauren T-shirts, and Nike sneakers who are the most anxious about this new form of
cultural colonization. They sure love American products, but they distrust the tidings
that accompany them. When asked what it is exactly that they like or dislike about
them, they make a face, bite their lips, cross their arms on their chest, and look down
at their shoes. They won't tell. It's something way beyond your average love-hate relationship—it's more like a fatal attraction.

American culture has always made Europeans nervous, but these days, with the
unification of Europe becoming a complex reality, there is a different quality to their
trepidation. For Europe, America is both a role model and a warning. It's what you
want to emulate—and what you want to avoid.

My niece does not object to the quality, the design, or the taste level of the
American goods she buys. In fact, she loves them. We've come a long way since the
days of the "ugly" American. The aesthetics of U.S. products and advertising campaigns are just as sophisticated and smart as anything that comes out of Italy,
England, Spain, Holland, Germany, or France. What annoys my niece about
American products versus, let's say, German products, is their emotional context. The
stuff is more than simply stuff—it's a concept, an attitude, and a value system. In
other words, it's a brand.

Branding a product and marketing its brand above and beyond the product itself is a uniquely American concept—one that isn't popular on the other side of the Atlantic. Heirs to Francis Bacon, Copernicus, Galileo, and Descartes, Europeans believe that selling an image is something along the order of idol worshipping—a practice for heathens, savages, and fetishists. Three hundred years of rationalism have taught them to celebrate reason, not emotions. For them, Coke is simply a beverage. Any subliminal message intended by the use of that ubiquitous red swirl silk-screened onto the can makes no impression on them. Or at least that's what they would like to think.

It comes as no surprise that European brands are much more demure than American ones. But so what. We'll still have Paris, right? Well, maybe not. As multi-nationals take control of the playing field, even the City of Lights is starting to look like an American suburban mall. Local brands cannot protect their territory against the likes of IBM, Philip Morris, Procter and Gamble, Colgate-Palmolive, Paramount Pictures, Mattel, or Disney—or even smaller American image merchants like Ralph Lauren, Gap, or Donna Karan, relative newcomers to the Euro scene. There are a few notable exceptions, such as French cosmetics giants Lancôme or Chanel, that have developed American-style branding strategies in order to compete in the States among U.S. rivals like Estée Lauder or Revlon.

Who would have guessed that, as the dust settles at the end of this American century, marketing—not literature, pop art, movies, music, or even television—would emerge as the defining medium for an entire nation. Today, the real American folk heroes (or villains) are not the John Waynes, James Deans, or Liz Taylors of the silver screen, but the Nike ads, Coke commercials, *Lion King* toys, Barbie dolls wearing Calvin Klein outfits—and the emaciated Calvin Klein models themselves. As far as the world at large is concerned, that's what this country is all about. Not people, but logos. Not principles, but trademarks. Not democracy, but brands.

Too many brands, too little time. The one thing Americans understand better than anyone else on this planet is how to create desires for things no one needs or even has time to use. They make it almost impossible for folks to be satisfied with what they already have. They don't simply ignore other people's cultures and traditions—they make the very concept of history obsolete.

To distance yourself from your past, develop brand awareness. The Cambodian priest who sips from a can of Pepsi, the Chinese toddler wearing a Joe Camel sweat-shirt, and the Iranian youth with the Converse sneakers are deliberately trying to break away from their traditions. The right logo embossed, silk-screened, or stitched onto a piece of goods becomes the official stamp on a new passport that gives you per-mission to put your identity as consumers before your national pride.

The increasing pervasiveness of American brands in Europe is probably a sign that future members of the European Economic Community (the EEC) are ready to let go of their most jingoistic instincts in order to come together as one united tribe. In *The Americans: The Democratic Experience,* author Daniel Boorstein tells how, 200 years ago in America, the development of commercial trademarks helped create a coherent culture. Back then, brands gave immigrants who had nothing in common a shared medium. He notes that brand names "drew together in novel ways people who might not otherwise have been drawn together at all. . . . The particular importance of

American consumption communities made it easier to assimilate, to 'Americanize' the millions who arrived here since the Civil War."

The branding phenomenon sweeping Europe today is not unlike the phenomenon that helped create a sense of commonwealth among American pioneers. There is one important difference, though: The new Europeans are more likely to rally around an American brand than around one of their many local favorites. It's a lot easier for people of different backgrounds to love—or hate—Big Macs than to combine the subtle flavor of French Papillon blue cheese with a sip of Italian Barolo red wine.

Unlike European brands that demand prior understanding of the local cultural moiré to be appreciated, American brands are simple narratives based on universal emotions. Take Joe Camel, for example. Where did he get that insolent and haughty temperament that appeals to smokers with a rebellious mindset? It was purely accidental. The original logo was drawn from a photograph of a Barnum & Bailey dromedary when the circus happened to pass through Winston-Salem in 1913. During the photo shoot, Old Joe, as the beast was called, wouldn't keep still, so his trainer hit him on the nose—thus the outraged look and raised tail of the one-humped mammal on the package. The genius of the marketing team at Reynolds Tobacco was to exploit this incident, turn it into a major component of their brand, and develop a consistent stream of imagery to support it.

Like Joe Camel, the most resilient American brands are living entities. The story of Levi's, a beloved American brand if there ever was one, is a twisted yarn—no pun intended. The concept was twenty years in the making before receiving its first patent in 1873. Levi Strauss, an immigrant from Bavaria, began selling denim jeans in California during the Gold Rush in the early 1850s. What made his pants different at first was the fabric, a sturdy imported twill; still, that was not enough to make them distinctive. In 1860, he added the rivets. But it was in 1873 that he put the final touch on his product: a double arc stitched onto the back pockets with orange thread. Only then did it all come together. Only then did Levi Strauss & Co. become a brand.

The powerful supermarket brands of today all have humble origins as well. They were created by people who sought easy solutions to everyday problems. Band-Aid came about when the young wife of a Johnson & Johnson employee kept burning her fingers on her kitchen stove. Her husband sat down one night and devised a bandage even a klutz could apply. The Gerber Baby was born in Fremont, Michigan in 1928, a couple of months after Dan Gerber's own baby was switched to solid food.

Dr. Pepper was the name of the father of the inventor's sweetheart. Wade Morrison, a young pharmacist from Virginia, named his soda fountain experiment after his fiancé's dad in a vain attempt to win the old man's approval.

Ivory Soap was a gift from heaven. Harley Procter, of Procter and Gamble fame, was sitting in church listening to the minister's sermon one Sunday in 1878, trying to come up with a name for his new white soap, the one that's "so pure, it floats," when he heard the preacher's words: "Out of the ivory palaces. . .whereby they have made thee glad." America's most popular soap was named after Psalms 45:8.

Aware of the powerful impact of the anecdote, American marketers today create fantasy narratives for their brands, deliberately incorporating odd, trumped-up biographical or historical details into the symbolism and iconography of their visual vocabulary. Their methodology combines an intuitive approach with daring *faux* rationalization—in ways that would make Descartes and his cohorts of enlightened philosophers and historians turn in their graves.

The ambivalence of European consumers toward marketing in general, and brands in particular, is directly proportionate to their high regard for historical accuracy. One of the biggest brand success stories in Europe is probably Chanel, a fashion empire based on a minor historical figure who has been cleverly marketed into a legend.

Maybe it's time we drop our *Encyclopedia Britannica* approach to culture and adopt a deliberately revisionist view of history. For more and more people, traditional analysis of data does not tell the whole story any longer. Recently, a friend of mine mentioned that he was flying down to Miami on PanAm. "You aren't flying on PanAm," I said sanctimoniously, "you are flying in an airplane with the old PanAm logo painted on its tail. Don't be fooled: A small airline just bought the right to use the logo." I felt smug, but the look of chagrin on his face made me wish I had kept my mouth shut. In this day and age, you don't belittle someone's brand choice. It's like denigrating his or her family values, belief system, and aesthetic judgement. For my friend, flying PanAm was a profound reality that had nothing to do with my linear view of the facts.

Next time I go to Paris, my hometown, I will go to the *faux* Danish Häagen-Dazs café on the Champs Elysées and I'll have a scoop of the same Vanilla "Swiss" Almond ice cream I can get around the corner from where I live in Brooklyn. The brand originated in the Bronx, the brainchild of a Polish immigrant called Reuben Mattus. Across the Parisian avenue is a the hugely popular McDonald's restaurant— "Mackdo," as the French call it—a far cry from the original 1954 hamburger stand in the San Bernadino valley, a profitable little business owned by two Scottish brothers.

So, this is Europe for you. America? It's the place we go to get permission to reinvent the past.

First published in *Communication Arts*, August 1997.

Thoughts on Identity
at the Century's End

Ellen Lupton

Graphic design's respectability as a profession is indebted to the rise of the corporate identity in the 1950s. Led by proselytizers like Paul Rand, Lester Beall, and Raymond Loewy and brand-building empires like Landor Associates and Lippincott & Margulies, the builders of corporate image lifted graphic design out of its lowly origins in artistic bohemia and the blue-collar trades. Design became both a science and a service.

Modernist designers rejected the ornamental detail and literal illustrations and centered on typography found in traditional business communications. The printer's vernacular at midcentury can be seen in the work of the William T. Manning Company, a Connecticut photoengraver that produced stationery for businesses across the country. Between 1940 and 1965, in-house designer Joel Anderson created meticulous renditions of factories, corporate headquarters, and industrial equipment that exploited the ability of the photoengraving process to reproduce minutely detailed photographs on soft-bond paper.

The new science of corporate identity rejected such literal representations in favor of the consistent use of bold, direct symbols, and logotypes, applied in a rigorously controlled manner to objects and environments large and small. The grandest ambition of design for corporate identity was to encompass an entire architectural setting with a coordinated language of colors, materials, symbols, and typography. The corporate headquarters of companies like IBM and Westinghouse—designed by Rand and architect Eliot Noyes—became landmarks in the culture of business, symbols for the sophistication and stability of the management community, as well as for the professionalization of the design field.

Several identity programs designed by Chermayeff & Geismar Associates in the early 1960s maintain their essential elements today. The firm's logotype for Mobil, typeset in blue with a round red o, is familiar around the world. Even in languages written in non-Roman characters—in Arabic, for example—a flash of red calligraphy still stands out from its blue surroundings. Chermayeff & Geismar Associates had designed the Chase Manhattan bank logo in 1960. Even after the recent merger of

Figure 1.

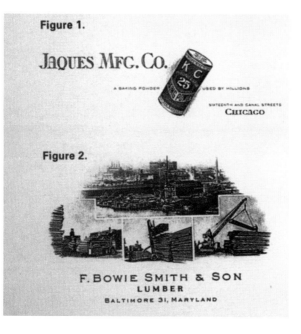

Figure 2.

F. BOWIE SMITH & SON
LUMBER
BALTIMORE 31, MARYLAND

Chase Manhattan and Chemical banks, which yielded one of the nation's largest banking companies, the Chase name and logo were retained to identify the new conglomerate, even though Chemical was the larger and stronger institution.

While such classics of corporate identity are directed largely at the business community, product identities speak to consumers. The logo for Betty Crocker, introduced by Lippincott & Margulies in 1954, uses handwritten letters on a red spoon to invoke the spirit of home cooking in the context of packaged foods. And what would a cake mix be without the box? It would sit there, gray and lifeless in its waxy bag, a mere sack of premeasured powders. But the crisp, rectilinear package offers an alluring four-color rendition of the cake-to-be. Betty Crocker herself is a fictional personality, embodied at the corporate headquarters in a series of oil paintings that have evolved to reflect changing images of the housewife, who, in her 1965 and 1980 renditions, was permitted to be a little bit sexy as well as sensible.

Andy Warhol tapped into the energy contained in supermarket vernacular when he started making paintings and objects in the late 1950s based on nationally branded products. He bypassed quaint and folksy forms of packaging—charming fruit-crate labels and cheerful biscuit tins—in favor of blandly contemporary consumerism. A brand name is often a company's most valuable asset, distinguishing generic goods such as detergent, toilet paper, or peanut butter with the mystical rune of the trade-

mark. A Kraft ad published in 1989 shows its famous red, white, and blue package erupting from within a block of cheese. The ad showed how packaging—normally viewed as an external, protective shell for the product wrapped inside—is, in the experienced reality of the marketplace, the driving motor of sales. Any cheese will do, as long as it's Kraft.

An amusing clash of cultures arises where the product vernacular intersects with the more staid and dignified language of corporate identity. A recent annual report for Lever Brothers opens with a photograph of neatly dressed executives, standing in the company's famous modernist high rise on New York's Park Avenue. But, this scene of perfect executive poise is undercut by the brashly domestic presence of brightly packaged cleaning products sitting on the table in front of them.

In Madison, New Jersey, stands a windowless, white corporate building for Tropicana; the huge green logo emblazoned across the building's top invokes a giant white juice box or refrigerator standing in the semi-industrial suburbs. The omnipresence of corporate identity has generated a heightened literacy of the eye. To be literate in contemporary culture means not only to know the letters of the alphabet but also to recognize a vast range of logos, brand names, and product images. This vocabulary of corporate symbols constitutes a "second alphabet," a set of symbols that we thoroughly internalize, that becomes second nature. When the Walt Disney Corporation bought ABC Television in 1995, the *New York Post* put mouse ears on Paul Rand's 1962 logo for ABC, creating a visual "sentence" in the alphabet of corporate image.

In New York's East Village, the band Lotion has made street posters that recast familiar product identities with the band's own name. Meticulously designed by band member Tony Zajkowski in 1992, these posters exploit the insistent familiarity of the second alphabet.

Metro-North Railroad

What is happening at the higher end of design for corporate identity today? I see a move away from the monolithic programs of the 1950s, '60s, and '70s, which sought to clean up the illustrative character of conventional business printing in favor of flatness, abstraction, and a reduction to essential forms. Landor Associates's 1994 redesign of the Federal Express corporate image overturned the tortured, abstracted letterforms the company had used since the early seventies. Some may dismiss the new design as a "nondesign," but its genius lies in embracing the phrase "FedEx," a piece of international slang whose clipped, telescopic form is familiar around the world. Landor Associates preserved the equity of the purple and orange color scheme, making the transition to the new design smooth and nearly unnoticeable to the general public.

Recent logos created by Siegel & Gale have introduced depth into the realm of corporate trademark design. For New York's Metropolitan Transit Authority, the firm created a logo that recedes into space, suggesting a moving train or bus. In 1995, the firm picked a new name for Northern Telecom—NORTEL—and turned the letter o into a globemark that, according to a promotional brochure, communicates "strength, dynamism, and global reach." In contrast with the abstractly suggestive sphere designed by Bass & Yager Associates for AT&T in 1984, the NORTEL mark is an overtly figurative reference to a globe, yet it employs a subtle, visually sophisticated vocabulary of arcs and curves that hovers between two- and three-dimensional modes of representation.

A figurative globe also enlivens the graphic identity created by Lippincott & Margulies for Continental Airlines in 1990. The new corporate symbol—a gold and white wire-frame drawing of a globe floating in a deep blue ground—finds its most dramatic setting on the tail of an airplane, where its complexity and dimensionality is an astonishing surprise amongst the drab, dreary, and obsessively "safe" context of airline identities.

NORTEL

Contemporary graphic designers use the term "vernacular" to refer to popular styles of typography and layout generated outside the profession. As an institution in search of legitimacy, design has long defined itself in opposition to commonplace commercial styles and do-it-yourself printing and publishing. Today, the lines between official and vernacular codes are becoming increasingly blurred. As a corporate identity or product image gains currency throughout the culture, it becomes open to appropriation and reuse. At the same time, the creators of major identity programs are allowing forms of everyday communication—from verbal slang to illustrative icons—to enter into their own languages.

First published *Communication Arts*, December 1996.

Protecting Corporate
Identity

Hugh Dubberly

If we took a survey of the steps people follow when starting
a new business, we would probably find that creating a logo is in the top ten. From
coffee shop to computer company, almost no self-respecting business goes to work
without a logo.

One reason there are so many logos may be that designing logos is fun. Design
problems do not get much more focused, visual, or direct. The possibilities for exploration and iteration are broad and deep, and few things in design are so pure and
clean.

But things don't remain pure and clean for long, because logos almost always end
up being used by someone other than the original designer. Most designers are concerned about how the logos they create will be used by others. They often provide
usage guidelines or standards manuals or corporate-identity policies or even branding
strategies to go with new logos. However, even if the rules are not spelled out, the
original and subsequent applications of the logo form a precedent and imply a set of
rules for using it.

Explicit or implicit, every organization has rules governing the use of its logo,
typography, photography, copy, layout, tone, and style. Together these rules, these
corporate-identity standards, constitute a house style, what some call a corporate
voice.

To me, the value of consistently applied corporate-identity standards seems self-
evident. Consistency makes communications clearer and reduces confusion.
Consistency ensures recognition. Consistency builds loyalty and brand equity.
Consistency builds wealth for shareholders. That's really the bottom line.

This monotheistic view of corporate identity, in which the designer is a caretaker,
custodian, or curator of a system that will survive him or her, is hardly new. In fact,
it's quite conventional. It is surprising then, given the love most designers have for
making logos and the conventional view of corporate identity, that so many designers
seem to dislike following other people's corporate-identity standards.

For the last nine years, I have worked as a design manager at Apple. During that time, I have often seen designers produce work for Apple that does not follow Apple's corporate-identity guidelines. Some of these designers are freelancers, relatively inexperienced, and may not know any better. But some work for large firms, are very experienced, and not only know better but also have consciously decided to break the rules.

Here are three examples in which reputable firms, firms that consistently produce high-quality work, knowingly chose to break Apple's rules.

Example 1

A Los Angeles firm produced a system of signs for a group of new Apple buildings. Instead of using Garamond, as called for in Apple's corporate signage manual, the designers used Gill Sans. Choosing the wrong typeface might seem of little consequence, but a system of signs is not a piece of ephemera. It will last for years. Hundreds of people—customers, vendors, and employees—see it every day. Using the wrong typeface sends a message that consistency doesn't matter. It makes it a little easier for others to break the rules.

Example 2

A Seattle firm produced a series of pieces for the Apple Developer Conference. The designers made use of a comic-book character, colored backgrounds, and typefaces never before seen on Apple materials. Inconsistent communications from Apple to its developers hardly helps convince them of the importance of consistently following interface design standards—a principle on which rests much of Apple's success.

Example 3

Even Apple's advertising agency is not beyond reproach. In a recent series of ads aimed at the design market, the agency distorted and mangled type in ways that might make David Carson proud. In fairness, I must admit that the Apple corporate-identity guidelines don't actually include a section on distorting and mangling type—at least not yet. While the agency argues that mangled type appeals to the design audience, I believe the mangled type makes the ad's sponsor less likely to be recognized.

The problem is not Apple's alone. When design firms show me their portfolios, they often include projects they have done for other companies—projects that violate those companies' standards.

One design firm proudly presented slides of an IBM tradeshow booth. This firm had created signs that abandoned IBM's traditional use of Bodoni and featured purple script running across the IBM logo. Paul Rand would not have been pleased.

More than a few design firms have presented work they have done for Hewlett-Packard, whose offices are near Apple's. Often these firms tell stories of how they avoided the HP design standards and the "design police."

Why they confess these sins to me, I cannot say. They seem not to have considered how a corporate design manager is likely to view design standards—whether the manager's standards or someone else's. My fear is that having violated someone else's standards, a designer would be likely to violate Apple's as well. I expect that any corporate design manager would be reluctant to hire or recommend someone who has violated another company's standards.

Having witnessed so many design firms ignoring design standards, I raised the subject at a recent American Institute of Graphic Arts (AIGA) board meeting. The board was discussing revisions to the AIGA Code of Ethics. I suggested including the following sentence: "A designer shall acquaint himself or herself with a client's design standards and shall follow those standards."

I thought this statement was pretty innocuous and expected no debate on the subject. I was wrong. Several members of the board were uncomfortable with the idea that not following standards might be called unethical. They made it clear that they do not wish to be bound by standards and view their role as design consultants to be one of changing design standards. After some debate we agreed on this ambiguous revised statement: "A designer shall acquaint himself or herself with a client's business and design standards and shall act in the client's best interests within the limits of professional responsibility."

Perplexed by the controversy over the proposal, I have raised the subject with several other designers. On a recent trip to Boston, I discussed it with three people who run their own design businesses: Marc English, Marc English Design; Judy Kohn, Kohn Cruikshank, Inc.; and Karin Fickett, Plus Design, Inc. They had some interesting insights.

First of all, they pointed out that the client who calls the design consultant is not necessarily the corporate design manager.

Judy Kohn said, "You have to decide if your client is the person who hired you or the corporation which employs him or her."

Marc English concurred, "It's got to be the end-user that you're really working for."

Karin Fickett added, "You have to assess whether what the client is asking for is in the corporation's interest or is driven mainly by the client's ego."

More often than not the client is a marketing manager with relatively little design experience and little branding experience. Often the marketing manager's job is to make as much noise as possible about the product, and the manager is often rewarded for optimizing communications for the product alone. That is, the marketing manager's product competes not only with products from other companies but with other products from the same company. A marketing manager's local concerns often put the manager in conflict with more global or corporate-wide concerns.

Judy, Marc, and Karin agreed that part of the solution involves educating the client. "If you design a corporate-identity system, it's your responsibility to teach the client how the system works," Judy said.

The responsibility for educating marketing managers does not rest with consultants alone. It is largely the role of the corporate design department. Bonnie Briggs, who manages Caterpillar's corporate identity, has put together a program of workshops to educate everyone at Caterpillar who buys design services. The program serves as an excellent example of how support for design consistency can be developed throughout an entire company.

Of course, being able to educate clients requires that design consultants know their clients' standards. Karin believes, "It's the designers' responsibility to ask for standards when they start work with a new client or when they start a new kind of project."

Educating the design consultants is another increasingly important function of a corporate design staff. This function becomes more important as businesses restructure—laying off staff or doing more with the same resources—and consultants take on a larger role in corporate design programs. The corporate design staff also needs to forge alliances with the other people within its corporation who deal with design consultants. The lawyers who write the contracts and the finance people who approve the purchase orders can help put in place controls that require consultants to complete training on the corporation's standards before beginning work.

Judy, Marc, and Karin also felt that many designers have a limited understanding of corporate identity. "You're assuming that all designers understand identity," said Marc.

"A lot of young designers think an identity is a logo," added Karin.

"I have done identity systems, and within a month, someone bastardizes them. Then they send me a printed piece, like I should be happy about it," Marc explained.

They also pointed out that sometimes clients simply get bored with their house styles and lose sight of their value. "The people in-house get tired of the same look," Karin said.

"It is a constant battle to sell red to Harvard. It is the same with blue at Yale," Judy asserted.

After about an hour of talking around the subject, I pushed each of them to tell me whether they would knowingly violate a company's corporate-identity standards if pressured to do so by a client.

Judy explained, "You try to redefine the problem. You try to find a solution that does not violate the guidelines. It can be difficult to negotiate the difference between what the client says he wants and what he probably needs."

Marc asked, "Why don't you come back with an alternative?"

Karin countered, "I would always come back gently to the standards. But you can't say 'no' to a client."

"When a client says, 'We want something fresh,' it's not politic to answer 'No, you don't.' Of course, there are times when you say 'that's not appropriate,' or haul out phrases like 'in my professional opinion,'" Judy added. "But it's presumptuous for a designer to tell a client, especially a new client, that his or her approach is wrong."

Marc said, "The issue is not what a piece looks like. The issue is the idea. Why don't you come up with a great idea? You need to define the message, present it clearly, and dramatize it. If you have a great idea, a great way to visually convey the message, you can make it work within almost any set of standards."

They all acknowledged the economic reality of the situation—that clients pay the bills. They also acknowledged the greater difficulty of pushing back on new clients. "There's a big distinction between a first-time client and one with whom you've had a long-term relationship," Judy stated.

"What do you do when you're just starting your own business and a client asks you to do work that violates his company's design standards? You try to stay within the standards, but you work with him," said Karin.

Finally, Judy pointed out that the real value designers add is their ability to define problems and present options, "Wouldn't it be awful if someone handed you something and said, 'I want a piece just like it.' What would you say?"

I was pleased to find that these designers expressed a great deal of concern about their clients' identity standards. Their observations reinforced my conviction that consistency cannot be legislated and that standards manuals are, at best, only part of the solution. There's no way to foresee every possible design option, let alone include them all in a standards manual. In a world of shrinking budgets and shrinking staffs, a corporate design manager's role involves not only defining standards but also educating and motivating both the firms that supply design and the marketing people that buy it. Ultimately the standards will not be used unless the consultants and the marketers see them as their own.

During the course of our conversation I was also reminded that another part of a design manager's job is to make sure his or her identity system has the right level of flexibility. A good system will have processes built in that allow for review, growth, and change. A good system must be able to keep pace with product and market changes.

Designers have to decide whether to work within their clients' identity systems or to reinvent them. Producing individual projects outside the system seems to me, if not unethical, at least irresponsible. If one believes the identity system is flawed, then the responsible course is to change it.

First published in *Communication Arts*, January/February 1995.

Identity Imperatives for the
Information Age

Phillip Marshall Durbrow

Definitions

Image: the way a company is perceived
Identity: the way a company really is
Identity expression: how a company communicates its identity

Imperative #1: Rule Breaking

The business environment, in which corporate identities are being created and communicated, is undergoing unprecedented change. We must aggressively question all that we know about identity and be prepared to break old identity rules, no matter how tried and true in the past, if we are going to develop and communicate identities in a way that is relevant and effective in the changing environment.

The only thing we know about the future, for sure, is that it will be different than today. Companies will face new types of investors, employees, customers, alliances, competitors, products, services, and media. CEOs must lead their companies forward in the face of increasingly swift, massive, and unpredictable changes in geopolitics, economics, technology, and regulatory or deregulatory climates.

How, then, can we continue, as we have in the past, to insist that companies express their identity "in one consistent way, without change or modification, as stipulated in the corporate-identity guidelines"? On the other hand, if we allow a company's identity expression to vary, or morph, to accommodate changes in the business environment, how can we build awareness and image over time? This will require new, thoughtful, and creative kinds of identity-communication systems that test the familiar identity rules.

Imperative #2: Strategic Ambiguity

Over the past forty years, among Fortune 100 companies, there has been a 70 percent decline in corporate names based on a specific location or product (U.S. Steel) and a 450 percent increase in abstract corporate names (USX). This is largely because it is hard to grow big enough to be on the *Fortune 100* if a company is restricted to one location or one product.

In today's globally competitive environment, identities must stand for something relevant if they are to hold a place in people's minds. Identities must be expressed in a way that seems understandable and is appealing without being so specific that the company's business opportunities are restricted.

This is called "strategic ambiguity." For example, the company named Oracle (a person of great knowledge), which produces databases, is committed to "enabling the information age." The name and tagline give one the sense of Oracle's reason for being, in a way that is suitable for its existing business yet that doesn't restrict its ability to grow and change.

Imperative #3: Visibility and Audibility

Unseen is unsold. Most people assume, if they have never seen a company nor heard of it, that it must not matter. People are most enthusiastic about the companies they understand best, and they cannot understand a company they have never seen nor heard.

It is not enough to create compelling identity expressions. We must find new ways to assure that a company's identity expressions are encountered by key audiences. Identity expressions must still be designed to work on stationery, signage, and vehicles, but new media provide opportunities to gain visibility and to imbue identity expressions with additional elements of visibility and audibility, such as dimension, movement, and sound.

Imperative #4: Integrated Media

The U.S. television audience can no longer "be delivered," as in the past, by three major television networks. Today, the U.S. market watches more than 50 (soon to be 500) television channels, and eventually we will have television programming on demand. Companies must create "virtual" mass audiences by developing identity systems that integrate the visibility and audibility of traditional and new media.

In our overly communicated environment, people have developed ways to screen out messages. They can choose to not see or hear a TV commercial by surfing channels or by leaving the room. They can choose to not pay attention to a TV commercial by talking or reading. And, even if they saw and heard a TV commercial, they can choose to not remember it. Integrated media can help penetrate these barriers.

There is evidence suggesting that people who receive the same message five times in the same medium are less influenced than people who receive similar messages in five different mediums. For instance, one is less likely to be influenced by seeing the same ad five times in the same newspaper than if one sees a newspaper ad, a Web banner, a company truck, and hears a radio commercial and a word-of-mouth endorsement. The cross-referenced messages seem to validate each other, resulting in greater overall impact and persuasiveness.

To be effective in integrated media, identity expressions must be designed to work in traditional and new media. Integrated media does not require that all identity expressions look or sound exactly alike, but all identity expressions should be driven by the same strategy, and each identity expression should resonate with its audience and maximize the potential of its medium.

Imperative #5: Identity Arsenals

Companies are proliferating themselves. To get closer to customers and to increase their relevance, companies are dividing into multiple entities focused on target markets. To extend their competitive capabilities, companies are creating joint ventures, strategic alliances, international partnerships, technical consortiums, wholly or partially owned subsidiaries, and spin-offs.

Logos aren't enough. New identity systems must have an arsenal of graphic and policy tools for appropriately communicating the company's involvement in these initiatives, without diluting, distorting, or losing control of its image. Such tools must also anticipate the identity needs of the partners involved. This requires serious thinking and creative innovation.

Additionally, the new forms of media that technology is creating, such as e-mail, faxes, interactive audio/video, and Web banners, make different demands on identity expressions. Different demands require different expressions. New media is digital, flexible, nonlinear, randomly accessed, interactive, audible, animated, deep, and rich. Today, companies need a range of identity expressions to convey a range of qualities and to come alive with the power of new media.

Imperative #6: Entertainment Values

We are in an "entertainment era." This is a time in which the themes and production values of movies, television, music, and sports are permeating business, marketing, the economy, culture, education, religion, and politics. The best communicators are not on Madison Avenue. They are in Hollywood. We willingly pay to see their stories.

Larry King Live has become the critical forum for national political campaigns. Jay Leno's jokes are carefully analyzed to seek clues to changes in the nation's mindset. Country music is recognized as another key indicator of mainstream opinion. Coca-Cola switched from an advertising agency to a theatrical agency to develop its advertising. Microsoft has acquired 11.5 percent of Comcast, the nation's fourth-largest cable-TV company. The Secretary of Defense was recently asked, by a member of the press, if our attack on Sudan was a Wag the Dog strategy. Entertainment has replaced defense as the driving force for new technology.

Why is all this happening? Because people are drawn to entertainment media that has been created to attract them, hook them, stimulate them, and reward them. Our institutions are learning that it is no longer enough to simply communicate. Educational institutions, religions, political parties, and businesses must compete for their audiences against powerfully appealing competitors. Annual reports must compete with *People* magazine. TV commercials must compete with HBO's uninterrupted Saturday-night movie.

The communication of identity in this arena presents new challenges. Identities must have relevance to the audience. They must be less rigid, singular, and structured and more interesting and thematic, with variations in imagery and qualities conveyed.

Look at the wonderful ways that MTV keeps its identity fresh and appealing. Entertain them and they will respond.

Imperative #7: Sympathy

Think about the people you know who are overwhelmed, overloaded, multitasking, and buried under e-mail, direct mail, voice mail, newspapers, magazines, memos, and meetings. People are having to grab information, assimilate "factoids" and sound bites, surf media, scan messages, and scroll text or "drill down" in hypertext. These are new ways of getting, and delivering, information. Work with them, not against them.

Have some sympathy in your identity communications. Explore ways to creatively help people deal with identity expressions and messages in the context of the world they live in.

Imperative #8: Leadership

There are three reasons, related to corporate identity, that Winston Churchill was such a compelling leader. First, he was born with a speech impediment, so he had to work hard to develop his voice, with the result that he developed a more powerful voice than those of us who have never worked at it. Second, he wrote all his own speeches, and there are preserved examples showing the pains he took to get just the right phrase. Third, he had certain things he believed in, and those things didn't change throughout his lifetime.

As a result, when Churchill spoke, you had a man with a powerful voice, speaking in his own words, about things he truly believed in. This was a powerful identity.

By comparison today, our politicians hire researchers to find out what people want to hear, have speeches written for them, with hot buttons for different audiences, and deliver their speeches with so little credibility we wonder, "who are these guys, and what do they stand for other than getting elected?"

It is disconcerting to see identity professionals leading corporate CEOs down a similar path, saying their identity must be responsive to huge research projects exploring key audience attitudes, needs, and perceptions and future trends. It is as though these corporations, like today's politicians, are running around saying, "Who do you want us to be? We'll be whatever you want; just tell us what we should be."

If all the companies in an industry poll the same audiences, they will get the same answers and come to the same conclusions, resulting in responsive but boringly similar and unmotivating identities and messages. This is called "the iron law of emulation" which states that companies that compete with each other become more and more like each other (e.g., United and American, Hertz and Avis, Exxon and Shell, AT&T and Sprint, and Compaq and Dell).

The role of identity, in this new era, is to find core beliefs that are powerfully motivating and differentiating and to convey this character with clarity and conviction. The real power of identity comes from within. It comes from being and doing what you believe in. It does not come from being what others want you to be.

We should help leaders to lead, develop a vision, and inspire others to pursue that vision, invest in that vision, and buy that vision. Certainly, companies can't alienate their key audiences and ignore future trends, but their key audiences don't have the perspective and the responsibility that the leadership of a company has. Through identity expression and communication, companies must make their vision clear and appealing to key audiences. It must be based on things the leadership believes in, and it must be delivered—as did Winston Churchill—in a powerful voice and in their own words.

- Rule breaking
- Strategic ambiguity
- Visibility & audibility
- Integrated media
- Identity arsenals
- Entertainment values
- Sympathy
- Leadership

These identity imperatives are meant to remind us that the world is changing and the way we think about developing identities and communicating them also must change. There is an opportunity now for a quantum leap in the art and science of corporate identity. Those who are prepared to observe carefully, think deeply, and innovate creatively will have stimulating and satisfying professional relationships and careers.

First published in *Communication Arts*, December 1998.

II | Critical Design

The extraordinarily broad vocabulary and application of visual communications has vast implications. In this part of the book, the graphic designer's responsibility to society and, ultimately, to history is discussed.

What's Bad About
Good Design

Véronique Vienne

Call for entries—how we love to hate them. The huge folded posters are invitations to partake in intimidating rituals of assessment and rejection. Despite the fact that the judging is done by people who know very little about the projects they are supposed to evaluate, designers are nonetheless compelled to seek the approval of these impromptu juries. In our field, we seem to depend on design competitions to define what's good and bad design. This behavior is particular to our profession. Other creative types, from decorators to writers, have their competitions— their games and tournaments—but being "good" is never the issue. Brilliance, originality, and proficiency are what matter. These artists don't have to stand on a high moral ground to get validation from their peers. Unlike us, they can be "bad" and still get a standing ovation.

Designers developed this strange do-good dependency in the early 1950s, when the modern design movement was still in its infancy. For five years, between 1950 and 1955, designers were subjected to a grueling evaluation exercise sponsored by the highest authority in the field—the Museum of Modern Art (MoMA). In collaboration with the Chicago Merchandise Mart, the Museum developed one of the most ambitious competition agendas to date—the prestigious Good Design program.

Reading about this amazing postwar brainwashing campaign is an eye opener. Recently, at the New York Public Library, I came across an essay on the subject, written by Terence Riley, chief curator of Design and Architecture at MoMA since 1991, and Edward Eigen, an advanced student at MIT. Part of a series of studies on the role of the Museum at midcentury, the well-documented article, titled "Between the Museum and the Marketplace: Selling Good Design," explains in great detail how the design community was systematically and deliberately conditioned to equate Modernism with good design—and good design with good business.

Indeed, the Good Design story is steeped in Modernist romance. The idea was the brainchild of Edgar Kaufmann Jr., the son of the Pittsburgh department-store magnate who had commissioned Frank Lloyd Wright's Fallingwater masterpiece in Mill Run, Pennsylvania. In 1946, the young Kaufmann, then in his thirties, was appointed director of the Museum's Department of Industrial Design. A proponent of the arts—he had studied painting in Vienna, typography in Florence, and architecture at Wright's Taliesen Foundation—he turned out to be a marketing genius ahead of his time. Trained in his father's store, he orchestrated the Good Design exhibitions with the enthusiasm of a retailer and the optimism of a merchant.

The originality of his scheme was to turn a curatorial feat into an unprecedented and well-coordinated merchandising and media event. His goal was ambitious: to stimulate the postwar economy by convincing the American people to buy new products because they were better than old ones.

The program consisted of three exhibitions a year, each displaying anywhere between two hundred to four hundred objects. The shows presented a comprehensive selection of what Kaufmann and his juries believed to be the best examples of modern products designed during that period. One of the originalities of the program was its classification—instead of presenting gold, silver, and bronze medals as well as prizes, a practice popularized by international exhibitions in the late nineteenth century, the jurors only awarded an unassailable Good Design stamp of approval. This democratic system of classification allowed them to dodge the difficult issue of defining by what standards they were assessing each entry. It gave the word "good" an aura of wholesomeness, elevating it above the realm of human frailties. To this day, good design is a lofty concept that evades definition.

Back then, arbitrary and unqualified pronouncements by patrons and pundits went unchallenged. A case in point is the Great Ideas of Western Man campaign launched in 1950 by Chicago industrialist Walter P. Paepcke, the enlightened advocate of Modernism who founded the Container Corporation of America and the Aspen Design Conference. Still hailed as one of the great advertising coups of all times, the Container Corporation's institutional campaign celebrated the concept of justice and liberty as defined by the likes of Alexander Hamilton and Theodore Roosevelt. In the perspective of today's political correctness, Paepcke's white-male-establishment point of view would probably come under attack. So would Kaufmann's somewhat capricious definition of goodness. But those were innocent times.

The overt commercialism of the Good Design venture didn't seem to raise many eyebrows. Exhibition catalogs were explicit service guides, listing the objects on display, their price, and where they could be purchased. The installations, designed by celebrated architects and designers—Charles Eames and Paul Rudolph among them—were laid out like department stores, with housewares, accessories, wall coverings, furniture, appliances, and linens featured in separate areas. The artists' singular vision was de-emphasized; the objects alone were the stars. To further reinforce the authenticity of the program, the products selected by the Museum of Modern Art were awarded bold and distinctive Good Design tags, easily identifiable from a distance when displayed in a busy retail environment.

The first two shows of each year were held in Chicago at the Merchandise Mart during the winter and summer housewares market; the third, timed to coincide with the Christmas buying season, was held in New York at the Museum of Modern Art. A two-month-long media blitz, this last extravaganza was supported by carefully synchronized magazine and newspaper articles, symposia, advertising, consumer-opinion polls, radio interviews, and television appearances by Kaufmann. There was even a MoMA TV game show.

The synergy between education and consumption was irresistible; at the time, you had to be a curmudgeon not to applaud the success of Good Design. Architect Philip Johnson was one of Kaufmann's few antagonists. Elitist by nature, the architect of the Glass House was annoyed by the Good Design program's populist approach—and by Kaufmann's evident endorsement of Frank Lloyd Wright's pragmatic philosophy. But there was more to his uneasiness than just rivalry. Johnson believed that only a formal definition of Modernism could "end the divorce between industry and culture," whereas Kaufmann preferred to keep things vague, professing no apparent ideology, "no ax to grind." For him, good design was a euphoric concept that equated aesthetics with "eye appeal" and newness with innovation. His only bias was against decorative vocabulary borrowed from the past. He made no distinction between machine-made or handcrafted objects and only excluded from consideration things that were not readily available on the U.S. market.

As it turned out, the Good Design domesticated form of Modernism was fraught with subliminal messages, some of which we are still trying to decipher today. Back then, the word "good" was linked with the notion of ethics and morality. Milton Glaser remembers how, in the early fifties, "good" referenced things that were supposed to be honest and truthful, like abstract art. In contrast, today, "good" has no moral, spiritual, or redemptive agenda; "good" simply means effective. "Good" means "that which sells." For him, as for an increasing number of designers, the idea that problem solving, in and of itself, is enough to generate good design is wearing thin.

In "Design and Business—The War is Over," an article published in 1995 in the *AIGA Journal*, Glaser elaborates on why he believes the design community got shortchanged in the struggle between commerce and culture. "In the United States, the social impulses that characterized Bauhaus thought began to be transformed by our pragmatic objectives, such as the use of design as a marketing tool and the elevation of style and taste as the moral center of design," he writes. "It occurred so swiftly that none of us was quite prepared for it."

But another witness to the period, ceramist Eva Zeisel, who won countless Good Design awards for her elegant and witty crockery, challenges the very assumption that good design—as defined by the Museum of Modern Art—did, in fact, sell. "Good Design was never good business," says the spirited, ninety-year-old artist. "It only appealed to a very narrow elite. For the majority of Americans, it was okay to have modern appliances in the kitchen, but in the rest of the house, particularly in the living room, traditional styles prevailed." She maintains that what Kaufmann called Good Design was nothing more than lack of applied ornamentation. Milton Glaser would agree. "Good Design stood for the elimination of storytelling," he now says.

But Kaufmann was a staunch Modernist who conducted a one-man campaign against what he sincerely believed to be the bad taste of the public. In his own words, he wanted to see "a more extensive repertory of shapes, textures, and, above all, surface patterns not imitative of the past." He held a highly publicized panel discussion at the Museum on the subject "Is Ornament Good Design?" Zeisel remembers with a chuckle that she was one of the panelists.

She couldn't be bought. After viewing one of the Good Design shows, she wrote: "Nothing could be said to have been made for glory or for the admiration of the people. There were no lapis lazuli glazes, no silver colored pottery, no sumptuous yellow tiles. Dishes were white, with severe, straight sides. . . . The call to reduce sounded almost as if calling out to us sinners to repent, repent, repent. . . . Why not call out rejoice, rejoice, rejoice?"

Postmodernism was a gallant attempt to bring joy back into the design process. It did succeed up to a point, but it didn't release us from nagging assumptions about "good" and "bad" design. Its over-the-top historicism didn't help us sort out the difference between what's modern and what's dated. Its wasteful eclecticism didn't promote a new understanding of the role of ornamentation. Most disturbing, postmodernism never challenged the notion that the measure of excellence of a design solution is its commercial success.

Let's put the Modernist agenda and its good-versus-bad dialectic behind—once and for all. Nature is suggesting we do. At the Museum of Modern Art, a number of objects from the 3,000-piece prestigious Design collection are beginning to disintegrate on their own. Plastic bowls are collapsing into toxic blobs; foam cushions are turning into sand; and acrylic parts are becoming an untidy mess. All good things must come to an end.

First published in *Communication Arts*, January/February 1997.

The Written Word:
The Designer as
Executor, Agent,
and Provocateur

William Drenttel

Late last year, America elected a reader as president. Bill Clinton read throughout the campaign to ease stress and to save his voice (ironically taking in words to keep himself from uttering words). A chief campaign spokeswoman then caused a stir by noting that his favorite book was the *Meditations* by Marcus Aurelius. Clinton usually reads a couple of books simultaneously: a work on contemporary politics or economics and a spy novel. As of this writing, he is reading Martin Cruz Smith's *Red Square*, a novel of black-market intrigue in contemporary Moscow. He is also reported to have asked the CIA to turn over its vast collection of spy novels to the White House for his private library. Some reporters have remarked that they felt better knowing that the president was readying himself for the challenges that lay ahead.

Compared to his predecessor, President Clinton is a bookworm. William Honan of the *New York Times* reported that in 1984 George Bush was innocently asked to name a book he had recently read. He stumbled, eventually naming the twenty-two-year-old best seller, *The Guns of August*, by Barbara Tuchman. During the 1992 campaign, the same question was asked, and President Bush floundered again, not remembering a title. While hardly illiterate, President Bush just was not a reader. And after the infamous "potatoe" incident, it was clearly established that his running mate just was not a speller!

I feel more comfortable knowing that the president is a reader, that he is both capable of reading policy reports and reading for its sheer pleasure. With all the discussion about literacy in America, the truth seems to be that much of our country is losing its taste, perhaps even its appetite, for the written word. The issue is not what you read so much as whether you read—and if the illiterate can't read, the literate increasingly don't read. If the illiterate don't know where Burma is, the literate probably don't know that Burma is now named Myanmar. In either case, the new atlases read like Greek to many of us. Who, after all, can remember the eleven new countries that comprise the Commonwealth of Independent States (the former U.S.S.R, without Georgia and the Baltics) much less the emerging cacophony that makes up the rest of the former Ottoman Empire? In this context, it is no surprise that few understand the historical complexity of the crisis in Bosnia or that public discourse on the economy is at best shallow. Our reliance on the written word seems to be at an all-time low, and with dramatic effect on general knowledge and communication.

For this state of affairs, we hear many explanations: the influence of television, in general; the rise of MTV; the rise of the sound bite and the corresponding decline of television news; the expansion and complexity of new forms of media; the popularity of Nintendo; the decline in educational quality; the proliferation of languages in a multicultural society; and the propensity to engage in other forms of leisure activity. Among my contemporaries, I most often hear that reading and having children just don't mix. The explanations are many; more concerning is the facile way in which they are invoked to explain away the issue. The very acceptance of these rationales has become self-fulfilling, the prophecy of a dead end.

This evolution of the role of the written word is having a profound effect on graphic designers. The fodder of graphic design is, after all, words and pictures. Yet how many times have you heard "Well, people just don't read anymore" offered as a rationale for deemphasizing the role or amount of writing (copy, text, language, whatever it's called) in a design project? Some designers seem to acquiesce to the logic of this statement. Other designers seem more cynical, taking this situation as license to render words fundamentally illegible, engaging in dense shenanigans under the guise of avant-garde typography. Still others view this as one of the challenges of being a designer today.

Of course, it is true that reading seems more and more a luxury given the frantic complexity of modern life. In a commercial sense, these changes are equally extreme, affecting the nature and form of business communication. How do designers produce brochures or promotional literature for their clients, yet trash most of what they themselves receive? (The answer that "my work is different" doesn't, of course, get the profession very far.)

When was the last time you saw someone actually read CD liner notes or an employee handbook? When a magazine editor or publisher says he wants his magazine to be easier to read, more scannable, he should be taken literally—he is praying that readers actually do scan it. If you are a graphic designer producing such brochures, leaflets, magazines, or direct mail, wouldn't you rather just go home for the day? Doesn't this feel like a professional dead end? Alex Isley, the principal of Alexander Isley Design in New York City, succinctly noted, "I just have to believe that people still read."

Many people, of course, still do read, especially the staples of books, magazines, and newspapers. I believe the reason is simple and that hidden within this reason is a way for graphic designers to approach this issue. These books (or magazines or whatever) were meant to be read. They were written to be published, sold, taken home, and read. Generally, the better they're written, the more they're read. If some of them become decoration on the coffee table, that's okay, too. Books have a way of taking on a life of their own; someone else picks them up off the coffee table, and a new reader is found. It is this glow of an afterlife that makes a good bookstore interesting and a large urban magazine shop exciting. There is the assumption that these objects of commerce are for you—that you might be interested, that they're worth your time, and they might educate, entertain, or just relax you.

The crux of this equation is their good intent—that they were meant to be read. Roland Barthes, the French critic, has written of the implicit contract between the writer and reader—that despite the image of the solitary artist, there is always a reader in the mind of the writer. Designers seem to have the image of a "viewer" in mind, even as they produce printed materials. The catch is that the "viewer" is a generic category, a composite consumer of imagery. The same can be said of "audience" and "public," perhaps even of "readers." As the novelist Paul Auster recently observed, "I don't think of 'the public.' 'The public' doesn't exist, because books are not a communal experience. They're a private experience. Every book is read by one person. No matter how many people read it totally, it's always one person reading the book. So I don't think of the physical mass of the reading public." Designers, too, can imagine a single reader and then set out to create work that is intended to be read. It is here that something like a contract can occur.

Instead, the intent of graphic design is usually posited as having something to do with "communication," another term more generic than specific. As the editor of this column, DK Holland, has written, "The graphic designer is a key player in the development of intelligent communication tools. . ." If one designs something and never really expects it to be read, then what kind of communication is being created? Why does so much award-winning design include language that was never meant to be read, and why does any text longer than a byline, caption, or design credit seem too long? "Well, people just don't read anymore."

These are traps for contemporary graphic design. The use of the word "communication" often sounds hollow, a camouflage for delivering sales points without an idea on the page. Look through a design annual and try to read the words—most of the time they're just a surface, a façade. This is what wins awards, and it's this level that other designers then try to emulate. Design-firm self-promotions suffer from the same affliction—one is seldom supposed to look further or to actually read anything shown. Recently, I was pleasantly surprised by a self-promotional book by MetaDesign of Berlin—one caption said to simply read the work pictured, which could be read and which explained itself.

It is as if some designers have grown fearful of language and are, like some audiences, only capable of thinking in visual terms. As one designer told me, "We may argue endlessly over the copy, but when it's done, the comment is always just that it 'looks good.'" If editors sometimes play the role of the visually illiterate, then there is something out there like the "dumb designer" syndrome, the desire to hide behind the right side of the brain. This, in some cases, flows directly from the historically inferior position designers hold in many worlds; magazine art directors seldom have the power of editors; advertising art directors are often not equal to their copywriting counterparts, who create the slogans of the industry; corporate art directors are usually in staff positions without line responsibility.

Nonetheless, many of the best graphic designers working today are or have been editorial designers. Learning from books is obviously the longest tradition in design history. In magazines, the structural link between editorial and art departments rewards talented designers who are comfortable with the written word. Also, the editorial process, even at its worst, still seems to focus on the reader as reader.

In corporate communications, other tendencies are apt to predominate. Paper companies are a case in point. Designers aspire to have the freedom and printing budgets of paper promotions, and then often produce homages to collections of dusty objects or meaningless explorations on vapid themes. They are meant to be printed but seldom meant to be read. Recent environmental concerns have resulted, at least to some extent, in sensitivity about how much paper and ink is used to produce such fluff. A few companies are grappling with these issues by encouraging promotional efforts that have enough content to be worth printing, with some recent promotions placing greater reliance on quality writing.

In the business world, writing incorporated by designers in corporate-communications projects is seldom well written, much less communicative. The usual recipes include idyllic fluff (flowery metaphors that say nothing), the hyperclarity of bullet points (well-thought-out snippets of services, features, and capabilities that numb any reader), or strategic hard sell (barely rewording client strategies and pretending this is the way people speak).

Yet, designers frequently control the editorial content of such projects. They are given a business need, an audience, and a budget, and then the creative juices are supposed to flow. They become, in effect, editors, determining the "story," hiring the writer, assigning the artwork. It is sometimes instructive to define a project in these terms, to think of the strategy as requiring a story. For a good editor, telling the story is the key thing, and writing and visualization are both important. Designers often put photographers and illustrators on a higher plane, with the writer considered just another freelance function. When designers describe their favorite writers, the compliment used most often is "professional"; i.e., the manuscript is delivered on time, ideally on a disk, with a flexible attitude about changes necessary to fit into the design. This is writing on demand, filler that fits. Used in this way, writers have as much importance as mechanical paste-up. One way to raise the importance of writing in an everyday office environment is to change the vocabulary. Referring to "writing" or "text," as opposed to "copywriting," is a way of signaling that the writing you use in your work must be real writing. (One step further is to hire real writers as opposed to copywriters, but here the argument becomes unintentionally inflammatory.)

For most of us, there is much to learn from the editorial world. Respect for editors leads to an understanding of what is a good story, what is a tightly written argument, and the power of a concise headline. Just as designers need a good brief and then a lot of freedom, so too with writers. Designers who work with writers often are also more comfortable with longer texts and more complicated, in-depth arguments. Some designers find that occasionally trying their own hand at writing is a way to get close to the words; it also helps to integrate writing and design. These and other efforts can be made by designers to elevate the role of writing in design projects and to grow more comfortable working with writing and writers.

In the end, though, writing that gets read must be intended to be read. Using the written word does not solve illiteracy, but it at least speaks to the literate as if they were living and breathing—rather than assuming they are brain dead. If Roland

Barthes was right about the contract between writer and reader, then perhaps there is also an implicit contract between client and audience, with the designer as executor, agent, and provocateur? This is perhaps where one can speak of responsibility, of the need to take seriously the written words that are used in graphic design. It is here that communication starts to happen, when a reader knows that you mean it.

First published in *Communication Arts,* March/April 1993.

Everyday at work, designers reshape the details of our lives. **73** "Human beings, like animals, are extremely sensitive to small signs, to tiny noises in the night, to small discrepancies in the customary layout of their environment, for these may be the only warnings received before hidden danger strikes," warns Canadian classics scholar Margaret Visser in *The Rituals of Dinner.*[1] Danger is not the main concern of designers' work on toasters, the cereal-box logo, and the spoon, but each of these microcosms fits together to build bigger cosms: the table, the kitchen, the house, the town, the country, etc. A designer's job is to be concerned with both the tiniest details and the broadest cosmological abstractions, and how they affect each other—as well as what looks good. An itsy-bitsy detail has no meaning until it fits into the big picture. In short, designers are naturally concerned with ecology.

Designers see that things no one seems to care about, like the white space in that classic VW advertisement, actually have important effects; the white space helped focus attention to sell more cars. But making things function and "appropriate for their context" is no longer enough; designers have to be concerned with how their designs affect their environment. It's an ecological view that goes beyond recycling. As with the results of our design work, we can imagine how a puff of wind created by some butterfly's wings in Mexico can, through a complex chain of events, cause a tornado in Kansas. Through another series of connections, the tornado can become a Hollywood icon that will continue to cause millions of nightmares in little heads way into the future.

So with my special designer micro/macro glasses, I am searching for a new kind of ecology. My old "green" ideas of conservation and sacrifice don't fit the reality of modern human living or the artificial opportunities offered by new technology in the future. Stuff like fashion design flies in the face of reuse imperatives. Sorting our garbage for recycling seems like too much trouble for most people (even putting litter in a waste bin seems too hard for many Americans). The natural objective of the design process is to make things easier, reduce the dangers, improve the way things work—efficiency, sustainability, and "beautility"—thus improving the quality of life.

This could be the basis for a proactive ecological design movement.

Commercial designers have two constituencies: the business people who most of us work for and the end users we are all concerned with. That adds up to three points of view: business (manufacturer, producer, distributor, and marketer), the user (concerned with function, ergonomics, ease of use, maintenance, symbolic value, etc.), and the designer (the creator, artist, conductor, and negotiator). Design is a generalist activity involved in everybody's business! Although today we emphasize the commercial benefits where the producer may gain the most monetarily and the users may have the longest relationship with the product, it is the designer who gives of his own person. Like a mother, we give the ideas life.

Design is not just a profession. Design is a manifestation of wisdom. "Homo sapiens" means "wise human being" in Latin. The ability to design is basic; it's what separates humans from animals. Scientists define the difference in many ways: We're smart; able to make abstractions, to reason, to speak, and to collaborate; and we write, make weapons and tools (our thumbs also help), and have intent. It seems like animals exhibit some of these traits. Bees build wonderful hives—but it's their instincts, not their reasoning, that make them do it. Squirrels save nuts, and birds fly south for the winter, but they don't know why. Humans do these things too, but we have an ulterior motive: planning. Design gives raw action purpose. Design is connecting abstract discussion with real-world building. What science does not acknowledge is that when you cluster the various particularly human attributes they add up to the design process—to make and apply abstraction and then doing something about it. Design is communication on the most intimate level. We make things happen; it might not always be a good design, but it's definitely better than a monkey can do.

Doing design separates our kind of animal from the rest of nature. In the beginning, during prehistoric times, it was easy to define the relationships of humans to their environment—it was us against it. Basic survival was the goal. When it rained, we had to find a cave for shelter; when the caveman's cave got too full of garbage, he just moved into a new one. If he found a saber-toothed tiger, "Run away!" was a really good response. Up until very recently (geologically), humans were the little animals fighting for survival against big ferocious animals, powerful weather conditions, and ugly diseases.

Using design ingenuity, we built stone houses to protect ourselves from nature's storms and cold, made metal weapons to protect ourselves from wild animals, cleared forests to grow plants to feed our hungry selves, and discovered medicine to fight nasty diseases and wrote the formulas down so others could learn how. Soon, cities and buildings were covering the earth. During the Industrial Revolution, the roles of nature and man reversed; we became the threat to Mother Nature. Although strictly speaking, humans are part of nature, there is a difference between a buffalo standing on the Great Plains eating wild grasses and a Holstein standing in a barn getting milked while listening to Elvis on the radio (especially since we exterminated almost all the buffalo to make room for our cattle).

We have graduated to a new plateau where we are in the driver's seat. We have evolved beyond primitive people who were in a battle against nature for their lives to being able to define what "survival" means and what nature is. Now, it seems as though most wild animals live in zoos. Modern science is creating a new world and modern medical science is filling it with a human population explosion. Huge machines grow our food and send it to shopping centers, and most Americans, without much effort, eat too much of it. Humans have not been handling our ecology well. We are evolving faster than the ecosphere. Our lives are just as natural as a spotted owl nesting in the wetlands, but it doesn't seem "natural" because we are making a mess.

"In our minds, nature suffers from a terrible case of acne or even skin cancer—but our faith in the essential strength remains, for the damage always seems local. But now the basis of that faith is lost. . . . We have changed the atmosphere, and thus we are changing the weather. By changing the weather, we make every spot on earth man-made and artificial. We have deprived nature of its independence, and that is fatal to its meaning. Nature's independence is its meaning, without it there is nothing but us," writes Bill McKibben in *The End of Nature.*[2]

We live in a watershed time and it's scary. We passed from a defensive posture to an active attack. Basically we have only recently reached the end of the Stone Age. Smashing the head of a mammoth to eat isn't that much different than slaughtering a black angus steer, cavemen banging rocks into tools is not substantially different than casting plastic into Lego blocks, and pounding leaves into sheets of papyrus is simply a primitive version of a modern paper factory. But it was revolutionary when we figured out how to make copper into telegraph wires, which transformed raw materials into conduits for information—copper electrical wire is fundamentally different from a copper dish. Like Muzak is to Elvis, when the telegraph wire is electrified it does something the dish doesn't do. Telegraphs and phonographs make materials do supernatural things. Humans took raw materials and made vacuum tubes, transistors, and silicon chips that can calculate. It only took about fifty years to go from carrying data to transforming information with computers, and now we can make those things think for themselves.

Not only are humans attacking nature, we are creating a new kind of nature. We can make intelligent objects, ones that seem alive and ones that actually are alive. Not only can we make smart products, we can grow objects to our own design. Forget about the moral dilemmas of the birds-and-the-bees, cross-pollination, virtual sex, or even cloning. We have made a really big step where humans have gone beyond natural selection to take control of evolution, to make things happen by our own design, for our own ulterior motives. We are now able to create animate objects that have an intangible existence of their own. This is not necessarily a comforting development, but it is a totally new level of ecology.

We could not even live without most of our new technology. It's another example of what separates humans from the rest of living things. It's not a new predicament—how could our prehistoric hairless ancestors live without clothes? We make prosthetic devices to remedy our handicaps; pirates used all the classics: peg legs, eye patches, wigs, and hooks. In the not-too-distant future, it will be possible to implant artificial devices into the human body that will create super intelligent and powerful posthuman beings, like the Six Million Dollar Man. Wait a minute! The *New York Times* revealed that this year, forty of the fifty-one contestants in the Miss USA beauty pageant had breast implants, twelve had tattoos, and four had navel rings. Those contestants are primitive cyborgs! They are not so unusual; most of our parents already fit artificial teeth into their heads, many have synthetic hip joints, some have prosthetic valves in hearts, and almost everyone has mood enhancers running around our brains (wake up and smell the coffee). Victor Margolin, the design-history teacher at the University of Illinois, Chicago, thinks that soon we'll be able to grow computers inside our bodies.

As the machine-man meld progresses, we can call ourselves supernatural, superhuman, or posthuman. Now we can really redesign ourselves—everything is on the drawing board. We no longer have to do what our chromosomes say. With some implants, we can be stronger, and if we take some smart drugs, we could all be happy Einsteins. Nature used to offer some discipline for human activity; now, either we create our own artificial restraints (rules, laws, morals, and ethics) or we go completely wild, anything goes—posthumans with silicon-chip implants and micromachines running around their veins. Posthumans will be even more different from us than we are from prehumans. Bioengineered and digital replacement body parts will be stronger, more durable, and better looking than the pumped-up muscle men in Calvin Klein perfume ads.

Sci-fi badboy Bruce Sterling writes, in the year 2291 entry of his epic *Schismatrix*, about the conflict between the Mechanists (who favor improving humans with prosthetic hardware devices) and the Shapers (who are into softer bio- and social-engineering):

> The boy looked suspicious, "Are you on the side of life, or aren't you?"
> Linsey smiled. "Is this political? I don't trust politics."
> "Politics? I'm talking biology. Things that live and grow. Organisms. Integrated forms."
> "Where do people come from?"
> The boy waved his hand irritably and caught the kite as it swooped. "Never mind them. I'm talking basic loyalties now. Like that tree. Are you on its side against the inorganic?"[3]

It's good to grow—it's American! It's good to go from the simple to complex. It's good to colonize the moon and Mars. Why not transform those dead environments to support life? It's good to be more interesting, to fertilize and nurture life. It's good to design. See, our intelligence has driven humanity past simply being "organic."

Now that we are stuck in the Postmodern era (in one era, out the other!), we are realizing that we can neither go back to Eden (remember the saber-toothed tiger?) or go on ravaging our natural resources (nuclear meltdowns like Chernobyl are too dangerous), because chopping down all the forests is making the air bad to breathe and dumping garbage is poisoning the water. But simply conserving resources is a dead-end street. We know that we will run out of oil someday, and more and more people using it accelerates the timeline. The basic reason for the environmental movement is not to preserve beautiful vistas of tree-covered mountains; it's to save our own lives. We can't wreck our natural ecological system without figuring out how to replace it with a new system that we can live in. We seem too worried to try that. I believe that we have the ability to design and build a new, sustainable, healthier humane ecology.

"Here, at the crossroads of the laboratory and the functioning of the human body, we find contemporary biometric materials research fulfilling the highest hopes—and, perhaps, some of the deepest anxieties—of a culture rapidly narrowing the gap between the organic and the synthetic, between humanity as the product of natural design and nature as the product of human design," writes Ivan Amato in *Stuff: The Materials the World is Made Of.*[4] Today, we have both the means and the inclination to reshape the world to our own image.

Change is not always fun. People are leery of making things "better" (look at the advantage incumbent politicians have in reelection results). History is full of examples of things that did not work out as expected. Fairy tales like *The Midas Touch* teach us that witches, sorcerers, and innovators usually mess up. But when the magic works, it is integrated into our lives and quickly redefined as "good" (like free-range chickens). The good news is, as Disney Imagineer Eddie Sotto says, "The public tends to prefer the artificial."

One of the definitions of comfort is predictability. People like order, and nature is not orderly enough for us. Order gives security. People are comfortable with McDonald's because they know that whichever one they dive into, they are guaranteed exactly the same fries. People like fast food, not just because it's easy and chewable; it's made by experts, and there might be something wrong with eating a mushroom you picked and cooked yourself. Disneyland and Hollywood present artificial thrills in a safe clean context. We need protection from the elements. The artificial world we are designing for ourselves tames natural chaos and transforms the wilderness into a protective and comfortable cocoon. Plastic is the perfect artificial material; it's inorganic and stable.

Most suburban people don't want contact with nature; they think it's dirty, slimy, itchy, and dangerous. My three-year-old daughter doesn't even want to touch a "smelly" dog! People all over the world like living with this kind of artificial design. Even with air-conditioned tractors, fewer and fewer people are willing to live off the earth. Who is going to tend the rice paddies in Japan after this generation of farmers retire? When only 8 percent of Texans live outside urban areas—where are the real cowboys in the Wild West? The desirable comfort level is constantly being ratcheted up until we prefer the totally artificial air-conditioned, sanitized malls and cruising in the air-cushioned, sealed-environment car to real interaction with nature.

Our appetites are out of control. People are more like Aesop's grasshopper than the squirrels storing away food for the winter. Through most of our history people have been hungry, so now when we have plenty it's normal to consume all that's available.

People will live a lot longer. I figure my daughter will live to be about 200 with probable advances in medicine and mechanical implants. She and her friends' bodies may be frail, but their minds will be able to connect vast experiences and knowledge. Those posthuman senior citizens will have a totally new perspective.

Moral dilemmas we face now about genetic manipulation of crops, drugs, wearing fur, abortion, and cloning are difficult. But in the future, Sterling says in another 2291 entry in *Schismatrix*, "the strain is everywhere. The new multiple humanities hurtled blindly toward their unknown destinations, and the vertigo of acceleration struck deep. Old preconceptions were in tatters, old loyalties were obsolete. Whole societies were paralyzed by the mind-blasting vistas of absolute possibility."[5]

There are three design issues: Where are the limits on the biohardware? Can we limit artificial organisms? Is it possible to restrict manipulation of human beings? Once we answer these questions, we can relax and enjoy the ride wherever it takes us; put up obstacles, create distractions, and enact laws necessary to control "progress"; or take an active role in designing our future.

The basic ethical laws for these new kinds of intelligent hardware were worked out by prolific science-fiction author Isaac Asimov, who devised the famous "Laws of Robotics" back in the fifties when it was inconceivable that the human race would splinter into posthuman factions: "First law: A robot must not injure a human being, or through inaction, cause a human being to come to harm. Second law: A robot must obey the orders given it by a human being unless such orders conflict with the first law. Third law: A robot must protect its own existence as long as such protection does not conflict with the first or second law."[6] As computers and robots become more complex, they start to have personalities and abnormalities. They will no longer be so accurate because they will be doing things that will incorporate value judgments and be based on experiences that will corrupt their logic. All this fuzzy logic will make them more human. My new computer is so smart that instead of having glitches or crashes, it seems to have mild cases of mental illness. It does things in different ways depending on its mood! (Luckily, I don't think it can read, can you?!)

So issue #1 (limits on the hardware) fades as the silicone melts into programmed artificial biology; like wetware, biological software is taking on a life of its own. Meanwhile domesticated animals are more like software, cows are running biological programs that make milk and vats of totally new bioengineered yeast are running wetware programs that can build all kinds of artificial cancer drugs. Both ends of our synthetic nature, totally artificial and supernatural, are converging in the middle.

Which puts more pressure on finding the limits of issue #2. With new skills melding ergonomics and psychonomics (my word for the mental mirror of ergonomics, the virtual world of perception, understanding, and cognition), designers will raise new ethical issues by creating things that incorporate our actual selves or things that have their own lives to live. Now we are taking life-forms and computers and stringing them together to create larger entities with longer life spans and more complex dependencies. But the special thing about wetware is that you can let it loose. UCLA professor of English, N. Katherine Hayles, points out in *How We Became Posthuman*, "Complex systems, when recursively structured, can spontaneously evolve in directions their creators did not anticipate."[7] This is really transforming nature.

Posthuman phase is the latest in a process that started thousands of years after humans first started designing. We are more capable of sophisticated thinking than cavemen, not because we are smarter but because we have built smarter environments in which to function. Now we don't have to think about which side of the road to drive on or need to consider what fruits are in season for breakfast. Our social structures and cultures are a more developed operating system than the Neanderthals had. Seen in this way, the posthuman "offers us a way to think about human-machine interfaces in ways that are life enhancing rather than life threatening," says Kate Hayles.[8]

Issue #3: Like free trade, illegal drugs, and now Microsoft, it is futile to try to curtail the development of human beings. Although the laissez-faire approach won't be comfortable, individual's desires and the benefits of getting posthuman are so great that it is impossible to regulate or control. And it's too late to construct a relevant code of ethics. So the only limit on the hardware, the wetware and ourselves, is physics, chemistry, and our imagination.

People are so afraid of the bioengineering of humans because they feel that they might be left behind and forgotten. So far, we've been on a pretty flat playing field—I can compare myself with Leonardo (da Vinci!) or Jerry Lewis and feel somewhat simpatico, but how do I compete with the likes of the Terminator or Michael Jackson? In the future when artificial circuits are implanted into someone's brain, they'll be different; they'll have an unfair advantage over me (and what's worse, they will look back on us as their loser cousins). Just because we might feel insecure doesn't mean we should attempt to hold back progress, handicapping future generations. It's not the Olympics where we can legislate limits. I want to be smarter! I don't want to die. Implanting artificial (heart) pumps, muscle boosters, or intelligence enhancers will create an inherent superiority—a new upper class based on substantially bigger brains and brawns.

When we start monkeying around with ourselves, we run into another big issue about cyborgs, a more subtle consideration. By allowing people to create their own characteristics, there will be more differences. Not just black, white, yellow, and red—but new purple blends with strange new body parts. That will reduce the basic commonality we share with our fellow human beings (and to a lesser degree with our fellow natural life-forms). It's like going from broadcast TV to having 500 cable stations. When the Big Three networks lost share, we also lost our communal "fireside" experiences like watching the Beatles on *Ed Sullivan*. That was what was so important about OJ's ride in the Bronco or Lady Di's death in Paris. The stories were carried everywhere. The whole world was electronically sequestered on OJ's jury. We did not realize until she died that we all grew up with Diana; we'd known her twenty years. She was one person who everyone in the whole world knew. We first met her in the courtship with Prince Charles, we watched the royal wedding on TV, we saw the pictures when the princes were born, we heard about the mother-in-law's dissatisfaction. We saw the marriage fall apart. Through the tabloid press, we went on her vacations and with massive media coverage practically rode with her that fateful night in Paris.

We were surprised when everyone sent flowers. In our modern global village she was "the girl next door." As we implement better-designed prosthetics, we will have less in common with each other. Like college roommates, over the years, we'll drift apart; it will be impossible to share feelings across the whole posthuman race.

"We hold these truths to be self-evident: life, liberty, and the pursuit of happiness . . ." aren't so evident some two hundred years after they wrote the Declaration of Independence. Not only as we change our bodies will the definitions of life and happiness diverge—even our sense of truth will change. When the human race splits into a strange menagerie of subcultures, will there be any universal events or feelings for all posthumans to share?

Underneath all the sequins, Elvis had the traits that are most important to being a model human: compassion, love, devotion, hipness, empathy, and truth. Maybe we need to add a corollary to the "Laws of Robotics" that defines some common good human traits that must be incorporated into all posthumans—so we make them super strong, super smart, and super good.

There are two options here: a futile one and an exciting one. Futility is on the side of the nineteenth-century Luddites, who believed that new technology was changing things for the worse so they smashed up machines in factories. It's too late for us to smash up the machines and go back. Almost everyone would be really upset if Disneyland burned down, its computers crashed, and all its electricity was turned off. Look how nervous everyone is getting about Y2K. So let's jump in! Let's figure out what these new intelligent, complex, man-made things are like! Even Henry David Thoreau was into it. He wrote in Walden: 'We are all sculptors and painters, and our material is our own flesh and blood and bones."[9]

Our Postmodern/quantum reality should embrace complexity and contradiction. The new artificial diversity will be a super-charged antidote to the homogenous meta-culture of McDonald's/Coke/Nike/Gap/Microsoft/Disneyland. Like the Web, big business won't be able to own it. We'll create a New World Order—not ruled by George Bush's multinational military-industrial complex. Through strategic cultural design (not cultural engineering) we can design a new humane village, grown from new technological abundance. Soon technology will fulfill all our ancient needs and desires. Then what?

Designers won't be squeezing circuit boards into plastic boxes or "solving problems" anymore. Plastic is a metaphor for this new opportunity; we can make polypropylene into any shape—soon we will be able to make anything into anything we want. We'll be able to squirt electrons as easily as we now squirt plastic. We'll be able *to live in* a virtual-reality world of our own creation. We will have a clean slate to create whatever we want. We'll have to design "desire."

What does all this mean for the design professions in particular? I think the designers of the twenty-first century (like ones in the past) are going to be making big things that don't do much and designing little things that matter a lot. But the big difference is that instead of charcoal, press type, laser prints, cast concrete, or touch screens, we are going to be using all kinds of new media, like DNA, nanotechnology, and band-gap engineering. Designers will need to apply their skill to broader issues than making beautiful shells for mechanical equipment and organizing information on a page.

In the past, it has mostly been scientists and science-fiction writers, movie directors, and, of course, lawyers/businessmen who have been creating the plans for the future. Now Hollywood and Wall Street are steering. But by definition, Homo sapiens (i.e., designers) should play the primary role. Designers are visionary leaders and creative team players, the ones who create desire and cast dreams into tangible reality. Design is a special profession of planners and innovators. We are the profession that gives form to the things the scientists discover by turning it into stuff that works and that people want. We make it look good. We are the generalists with a holistic, integrated strategic approach to make the social engineering concrete and fun. We have that special mix of art, science, and talent that encompass the mind, body, and soul.

We tap into client/customers' emotions as well as meet their functional requirements. As frog founder Hartmut Esslinger says: "Form follows emotion." Designers, literally, make our dreams come true!

What we need to realize today is that radical change will happen, so instead of wishing for things to stay the same, or trying to make the change seem familiar, we should turn around, face the new horizon, embrace the new possibilities. We can start charting our own course instead of stumbling along picking up every new invention that pops out. It's time to go beyond what's possible. We have to design what we want—not just what "they" can do. For the first time in history, we can dream without any limits—and make it real. Hardware, software, wetware, evening wear—hopefully with designers' vision, the vectors will converge in a nice world for everyone, a utopia in flux, where tomorrow could always be better than today.

Notes:

1. Margaret Visser, *The Rituals of Dinner: The Origins, Evolutions, Eccentricities, and Meaning of Table Manners* (New York: Grove Atlantic, Inc., 1991).

2. Bill McKibben, *The End of Nature* (New York: Random House, 1989).

3. Bruce Sterling, *Schismatrix*, Plus (New York: Berkley Publishing Group, 1996).

4. Ivan Amato, *Stuff: The Materials the World is Made Of* (New York: Harper Collins, 1997).

5. Sterling.

6. Isaac Asimov, *I, Robot* (New York: Bantam Doubleday Dell, 1950).

7. N. Katherine Hayles, *How We Became Posthuman: Virtual Bodies in Cybernetics, Literature, and Informatics* (Chicago: The University of Chicago Press, 1999).

8. Ibid.

9. Henry David Thoreau, *Walden,* (New York: Harper Collins & Row, 1965).

First published in *Communication Arts*, November 1998.

Is Functionalism
Functional?
The Relationship
Between Function
and Purity

Justin Vood Good
and Peter Good

Functionalism is a Style

In a gesticulating polemic titled "Long Live Modernism!,"
Massimo Vignelli states that "Modernism was never a style, but an attitude. This is
often misunderstood by those designers who dwell on revivals of the *form* rather than
the content of Modernism." This is in part true, but mostly misleading. The misunderstanding is not to be blamed entirely on the revivalists but rather on a problem
with the modernist belief that content and form could be so completely distinguished
from each other that form could transparently (i.e., with perfect efficiency) reflect
content. As we will see, it is precisely the modernist desire to separate form and function, in an effort to transcend the historical contingency of style, that drove it into a
rigid stylistic code insensitive to a given design's actual functional character. The urge
to purify the design practices of merely decorative or aesthetic considerations, in an
effort to create a new technological aesthetic based on the beauty of mechanical efficiency, thus ultimately led to a design theory limited by its narrow concept of function.

Take, for example, one of Jan Tschichold's early manifestos on functionalist
typography where he asserts that the new typography is purposeful, the purpose of all
typography is communication, and communication must be made in the shortest,
simplest, most definitive way.[2]

Thus, the *form* of typography, its mechanical methods and visual conventions,
follow from, or are determined by, the *function*, which is communication. But what is
crucial to note here is that the concept of communication, while claiming to be universal, is already highly specified. Tschichold appeals to communication as if it were
some quantifiable substance, some definite thing to be transparently reflected.

"The purpose of all typography is to communicate something" is an altogether
different kind of assertion. Only by positing a function as an abstract universal, i.e.,
"communication," could Tschichold justify a notion of form, a specified set of typographical conventions such as sans-serif fonts or total asymmetry in type layout, *as
following from* the function of communication. But as soon as one supposes that

communication *as such* can never be something definite but only abstract, then the direction of determination shifts. This is because what is definite will tend to determine what is indefinite. Tschichold tell us that "communication must be made in the shortest, simplest, most definite way." While he says little about what communication is, he tells us that it is something that should be accomplished in the most efficient way. But Tschichold does have a definite idea of what efficiency is and how to be as efficient as possible, even when he does not know *what* he is communicating. According to his design theory, the what that is communicated is always the same. The interesting effect that follows is this:

The goal is efficiency (the pure visual language of graphic design) of communication (an indeterminate content).

Efficiency is communication.

Hence, what is definite, rule for typographic design, determines what is indefinite, communication as communication. The form determines the function, *or function follows form.*

Functionalism Broadly Conceived

Functionalism is generally understood as a way of thinking about and practicing design in which the *form* of an object (or a graphic or building) is held to follow from its purpose, its "what does it do?" Significantly, the goal of this principle is a kind of *purity* of form. A distinction is made, based on the specified function or purpose, (e.g., "to drive nails" or "to communicate") on those aspects of the form that are intrinsic and essential to the function, and those aspects that are extrinsic and nonessential. Design involves reduction, whereby the form of the work in question is distilled to essential aspects, relative to the stated function. What remains, ideally, is a unity of form and content, an object that is at once *beautiful*, due to its formal purity, and *practical*, due to its economy of means. This much of the concept of functionalism is not only clear, it's compelling. It resonates with an intuitive sense of the rightness. There's even something *natural* about it.

The Form of Functionalism

What is difficult to square with functionalism generally conceived is that the designation "functionalist" conventionally applies only to graphic design exhibiting certain formal characteristics and utilizing a specific set of stylistic conventions. When searching for an example of functionalistic design, one thinks of Jan Tschichold's New Typography, Theo Balmer's International Style, Max Bill and Bauhaus functionalism, Armin Hoffman, or Josef Müller-Brockmann. Works by such designers express formal characteristics that in one way or another reflect the conceptual battle cry of Walter Gropius, *starting from zero*. They often exhibit an ascetic economy of means, disparaging any element not organically related to their purpose. Each aspect of the design is expected to have a rational justification for its presence, safeguarding the purity of function from the menace of gratuitous decoration. In their strict and rigid allegiance to a singular function, functionalist designs resemble machines. In fact, they strive to emulate them in that their beauty is directly proportional to the economy and efficiency with which they serve their function.

Between Functionalist Design and Formal Purity

A question that has arisen for many graphic designers is whether functional thinking is necessarily connected to this mechanical or formal purity, or whether this mechanical aesthetic is simply one interpretation of functionalism. For some designers, the latter seems to be the case. For example, in an article titled "Rethinking Modernism, Revising Functionalism," from *Looking Closer: Critical Writings on Graphic Design*, Katherine McCoy writes, "I have never lost my faith in rational functionalism, in spite of appearances to the contrary. The only thing lost was an absolute dedication to minimalist form, which is a completely different issue from rationalist process."[4] Speaking of the Bauhaus, Dietmar Winkler has noted that "the functionalist label applied only to the primarily technological area."[5] More to the point, in an article from the same compilation *Looking Closer*, titled "On Overcoming Modernism," Lorraine Wild observes that "despite those who would attribute functionalism solely to Modernism, functionalism can be seen as inherent in the definition of design itself: a series of actions taken to produce a desired effect. It may be time to detach the notion of function from the failed ideology of Modernism in order that function might regain its simplicity and clarity as a design value."[6]

The Equivocal Nature of Function

Ambivalent responses like these stem from confusion as to what might in fact count as *the* function of design. For example, a movement in the United States during the 1970s involved the usage of generic packaging. The sparse design was functional with reference to a strictly formal criterion. The packaging had been *purified* of elements extrinsic to its supposed function *to indicate the contents of the package* but failed to function from a marketing standpoint, which serves the function *to get sold*. And this constitutes the chief weakness in modernist functionalism: that its mechanical picture of purity, i.e., the economy of means that follows from, and that *requires*, a strict adherence to a specified function, undercut the more difficult task of ascertaining the meaning of function in the first place.

The most infamous example of this is Le Corbusier's worker housing projects. Le Corbusier, calling his buildings "machines for living," conceived of them in such a for-

85

Is Functionalism Functional? The Relationship Between Function and Purity

malistic way that such architectural features as high ceilings, wide hallways, colors, and casings or moldings of any kind were vigilantly designed away and thrown into the pile of architectural characteristics labeled extrinsic to the purpose of a building. Thus the purpose of the building, supposedly to live in, was absurdly reduced to a dehumanizing, unlivable purity. In this case, the process "to live" was, like in many other instances, interpreted in purely mechanical terms, i.e., eating, sleeping, sitting, etc. Le Corbusier's functionalism compelled him to design with a concern to remove all factors not mechanically integrated into the activity of living. Any architectural aspect not justifiable within the narrow mechanical function to live in was necessarily jettisoned.

The Difficulty of Ascertaining Criteria for Functionality

Function, like its sly synonym "purpose," is one of the most equivocal, philosophically slippery, and semantically fecund notions one can invoke. The modernist theoreticians claimed that their design was functional, implying that previous design was nonfunctional. But if functional thinking is taken in its most general form, then one could argue that every piece of design is, by definition, functional. Every piece of visual information, from a corporate logo to a tag sale sign, *functions* with respect to some criterion. Just consider some possible criteria for defining function for any given design project. Take the function of a chair: to sit on (modernist), to gaze at (aesthetic), to sell (economic).

Function, when not tied to a specific set of criteria, always threatens to expand, or to reveal, the many possible ways that it can be conditioned. An object or graphic that is *nonfunctional* in one context might be functional in another. Oddly enough, if one radically extends this thought, it becomes increasingly difficult to find an example of nonfunctional design, for every existing work of graphic design serves some function, however hidden. As commercial advertising proves over and over again, design that transgresses every principle of clarity and beauty can still *function* according to marketing principles. In this respect, even design failures have, like evolutionary mistakes in the natural world, a functional significance, since they can indicate choices or adaptations that lack efficacy (fail to find a niche) and should therefore be avoided in the future.

Function as Noun versus Function as Verb

So what did the modernists mean when they said that their design was functional and that previous design was not? They meant that modernist design was *self-consciously or intentionally* functional, that it was *intended* to have a specific *function*, whereas other kinds of design simply functioned in a blind and confused manner. Here, the distinction between function as a noun and function as a verb becomes useful to describe this difference. As a noun, we use "function" to mean the purpose for which a thing was designed or intended to serve. The function of a clothes iron is to iron clothes.

As a verb however, function is not tied to a particular intention. A thing designed for a particular purpose (e.g., clothes iron) or even not designed at all (e.g., a wooden log) can function in a number of ways. An old-fashioned iron that doesn't function that well as an iron can function very well as a bookend. What's important to note here is that the second kind of function is conditioned by the relationships the thing in question has with its environment, whereas the first kind, i.e., function as a noun, is conditioned by the intention of the designer behind its existence.

Determining What Counts as Function in Design

One gets a sense of the more difficult task of determining how functional the criteria themselves are by simply asking the question "why" over and over again like a precocious toddler.

In the 1970s Pratt & Whitney, the well-known manufacturer of jet engines, introduced a new (timeless) logo for the division, replacing the legendary Flying Eagle. The formal aspects fit nicely into the popular corporate graphic vernacular, logo sheets, and guidelines. Although a promising design from the rationalist point of view, the design failed in a very important way. Simply put, the employees missed the eagle. The belt buckles and pins just weren't the same without their eagle. Morale, unity, and the comradeship of employees become strategic factors that are influenced by corporate images and the loyalties attached to them. Maybe this is why sports teams maintain very uncorporate-like identities. The resentment and rejection became so strong that management decided to return to their beloved icon with all its wonderful (unnecessary) detail. A similar scenario could be written about the 1970s NASA identity, which was jettisoned by sentimental revivalists.

Q: What is the function of typography?

A: To communicate.

Q: What is the function of communication?

A: Good question!

As Tschichold came to see, midway through his career, functionalist typography and design had overlooked the question of how functional their principles themselves were in the larger cultural context. The principle reason for this blindness was directly caused by the angst-ridden desire for formal purity that surrounded the genesis of the modernist conception of functionality. In lucid self-defense of his midcareer volte-face against the reactionary attacks of Max Bill, Tschichold wrote, "The New or functional Typography is well suited for publicizing industrial products (it has the same origin), and it fulfills that purpose now as well as ever. Yet its means of expression are limited because it strives solely for puritanical 'clarity' and purity." He continues by stating that "there are many typographical problems which cannot be solved on such regimented lines without doing violence to the text." As Tschichold notes, it was the modern preoccupation with formal purity, as modeled by mechanical efficiency, which paradoxically forced functionalist design to disregard the ways in which design itself functioned with respect to the larger context.

What Purity Is

Generally, purity concerns the distinction between what is necessary and what is merely incidental and disposable. More specifically, it involves a process of reduction whereby the thing in question is distilled down to its essential and necessary elements; everything nonessential to its identity is shaved away. At this level of generality, purity appears to be integrally related to functionality. This is because functionalism concerns the design process, whereby elements that are not functional (with respect to a given goal) are distinguished and *removed* from the design in question so that one is left with a design that is solely constituted by elements that are absolutely necessary to the achieving of its goal. But this doesn't really get us anywhere in understanding modern rational functionalism because this is simply a description of practical reason, which operates under the rule "If you want to achieve X, then do Y."

The Urge to Purge

What is characteristic of the modernist approach to purity is the fanatical way in which it was pursued and the extreme criteria for what counted as truly pure. It is difficult to overestimate the philosophical angst that fueled this purification urge. In the spiritually, politically agonized climate of post–World War I Germany, the petri dish of modernist aesthetic sensibilities, a quasi-religious fervor was generated out of the need to purify so-called high cultural practices of the deadly shortcomings that led up to the Great War. The principle shortcoming under attack was, in the Marxian climate of the Weimar Republic, a value bifurcation caused by a socioeconomic stratification, resulting in an institutionalized separation between artistic practices and the rest of the activities that constituted society. According to the principal theorists of modern art and design theory, the economic stratification of society had created, on one hand, a small elitist class of bourgeois artists and intellectuals who spent their time indulging irresponsibly

Formal purity as a defining approach to visual communication can be highly successful, as shown in the brilliant solution for the identification for Canadian National Railways. Systems that require wide variations of reproduction techniques and materials are aided by simplicity of form.

in their own vain subjectivity, titillating either themselves or their wealthy patrons and clients with superfluous decoration. On the other hand, there existed the vast proletariat, the people—*the Volk*—who constituted the true essence of Germany, the essence that had been neglected and betrayed by the guardians of the culture.

Out of the ashes arose a torrent of indictments against art. For how could any practice be justified, went the argument, that had no obvious utilitarian value with respect to the reconstruction of society? Artistic or aesthetics-related practices concerned things that were valued in themselves, as ends, not as means. The response to this severe ideological interrogation was to reconceptualize all aesthetics-related practices, (i.e., fine arts, graphic and industrial design, architecture, etc.) in a way that would ethically and politically justify their existence. The cult of subjectivity became the cult of utility. Art moved from being a mirror to being a hammer, from a passive, contemplative character associated with bourgeois idleness, to an active ideological weapon in the service of social reconstruction.

Beauty versus Utility

The machine became the root metaphor for progress in every discipline because it was the logical embodiment of everything that seemed to transcend the old problems. One, the machine was *neutral*, which meant that it was apolitical and nonpersonal, hence transcending the divisive effects of individual, racial, ethnic, or national identities. It thus led to an international aesthetic, a Socialist ideal. Two, it was a model for utility, stripped of decorative baggage, a new ethical ideal based on the idea that the highest values do not concern things as ephemeral as beauty but rather concrete things like tools. Its designs exhibited obvious instrumental value. Beauty is notoriously difficult to square with utility. The modernist solution to this problem was to identify beauty as utility; what is beautiful is beautiful because it is practical. That is, beauty is to be found in the purity of means that come to be defined and organized around the serving of some function. The hand-carved figures on the handle of a medieval broad sword or a blacksmith's hammer might be beautiful artistic expressions, but what do they have to do with the function of a sword or a hammer? Remove everything not obviously and directly integrated into the function of pounding nails or killing foes, argues the rational functionalist. Then, that "purity" of function will reveal a deeper beauty in the tools.

When, however, as Tom Wolfe observed in *From Bauhaus to Our House*, the emphasis falls on purity itself rather than *what* is being purified, the process undergoes a twist. Consider: To purify means to separate the merely incidental elements of a design from the necessary elements, relative to a purpose. Hence, the very possibility of purification rests on the ability to make the distinction between necessary and incidental. Therefore, purity becomes more difficult when this distinction is not easy to make, and easier when the distinction is more obvious and explicit. Additionally, the degree to which the distinction can be made explicit is directly proportional to the discreteness of the purpose or function, or how well the purpose is defined. "To drive nails with the greatest efficiency" is easier to purify of incidentals than is the function "to drive nails while being enjoyed as a possession or reflecting the pride a carpenter has in his work." But the tendency to define the function of design in increasingly narrow ways, so as to facilitate the purification process, eventually impoverished the modernist conception of function.

Why a Theory of Graphic Design is Impossible

A theoretical treatment of graphic design must ultimately address two central questions: "What is graphic design?" and "What is good graphic design?" Broadly speaking, the modernist tradition attempted to ascertain a set of immutable principles that would not only explain what made a work of design successful but would also serve as a kind of recipe for creating perfect design. Such a theory would have two parts: a description of the *ends* of design, and a description of the *means* by which to bring about the ends. In other words, it would be able to define *the* function of design.

But as the examination of purity suggests, it is the very attempt to formalize function that makes such so-called functionalist designs nonreceptive or indifferent to the larger, and ultimately more significant, ways that design "functions" in the world. In the speculative design studies of evolutionary biology, ascertaining the comparative "design excellence" of organisms is notoriously difficult. Time and again, a given species of animal that seems to exhibit design defects, i.e., to exhibit design features that have no functional significance, turn out on closer inspection to express profound problem-solving ingenuity, *once the context within which their evolutionary adaptations occurred is taken into consideration.* In this respect, the blue-green algae that thrived on the earth for billions of years, while obviously less sophisticated than Homo sapiens from a design point of view, exhibit no less ingenuity and purity of function with respect to the particular functional constraints that determined their structural generation. Indeed, 3.5 billion years ago when prokaryotic life forms first emerged, the human form idealized by the Greeks as the most perfect unity of form and function would have failed miserably, given the tragic discrepancies between its organic structure and the severe functional requirements of the young planet Earth.

The excellence of a design solution is obviously dependent on the character of the problem. And modernist functionalism tends to disregard this contingency. Solving problems is never a matter of chance; reason is always involved in the process.

Chance, however, is often at work determining which problems get addressed in the first place. This irreducible organic element to graphic design must condition whatever is taken to count as function if form is going to follow it rather than loop around itself in a comfortable self-referential circle of cool formal purity.

Notes:

1. Massimo Vignelli, "Long Live Modernism!," *AIGA Journal of Graphic Design* (vol. 9, no. 2, 1991).

2. Jan Tschichold, "Elementare Typographie" in Ruari McLean, *Jan Tschichold: Typographer* (Boston: David Godine, 1975), 29.

3. This is the principle point of contention made by poststructuralist criticisms of modernist art and design theory who have attacked the notion of a universal master code to language, linguistic or visual. Their argument is derived from Jacques Derrida's deconstruction of Sausserian linguistics. While Derrida has attempted to show the self-contradictory character of Saussure's belief in the purity of speech in contrast to the contingency of written language, the same chain of reasoning has been used in typography criticism to show the self-contradictory character of the modernist belief in a pure syntactical structure to written language in contrast to the contingency of letterforms.

4. Katherine McCoy, "Rethinking Modernism, Revising Functionalism," in *Looking Closer: Critical Writings on Graphic Design*, eds. Michael Bierut, William Drenttel, Steven Heller, and DK Holland (New York: Allworth Press, 1994), 50.

5. Dietmar Winkler, "Morality and Myth: The Bauhaus Reassessed," *Looking Closer: Critical Writings on Graphic Design*, 40.

6. Lorraine Wild, "On Overcoming Modernism," *Looking Closer: Critical Writings on Graphic Design*, 57.

7. Jan Tschichold, p. 133.

First published in *Communication Arts*, September/October 1995.

The Current State of
Our Currency

J. Phillips Williams

What can we expect from 1999? Anticipate a new ten-dollar
bill. We have already witnessed the redesign of the hundred, fifty, and twenty; the year
2000 will bring a new five, and in 2001 the almighty dollar will reemerge. Much has
already been written about the evolution of this iconic design. It is a solid symbol of
the United States, firmly planted in the mind of the world.

I began thinking about our "new" money as I was looking through my design
library. I ran across a copy of a book long dormant: *Towards a Reform of the Paper
Currency*, particularly interesting because of its design by noted American type/book
designer WA Dwiggins. A mere 300 copies of this slim edition were published in
1932 by the Limited Editions Club. I pulled it out and found that I had placed a few
samples of paper currencies between its pages: a Swiss franc, a Dutch gilder, and an
American silver certificate from 1928. Reading Dwiggins made me smile. "It seems
to me that now—grown to the size we are, really a mature society with responsibilities and wherewithal to discharge them—it is time for us to wash behind our ears,
put on neckties, clean our fingernails, polish our shoes, and begin to take a little
pride in our getup." He goes on to say that the United States "would not borrow that
style of another 'period.' It would tell of speed, and of enormous electrical potentials,
of the air as a new highway, of a universe suddenly swollen to appalling size—it
would tell about these things, but not in pictures—by implication and through
'atmosphere'. . ."

Has that atmosphere changed? I think not. It has only intensified. The need has
arisen to alter our currency due to counterfeiting and technological advances. The
addition of microprinting, a special thread added to the paper, the integration of a
watermark—all this contributes to a more sophisticated and technical design problem. So why isn't the design itself more sophisticated? Why, as Dwiggins says, don't
we embrace it?

It occurs to me that the opportunity to design a new currency calls for us to look
toward the future and not draw from the past. If we look at the silver certificate, we
can see a sample of the paper money to which Dwiggins was referring. I remember

buying this particular dollar at a coin show with my father when I was about ten. Of course, I was familiar with the dollar bill, but I was especially fascinated by this one, especially the back. It seemed so different. I soon learned about the great diversity in U.S. paper currency. Our money was larger in size and even more ornate than the currency Dwiggins wrote about. Many of the earlier bank notes depicted scientists and inventors as well as the patriotic symbols. No matter how interested I am in our old bank notes, I—like Dwiggins—do not understand why we look to the past for inspiration. Is it nostalgia? Are we afraid of losing our identity?

We know that U.S. currency commands a special place throughout the world. It is hoarded, coveted, and accepted without question. Dwiggins himself states, "The paper currency is a key specimen of the quality of the product of the federal government as it expresses itself on paper. The currency is an instrument of contact between government and people of the most intimate kind imaginable." So what's missing?

Let me address this question by looking at the other pieces of currency I had stashed within Dwiggins's book. The Dutch gilder is certainly not mired in the past. It embraces modern technology and feels contemporary. Its design is complex, encompassing a richness in both form and technology. The latest printing techniques are utilized. The longer you gaze at this bank note, the more apparent the design becomes; the subtleties of the watermark, the layers of information . . . When you hold the note to the light, you can see how the design's two sides work in conjunction with each other.

The Swiss franc also embraces technology and the complexities of society. It depicts portraits that leave little doubt as to the date of their printing. Each denomination changes in size as it increases in value. The printing has layer upon layer, adding depth and richness. The complexity of the design relies on this layering, a result of the use of various printing and microprinting techniques. The design also encompasses metal foils that help prevent counterfeits. It appears that each of these techniques is incorporated to enhance the design of the bank note.

I don't propose that we look to these designs for inspiration. I simply want to ask why our own currency does not similarly reflect our times. I appreciate the mono-

chrome quality of our currency, and I like many of the design elements contained within each bill. But I don't understand why we have not evolved nor tested the waters for a richer design. As I have pointed out, the history of our currency has varied greatly. Surely we can do better now. Dwiggins thought so, back in 1932. He points out, "If it were necessary to 'sell' the idea to a consumer market, any advertising agency would reject the design—vehemently. The agency would say, in plain language, that 'the layout is rotten,' absolutely inadequate, and that a new scheme must be worked out on a totally different basis— from the beginning." Dwiggins makes a comparison I feel compelled to include: "The only comment I wish to make about the shapes of the numerals is to put one of them in a row with some others. The others were designed by (A) Fournier, (B) Caslon, (C) Baskerville, (D) Bodoni, (E) F.W. Goudy, (F) Bruce Rogers, (G) George W. Jones."

I smile when I look at this comparison. This illustration shows where the design has gone wrong. No matter how nostalgic we feel about our money, how fond we are of its familiar lines, it is made to look rather silly by virtue of this contrast. This sampling of typefaces shows several in an infinite array of possible directions I would pursue. Dwiggins's comparison also points out and questions where we are and where we should begin looking. He quotes an article from *Transactions*, October 1929, that dis-

cusses the bank in these terms: "And this document—this singular document—stands as the prime symbol of value in the infinite transactions of a great commercial nation."

This statement sums up my sentiments. The world, for good or bad, looks to the United States—our policies, our music, our movies, our freedom of expression . . . so why can't we have a bank note that adequately evokes all that we are? Why does the redesign of our currency come under the category of missed opportunity? The answer is leadership. We should take a stance and urge this country toward progress, taking our cue from the Swiss and Dutch notes. We should be advocating a stronger design, lobbying for a change in direction, moving forward rather than standing still. The current redesign falls considerably short of what our great nation has always promised.

First published in *Communication Arts*, August 1999.

The State of
Our Ballot

J. Phillips
Williams

The controversy in Palm Beach, Florida over the design of
the presidential-election ballot places the value of design importantly in the mind of
the general public. Overall, design awareness in this country is abysmal. The general
consensus is that something as simple as a ballot with a list of names needs essentially no design. In the *Wall Street Journal,* Thomas Weber cited Edward Tufte, the
design world's authority on the analysis of visual information: "Don't get it original—get it right." Specifically pertaining to the Palm Beach ballot, Tufte said, "The
user is never wrong, and the user is never stupid. In information design, only
designs are wrong and stupid."

"Drafting the Perfect Ballot," an article by Emily Oberman and Bonnie Siegler
of the design studio Number Seventeen, appeared in the *New York Times* and por-
trayed their version of the perfect ballot. "First, we'd use the sans-serif typeface
Interstate. Since it was designed for highways (hence the name), it is extremely legi-
ble and has an American feel to it—open and utilitarian. Logic dictates the position-
ing: the presidential candidate's name is the most important piece of information,
so it is the biggest. A large arrow points to the ballot boxes so the voters can't miss
them. Voting should be easy." I spoke with Bonnie Siegler, and she mentioned that
the obvious was completely ignored, referring to the fact that listing the candidates
in a single column clarifies and simplifies the ballot. It seems many of the ballots
she reviewed list the candidates in two columns. She went further, pointing out that
for "write-ins," the instructions for the category were printed on the back of the
envelope. She states, "this definitely discourages write-ins and made it more difficult
and confusing."

Paula Scher of Pentagram dissected the Palm Beach Ballot on the *New York
Times* op-ed page, pointing out the legal ramifications of the improper ballot. (She
tells us that Florida law actually specifies that voters mark the box to the right of the
ballot. The county election officials foolishly violated this law.) She goes on to state
that "many official bodies and corporations approve products or documents that are
incompetently designed. When a design causes problems for a significant number of

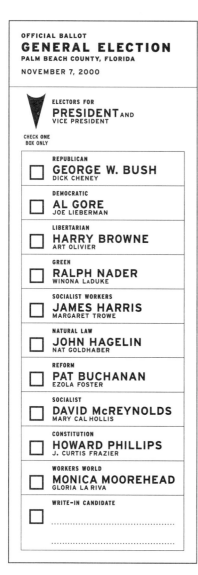

people, even if it was 'approved,' the product is usually recalled, and sometimes reparations are made."

USA Today asked "five of the world's best graphic designers to tackle the task of drafting a better ballot." Milton Glaser added color. Michael Bierut suggested "a quick, efficient scan." Roger Black wanted to "put the candidates names to the left of the holes to be punched, because we read left to right." Walter Bernard suggested using the same layout as the Palm Beach ballot "but only clearer." Even EDS, the information-systems company started by Ross Perot, posited an alternative. On November 17th, they placed a full-page ad in the *Wall Street Journal* with their version of a redesign of the ballot in question. The headline read "Nothing is too complex for us to solve." The ad's small print stated, "antiquated systems can cause mistakes, unsatisfactory outcomes, and unhappy customers. Fortunately, EDS can design, implement, and manage even your most complex systems to ensure the highest level of accuracy and customer trust."

The last time I was so enthralled in following the newspaper day to day and watching the news religiously was a result of the unsuccessful prosecution of OJ Simpson. My discovery of the chad in all its permutations—the dimpled chad, the hanging chad, the penciled chad, the pregnant chad, the swinging-door chad, the tri-chad, the incomplete detached chad, the trapdoor chad, the nondetached chad—opened up a whole new world. In checking the *Oxford English Dictionary*, I learned that a chad is not a chad unless it is completely punched out and in the chad box. Who knew? (What happens to the used chad? Or is it the unused chad that's in the chad box?) I found out that as recently as 1996, the "so-called pregnant chad gave William Delahunt a primary election victory for a Massachusetts seat in the House." I was sad to learn that, across the country, our voting system depends on antiquated equipment that has been manufactured more than twenty years ago.

By following the newspaper reports and the myriad details of the election, I became aware of Theresa Lepore, designer of the infamous ballot—not a graphic designer but the county's supervisor of elections. (She probably designs her own newsletter as well!) Her greatest virtue was her wish to make the ballot easier to read for the older residents in her county, certainly a laudable consideration. I read about the announcement made by a senate official that a commission with a budget of $10 million should be formed to look into our electoral process and a national ballot. I assume they will not be calling Ms. Lepore. The question is, who will they call?

What we need right now is to capitalize on the public's awareness of the dire consequences of ignoring design. (Paula Scher pointed out when the design causes problems for a certain number of people then often reparations are made. What will Al Gore's reparation be?) We go to conferences and attend lectures and discuss design for the public good. We get excited about our profession. The problem is that we are always preaching to the converted. When it comes right down to it, the county supervisor designs the ballot—a piece of design that quite possibly decided the fate of our next president. When was the last time you designed something which had such great importance?

Perhaps the American Institute of Graphic Arts (AIGA), rather than the EDS, should have taken out that full-page ad in the *New York Times*. The advertisement could have appeared across the country advocating the importance of better design—for ballots and beyond. I spoke with Michael Bierut, the president of the AIGA, and he informed me, fortuitously, that the next AIGA conference is scheduled for Washington, DC, in the fall of 2001; the theme—"Voice." He indicated that "at the conference we intend to explore the ways that design can affect the world for better or worse and how designers can take an active role in the process." He also pointed out that the first "save-the-date" mailing for the design conference "stars" the notorious butterfly ballot. He forwarded an e-mail stating that the Chicago Chapter of the AIGA had established a partnership with the Chicago Board of Elections Commissioner. The president of that chapter, Lance Rutter, explains, "The partnership's aim will be to address issues of education, experience, and mechanics and to use communication design as the tool for providing solutions to these three principle issues for Chicago voters."

We know that a small handful of industries have supported design and valued it, as we as designers define it. It seems evident that the government should be among them. Members of the studio Number Seventeen suggested that "our government could look at other governments and branches of government (like the Dutch Postal System PTT) [that] regularly commission good design and appreciate its importance in society."

Design for the greater good is that which is usually overlooked: airport signage, stamps, passports, the driver's license. It's time for our government to act publicly,

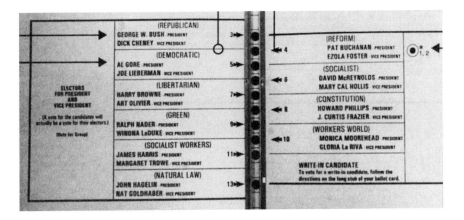

fervently, and adamantly in advocating the essential and necessary nature of design. Design should be valued and recognized for the power it holds. We should all press our associations, guilds, and institutions to—dare I say it?—lobby for design that makes a difference. Let us seize this opportunity to lead, demonstrating our expertise in all areas of graphic design.

The most obvious place to begin is with a national ballot design. The knowledge that the AIGA has scheduled its biannual conference for Washington is an opportunity to raise the bar! Instead of a save-the-date card going solely to the AIGA members, perhaps our focus should also be our target audience—the politicians and the government as a whole. We should engage them and make them aware! Ms. Lepore was not aware of our "value." Do we have any illusions that the politicians on Capitol Hill are any more aware than she is? Let us demonstrate! Let's pass out the perfect ballots in the hall of Congress. Let's rent billboards and advertise the benefits of good design. We know that design has benefited many industries. The *Wall Street Journal* pointed out that "any Web retailer that depended on a design as poor as that Palm Beach ballot's would find itself out of business in no time." Al Gore is out of a job and it's time for us to get to work!

First published in *Communication Arts*, March/April 2001

You Eat the Soup

Cecilia Holland

You eat the soup and throw the can away. Yet the soup is just a meal, while the can, like a fractal of a Mandelbrot set, recapitulates our culture in little.

The technology of the humble can, the rolled metal, the paper label, the pull tab, reveals an interdependent, specialized market economy whose resources are devoted largely to serving the mass of people, rather than an elite—which in turn implies a stable, peaceful culture. The size of the can hints at small families. The bright colors of the label and the cheery graphics, not to mention the staggering variety of flavors, demonstrate the soup company's need to compete for consumers' attention—hence an affluent society, where nearly everybody has a wide range of choices. The down side is that the can is one of identical millions, a clue to the relentless conformity and underlying angst of American life.

Compare this with an artifact from, say, Europe in the eighth century C.E. There are no soup cans from this era, although certainly people ate a lot of soup; but they made it themselves, from ingredients they found or killed or dug up with their own hands. What design from this era survives reveals a far different focus—such as Charlemagne's cathedral at Aachen.

The great Frankish king, conqueror of half of Europe, had seen and admired the cathedral of San Vitale in Ravenna in Italy, and, returning to his favorite home of Aachen, he undertook to replicate that building. Finished in 802 C.E., the cathedral is made of dark stone, its dome supported by massive marble columns dragged up over the Alps from Italy; fortresslike, its octagonal structure is so closed that I once walked all the way around it without being able to find the way in. Its most striking interior feature, besides the dark-veined marble columns, is Charlemagne's sarcophagus.

This design, clearly, springs from a culture focused on the power at the top, where God and monarchy conjoined, a conservative society trying desperately to defend and protect the legacy of a grander past, even if it had to borrow some of that legacy from another country. The dark, squat bulk of the building, hugging the ground, accessible only through narrow openings, projects the society's fear of a grim and uncertain present and a grimmer and nastier future. The building is consecrated to death, the Crucifixion of Christ, the burial of the great Emperor, who was the human linchpin of the whole society. Once Charlemagne was gone, that society began to come apart at the seams. Although Aachen's cathedral remained, and still remains, the design of the Romanesque was failing.

This is, of course, the broadest definition of design: not just the arrangement of elements on a page, but the construction of human lives. Still, the idea of design is at the core of all human creativity. We construct the world around us to suit ourselves, and the designs we make reflect the way we see ourselves. To know us, know what we design and why.

The urge to design doesn't merely reflect social values; it also drives social change. Some 300 years after Charlemagne's death in 814, a new design ushered in a sea change in the European worldview.

This was the design we call Gothic. The masons of the twelfth century basically took the old Romanesque plan for a cathedral and turned it inside out. To open up the interior space, they pulled the supporting columns outside the walls of the cathedral, extending the force lines of the vaulted roof out through the walls. On these flying buttresses they raised the vaulted roof up to a dizzying height, and between that roof and the walls they inserted a row of windows, the clerestory, where rows of stained-glass windows let in the sunshine and cast brilliant blades of color down through the whole vast, open interior. The result was a building that seemed all air and light, almost weightless, soaring upward toward heaven—a structure that reflected eleventh-century Europe's newfound hope and confidence. Where the Romanesque reflected a grim determination to hang on to the past, the Gothic spoke of optimism and the limitless power of God's grace.

The new style gave concrete shape and impetus to the explosive period of creativity of the High Middle Ages, when the foundations for our modern life were laid down. The new style spread throughout Europe, from Paris and Coventry to Prague. Nameless masons, traveling from site to site, spread and refined the techniques, working out the formulas by which the tremendous walls could be made to stand almost in defiance of gravity. Ordinary people, from serfs to noblemen and women, flung themselves into the work, hauling and laying stone and spreading mortar to raise the glories of Chartres and Durham and York.

These huge monuments took scores, even hundreds of years to build; their sheer size and weight seem to obliterate the average men and women creeping around their feet. Their builders remain mostly anonymous. Each cathedral was different, and yet the same in their imposing, almost arrogant reach toward God. If any design was oblivious to the mass of the people, surely it was the Gothic. Nothing could be more different than the soup can.

Walking around the York Minster recently, I marveled at the soaring height of the building, its harmonies of proportion, and its teeming ornamentation, the gargoyles and dragons and angels, bosses and plaques, the statues and chiseled stone heads of people that encrust the whole vast flamboyant edifice. There are hundreds of human faces ornamenting the outside and inside, and close inspection with binoculars revealed a startling fact: Every face is unique.

The nameless and forgotten stone workers covered the inside and outside of this building, dedicated to an omnipotent God, with individual images, putting them up where no living man could ever see them, clothing the monolithic harmony of the thrust toward God with an endless human variety, a thousand ordinary souls hitching a ride to heaven. By contrast, the soup can looks suddenly indifferent, inhuman, and stupid.

Life in the twelfth century was desperate and cruel; people died early of overwork and underfeeding, of brutal violence, of horrible diseases long since rendered harmless. In the last year of the twentieth century we live on average twice as long. We have in fact too much to eat. It's getting so hard to die that we're starting to talk about the right to do so. And yet we share with that earlier time a sense of helplessness, of powerlessness and despair. And the soup can is one reason why.

Marching off the assembly line in its dizzying millions, the soup can treats us all alike. And it isn't merely a matter of soup. Buying clothes now is like selling yourself as a billboard. Every T-shirt, every jacket, every pair of jeans comes blazoned with a brand name, be it that discreet little polo player or a huge OLD NAVY. Our clothes don't express us anymore. Some distant corporation uses our bodies to advertise themselves. We're being branded, like herds of cattle, trudging on to nowhere. We don't even get paid for carrying the advertising.

Like the Gothic cathedral, we've been turned inside out. The resources of imagination and initiative and identity that we can only find in ourselves we look for in externals—so beer commercials can tell us to "go for the gusto," and shoe sellers want us to "be like Mike" or Dennis or Venus or anybody but our poor mediocre worthless selves. The real people are those on TV or the big screen, leaving the rest of us in the audience as spectators of life. Yet all we have is who we are.

We tend to blame the corporations for all this alienation, displacing the guilt, but it's certainly our own fault. We have it easy, and so we've come to think that having it easy is the purpose of life. We sit back in our chairs and demand that more entertainment, more titillation, more excitement be brought before us for our delectation, not noticing that such a pose shrinks us down from real human beings to mere consumers, who know nothing, believe nothing, create nothing, and only buy.

Even interesting ideas, like the Absolut ads, *Alien* I, or the righteous indignation of Seattle, get done to death by repetition. One of the most horrible feelings of modern life is the knowledge that any interesting or successful new thing will be seized on by the commercial media and repeated and repeated until it puts your teeth on edge—a sort of prepartum depression. Yet the soup-can culture cannot escape from this wheel. It only values what can be replicated in an endless series. The whole notion of choice has become problematical. What's the choice when everything is the same? All books and movies have sequels, even though the originals worked precisely because they were original. Somewhere, even now, some movie studio is trying desperately to come up with a way of making *Titanic II*.

In the void left behind by the abdication of ourselves, the purveyors of stuff work desperately to make us happy so we will keep on buying. And everybody wonders why the quality of all that stuff keeps going down and why things don't make us happy anymore.

We need to redesign ourselves. Somehow in the stultifying sameness and ordinariness that surrounds us, we have to find that which is unique to each of us, and build on it. Fortunately there are excellent examples of this, and some of the best are skimming along the great wave of modern commercialism that seems so all-powerful and so depressingly mediocre, surfing like angels along the edge of the money and power.

There was Tibor Kalman, for instance, the master designer who had no formal training and yet who was behind so much extraordinary design. Who else is so loud, so brash, so fascinated by the ugly, the weird, and the unmentionable? The soup-can culture works toward simplicity, continuity, a sense of eternal sameness. Tibor went—with glee—for mess and transience, drawing on living bodies, jumping words all over a page or a piece of film, using pictures as text, and text as pictures, blood as ink, razors as drawing pencils. Best of all, he never seemed to repeat himself. Everything he did was straight from him to the moment.

Some of this is an inevitable response to the bland and boring stuff of the soup-can culture. In each of us there is some deep urge, when the storm rages outside and everybody else is huddling around the warmth of the fire, to open the door and let in the dark. More important is the invitation in Tibor's work to escape the boundaries and see things new again. A buoyant optimism underlies his work. He knew there was new stuff out there to see, and he knew that learning to see new is the way to freedom.

No professional creatives can better teach us to see than graphic designers. The very need to seize and hold the ever-restless eye requires a constant reinvention of the ideas of text and image. That can't happen by following the rules and obeying the law. Design of this sort could derive a sense of itself from Zen Buddhism. Zen and design may seem opposing concepts, but just as Zen aims to annihilate expectation and anticipation, bringing alive the moment, great graphic design wants to trick the viewer into seeing as if for the first time. Tibor Kalman delighted in doing this, and in so doing, invited us into a new world, the best of the soup can and the cathedral, a culture designed for everybody, in which every face is unique.

First published in *Communication Arts*, January/February 2001

III | We Struggle to Do the Right Thing

Because of the power of graphic design, it's crucial that we understand the potential use or abuse of design as a tool. This part of the book explores the designer's ethical responsibility to himself and as a professional.

Trapped in mouse-potato-dom, most of us are docile specta-

tors, our idle hands forever deprived of the tactile satisfaction of actually making things. This enforced passivity has dire consequences for the brain. There is evidence that toolmaking is linked to the development of language. Our hands are connected to our gray matter by a crisscrossing network of nerve pathways that travel back and forth from the right brain to the left hand and from left brain to the right hand. So, while manual dexterity stimulates our central nervous system, simple spectatorship numbs the mind.

But with nothing to fabricate, the majority of people are reduced to buying ready-made products—examining them, poking them, and fondling them in the process just to satisfy the yearning in their fingers. Shopping is a substitute for producing. When my daughter was a teenager, she would often say, like so many of her contemporaries, "Mom, I have nothing to do. I am bored. Let's go shopping!" It soon became a family joke. We worked out a couple of silly variations, including "Mom, my closet is full of clothes. I have nothing to wear. Let's go shopping" and "Mom, I have too many pairs of sneakers. I am confused. Let's go shopping."

From time to time, I indulged her shopping impulses, but I also suggested fun alternatives: fix toys, repaint the bathroom, make jam, wax the furniture. One of her favorite mood-uppers, it turned out, was doing the silver. I will always cherish the memory of her sitting at the kitchen table, a big apron secured around her chest, happily polishing our odd collection of forks and spoons.

"In his or her daydreams the passive worker becomes an active consumer," wrote John Berger, Britain's eminent critic and novelist, in his 1972 best-seller *Ways of Seeing*. Acquiring things, he believes, is a poor alternative for fashioning objects. The spectator-self, no longer involved with the making of artifacts, envies the consumer-self who gets to touch and use new gadgets, appliances, devices, and goods.

This perception is not new. More than forty years ago in Paris, an obscure group of cultural critics calling themselves "situationists" began protesting against the escalating commercial takeover of everyday life and against the artists, illustrators, photographers, art directors, and graphic designers who manufactured this fake gee-whiz reality. In his book, *The Society of Spectacle*, French situationist leader Guy Debord wrote: "In our society where modern conditions of production prevail, all of life presents itself as an immense accumulation of spectacles." Yet, by today's standards, the spectacle hadn't even begun. This was before the Cuban revolution, before the invasion of Tibet, before the Pill, before *La Dolce Vita*, before Pop Art. In the 1958 Paris of the early situationists, Edith Piaf was singing "Milord," François Truffaut was shooting *The 400 Blows*, and demure Danish Modern was the cutting edge.

Yet, with a clairvoyance that's startling in hindsight, the short-lived (1957-1972) Situationist International movement predicted our most serious current dilemma. According to the latest findings, we spend 58 percent of our waking time interacting with the media; people sleep less and spend less time with their family in order to watch more television; megaplexes and superstores are increasingly designed to resemble theme parks; and the Mall of America in Minneapolis hosts more visitors than Walt Disney World, Disneyland, and the Grand Canyon combined. In his new book, *The Entertainment Economy: How Mega-Media Forces Are Transforming Our Lives*, Michael J. Wolf asserts: "We have come to expect that we will be entertained all the time. Products and brands that deliver on this expectation are succeeding. Products that do not will disappear."

No wonder the situationists' ethos has become the mantra of critics and detractors of our imagineering culture. Everyone who is anyone these days is dropping their name—from Adbusters to Emigré magazines, from Greil Marcus to J. Abbott Miller. Debord's seminal book, *The Society of Spectacle*, is on the list of the trendy Zone Books, and MIT Press has recently published *The Situationist City*, a comprehensive investigation of the situationists' urbanist theories, written by Simon Sadler. Move over Paul Virillio. SI, as the Situationist International movement is now labeled, is the latest French intellectual import.

An underground movement that shunned the limelight—the members of this elusive group lived by the precepts they preached—SI's subversive ideology at first defies comprehension. Unless you understand the specific context of the period, many of their assertions make little sense today. Influenced by Lettrist International, a radical group of the 1950s that sought to revitalize urban life through the fusion of poetry and music, Debord and his colleague Raoul Vaneigem used Dada slogans to spread their message. "The more you consume, the less you live," and "Be realistic, demand the impossible," are two of the most memorable SI pronouncements.

Yet in spite of its so-called anarchist mentality, the SI methodology was precisely constructed. The name of the group was born out of the realization that participants had to create special conditions in their everyday life—special "situations"—in order to resist the insidious appeal of the pseudoneeds of increased consumption and to overcome the mounting sense of alienation that characterized the postmodern age. They conducted open-ended experiments that involved playful constructive behavior aimed at scrambling mental expectations. Most popular of these strategies was taking aimless strolls through a busy neighborhood, deliberately rearranging the furniture in their apartments to create as many obstacles as possible, systematically rejecting labor-saving devices and voluntarily disorienting themselves by consulting the map of

London when visiting Amsterdam. Called "drifting"—*dérive* in French—the technique was an effective way to "reclaim the night," to momentarily defy the white patriarchy of traditional space-time.

Like most rational people today, I too would find this approach naïve and dogmatic if I hadn't experienced it firsthand. In 1960, as a student at the Paris Beaux-Arts school of architecture, I was unwittingly part of an SI experiment. The very first day I showed up at the studio with a dozen other new recruits, the young instructor announced that we should reconvene at La Palette, a bistro across the street. At nine in the morning, the sidewalk had just been washed and the waiter was trundling the cast-iron tables out onto the boulevard. We each grabbed a wicker chair from a tall stack in a corner, picked our spot on the terrace, angled our seats to catch the morning sun, stretched our legs, yawned and ordered a round of black coffee.

"This is your first lesson in architecture," said the instructor, a gaunt young man in a black turtleneck—the trademark look of the avant-garde back then. "For the next three months, we will spend six hours a day sitting right here. I want you to learn about space-time—particularly how to use space in order to waste time. Unless you understand that, you'll never be good architects."

I now know that this is straightforward SI doctrine. Embracing Arthur Rimbaud's assertion that laziness is a refusal to compartmentalize time, situationists advocated "living without restrictions or dead time," and "never work—never risk dying of boredom." They wasted time deliberately, and playfully, as a guerrilla strategy against the sense of emptiness imposed by the relentless spectacle of consumption that was quickly subsuming French culture.

And so, for the first semester, we sat at the bistro from 9:00 A.M. to 2:00 P.M., five days a week. Except for mornings when we would drift through Paris, sketchbooks in hand, making detailed drawings of whatever caught our fancy—a stairway leading to the river bank, an abandoned gazebo in a park, the monumental gate of a hospital—you would find us huddled at the terrace of La Palette. This was in situ urban anthropology. I learned to observe how people choose the best spot to sit, how lovers fight, how couples brood, how friends compete, how everyone sits straighter when a pretty girl walks in, how people celebrate on payday—and how they scrutinize a menu when they are broke.

Sometimes we would get into conversations, sometimes we would draw, sometimes we would read, sometimes we would argue—and often we would simply daydream. As promised, the space-time equation became a reality, one rich in surprises and discoveries. We became familiar with the angles of the various streets, the movements of the sun, the sounds of the city, the rhythm of life around us. No two minutes were ever alike. As we sat there, absorbing what felt like vital information, we developed a perception of the human scale—a critical notion for architects. And then, almost reluctantly, after lunch, we drifted across the street to the studio where we worked late into the night to acquire the rudiments of the classical orders of architecture.

I never completed my architectural studies. Instead, I moved to the States and eventually became a magazine art director. During my career in design, I often used the *dérive* technique to avoid the pitfalls of linear thinking. Another situationist construct also came in handy. Called *détournement*, translated as "rerouting," it consists of transforming images by interpreting them to mean something of your own making. SI theorists liked to describe the method as "hijacking, misappropriation, corruption of preexisting aesthetic elements." I simply call it sticking words on top of images.

Rerouting images is the basic MO of graphic communication. The minute you put a caption under a photograph, place a headline next to a picture, create a collage, single out a pull-quote, or write cover lines, you subvert the significance of both word and image. I believe that most of the creative tensions between editors and art directors, or between clients and designers, evolve from a misunderstanding of how visual artifacts can be reconfigured into constructed situations.

Chris Dixon, art director of *Adbusters* magazine, the anticonsumerism publication that has wholeheartedly embraced the SI legacy, is probably one of the few North American designers to consciously use *détournement*. "Often the captions we use in the magazine are much more provocative than the images themselves," he says. "In fact, we deliberately use rather conventional photographs to let our readers know that we speak the same language they do." Even though its overall message is anticommercial and antiadvertising, *Adbusters* is surprisingly well designed, as if to mock the very aesthetic that drives the advertising community.

Where *Adbusters* and SI part ways is on the discourse they have chosen to promote similar ideas. "We link anticonsumerism to the environmental movement," explains Dixon. "Readers understand the correlation between buying too many useless products and depleting the natural resources of the planet." Concern for the environment never appears in the newspapers, journals, tracks, graffiti, or manifestoes left behind by the SI. They didn't have much of a social agenda, either. Their mandate was to resist the cultural imperialism that drains human beings of their *joie de vivre*, a very French concept, indeed. Boredom was their enemy; happiness was their goal. Another of their maxims was: "They are buying your happiness—steal it back."

The situationist idea of happiness is very different from the "hedonomics" of the buying experience, as defined by Michael J. Wolf in *The Entertainment Economy*. Whereas Americans equate feeling good with having "fun," the French in general, and the SI in particular, describe happiness as liberating—as being euphoric, mischievous, prankish. It's the feeling that swept over France during the first weeks of the May 1968 general strike when all Paris took to the streets in what was at first a festival more than a student revolt.

The situationists were responsible for initiating the construction of barricades in the streets of Paris that month. (Pull up some cobblestones, add a half-dozen trash cans, more cobblestones, some discarded lumber, maybe a broken bicycle. Borrow chairs from a café, sit and wait.) They also encouraged students to cover the walls of the city with Lettrist-inspired graffiti ("It is forbidden to forbid"). Last, but not least, they were credited with giving the rebellion its upbeat and high-spirited signature.

But the events of 1968—not only in France, but all over the world—were eventually "rerouted" by the establishment. As Thomas Frank, editor-in-chief of *The Baffler*, explains in his book, *The Conquest of Cool*, the anticonsumerism rebellion of the postwar era was "commodified" by Madison Avenue into what is now known as the

"Youth Culture"—one of the greatest marketing tools of the second part of the twentieth century. The Society of Spectacle was here to stay. Blaming themselves for their failure to change society, but also grieving for the millions of consumers who would only experience euphoria through shopping, Debord and his troops dispersed in 1972. Tragically unable to recapture the *joie de vivre* of the early days of SI, Debord took his own life in December 1994, soon after completing a documentary film on his work.

Five years after Debord's suicide, events would prove that the spirit he had championed still survived. On December 5, 1999, the front page of the *New York Times* featured a photograph that would have cheered him up. Taken by Jimi Lott of the *Seattle Times*, it showed Mr. and Mrs. Santa Claus being escorted home by four riot policemen wearing Ninja-turtle combat boots and padded breastplates. The violent protests against the World Trade Organization in Seattle had so disrupted holiday shopping, explained the caption, that the Yule pair had to be put under police protection.

As one flipped through the newspaper, one quickly realized that the former Saint Nicholas (a historical figure incidentally recast in 1931 by Coca-Cola as the beloved red-and-white icon we now identify with Christmas shopping) was not the only consumer icon that needed police protection. National Guard troops and riot paratroopers had been posted in front of all retail stores in downtown Seattle—guarding Starbucks, Banana Republic, Coach, Gap, and Gucci, just to name a few. The entrance of Niketown in particular looked like the set of *Star Wars*, with hooded figures in black armor standing at attention, their four-foot bludgeons poised to strike.

It looked like the police were confronting rowdy crowds not to protect civil liberties and political institutions—but to protect global brands. Though one didn't have to be a trend forecaster to feel that brand backlash was coming ("My wish for the New Year was to get through meetings without someone mentioning branding," joked Web-page editorial designer Jessica Helfand recently), most of us never expected it would be so sudden, so graphic, or so ready-for-prime-time television. "The revolution will not be televised," sang Gil Scott-Heron in 1974. Wishful thinking, indeed. The anticonsumerism, antibrand revolution, complete with demonstrators smashing store windows, was on the eleven o'clock news. Replays showing the same scenes over and over were aired every ten minutes, as if to "brand" the violent images in the mind of viewers.

Kalle Lasn, editor of *Adbusters* magazine in Vancouver, Canada and famous for advocating what he calls "culture jamming," was one of the few people who wasn't surprised by the Seattle uproar. In fact, the December 1999 issue of his magazine had an article predicting that the WTO conference would be "a historic confrontation between civil society and corporate rule." His book, *Culture Jam, The Uncooling of America*, had just been released. *Time* magazine had praised him for taking arms against our 3,000-marketing-message-a-day society. Still he wasn't prepared for what he saw when he went to Seattle to observe the riots.

"It was like a festival," he says. "Except for a few people confronting cops, demonstrators were laid-back, happy, having fun. There was a lot of street theater, spontaneous happenings, and cheerful pranks being played." It had a situationist ambiance, for sure. But then, unexpectedly, Lasn got his first whiff of tear gas. "I'll never forget that smell," he says. "Nor will I forget the savage look on the face of the policemen. They really didn't get it."

But who gets it? Why are the global brands a threat to our very existence—a threat so real it galvanized 30,000 protestors to take to the streets? "There were more than 100 different groups," tells Lasn. "Environmentalists, students, anarchists, but also musty old socialists, Christians tired of the violence on TV, critics of genetic engineering, and card-carrying union members—every single one of them worried about some unofficial global government body enforcing an elite corporate agenda."

During the WTO riots, the design community was in a state of complete denial. No one talked about what was happening in Seattle. Heck, we were still nursing our Las Vegas hangover following the "hedonomic" AIGA conference held two months earlier. There had been practically no references to the social or environmental responsibility of designers, let alone their role in "supporting, or implicitly endorsing, a mental environment so saturated with commercial messages that it is changing the very way citizen-consumers speak, think, feel, respond, and interact," to quote the language of "First Things First," the *Adbusters* manifesto signed by thirty-three prominent designers worldwide. In fact, when AIGA president Michael Bierut, in his closing statement in Las Vegas, had made a passing reference to this controversial call for moderation-in-marketing, some people in the audience had booed his comments.

But, as luck would have it, that same week—for the fifth anniversary of Debord's death—I had given my graphic-design students at the School of Visual Arts a series of *dérive* exercises directly inspired by my own SI experience and studies. First they had to draw a map of all their travel/wanderings/whereabouts in New York City during the last three months, plotting on paper their perception of time-space in the Big Apple. Their map, I told them, was supposed to be an "aid to reverie," a tool for "annexing their private space into the public sphere." Then, they had to explore and draw the Beaux-Arts colonnade at the Manhattan Bridge anchorage, with the idea that urbanism was in fact "the organization of silence."

No one really got it. But the discussions, laughter, confessions, and astute comments generated by my students as we reviewed their serendipitous maps and awkward sketches reaffirmed my faith in design and art education. As long as we encourage each other to observe, imagine, construct, and manufacture things—whether useful objects or useless situations—we will never become bored and depressed consumers. Let's not use design as an inducement to shop, but an inducement to *joie de vivre.*

First published in *Communication Arts*, March/April 2000.

First Things First:
A Second Look

Carolyn McCarron

The tear gas has dissipated, the shattered glass has been swept, and Seattle's chief of police has resigned. Yet, the concerns of peaceful protesters at the World Trade Organization (WTO) meeting in Seattle are still resonating, not only throughout business and commerce but in advertising and design as well. As businesses and the WTO are being lobbied to open their doors to the public and make information on trade accessible, the advertising and design professions are being urged to accept more social responsibility in promoting corporations via visual communications.

Despite unprecedented economic growth and low unemployment rates, citizens are becoming concerned about the increasing size and power of international corporations. Pulitzer Prize–winning journalist Haynes Johnson, who has written several books about American culture and politics, states: "This ought to be, objectively, the best time for Americans in history. But not everyone is sharing in the bounty, and many are uneasy about a general loss of trust in institutions."[1]

With this concern in mind, *Adbusters*, the antiadvertising magazine published by the Adbusters Media Foundation in Canada, issued a direct challenge to the international design community by publishing *First Things First 2000* and recruiting thirty-three world-renowned designers to sign the manifesto.

The entire issue of *Adbusters* (No. 27, Autumn 1999) was written and designed around *First Things First*, which advocates for a "reversal of priorities" from branding and commercial product promotion to "more useful, lasting, and democratic forms of communication." The publication opens with Nike's infamous swoosh juxtaposed with the question, "Isn't this what design is all about?," highlighting an issue that Tibor Kalman, founder of New York design studio M&Co., raised shortly before he died last year. "Isn't that what most design is about—making something different from what it truly is?" he asked. "That's the point at which I begin to worry about what we designers, who are very skillful and have powerful tools at our disposal, are doing in the world—what role we are playing—making the filthy oil company look 'clean,' making the car brochure higher-quality than the car, making the spaghetti sauce look like it's been put up by grandma, making the junky condo look hip. Is all that okay or just the level to which design and many other professions have sunk?"[2] In his career, Mr. Kalman used M&Co. as a platform to promote various sociopolitical issues and urged his design colleagues to take more responsibility for their work's impact on their surrounding culture.

To reach an international audience, the authors of *First Things First 2000* convinced six additional publications worldwide to publish the manifesto: *Emigré* and the American Institute of Graphic Arts (AIGA) Journal in the United States; *Blueprint* and *Eye* in London, United Kingdom; *Items* in Amsterdam, the Netherlands; and *Form* in Frankfurt, Germany.

A History of First Things First

Just as the protests on the streets of Seattle bring back memories of the 1960s, the language of *First Things First 2000* revives the spirit of dissension that is the hallmark of that time. In fact, the language is from the sixties. The wording was adopted from a manifesto also titled *First Things First*, written in 1964 by British designer and educator Ken Garland. As he wrote of the sixties twenty years later: "Manifestos were in, okay? It was, after all, a time to conjure up a cause, be self-righteous, take a stand."[3]

Alongside the political and cultural revolutions taking place around the world during the sixties, the Creative Revolution was taking place within the advertising industry in New York and London. Bill Bernbach, founder of Doyle Dane Bernbach (DDB), was one of the instigators of this new direction—exemplified in his early work for Volkswagen—in which visual execution played a critical role in creating a successful campaign. Many artists, inspired by Bernbach and other up-and-coming successful advertising creatives, began to join the glamorous world of advertising, which was also becoming a well-paid line of work. Garland confirms, "Far more money was being hurled at the 'creative' side of the advertising biz. Almost overnight the agencies had twigged that graphic design was a good thing after all and had begun to offer all manner of temptations to talented, young hopefuls. Was this flattering attention itself a good thing or bad thing? The sixties had become the scene of such a hectic, exuberant, optimistic, burgeoning economy that it seemed ungenerous and churlish to question the priorities involved in spending several kings' ransoms on the marketing and promotion of so many superfluous products . . . However, I did."[4] Thus, the original *First Things First* manifesto was born.

Garland wrote *First Things First* in December 1963 while listening to speakers at a meeting of the Society of Industrial Arts (SIA) persuade potential members to join their professional organization. "I was, I thought, composing an argument against joining a society that was myopic and misdirected," he states. His insult to the SIA, however, turned out to be a statement of what Garland thought the profession should become. At the end of the meeting, he read it to the audience. He remembers: "As I warmed to the task, I found I wasn't so much reading it as declaiming it; it had become, we all realized simultaneously, that totally unfashionable device, a manifesto. Towards the end it seemed to have acquired the ringing, rhetorical pitch of the pre-Agincourt pep talk from Henry the Fifth."[5]

Nevertheless, the audience cheered. Twenty-two people signed it that night. Many periodicals reproduced and debated it, and it was translated into other languages and distributed throughout Europe. Garland was even invited to a television news program to discuss *First Things First*.

Garland's manifesto was reprinted in *Adbusters* in 1998. According to Chris Dixon, *Adbusters*'s art director, the idea to "update" the 1964 manifesto and collect new signatures of contemporary designers was born when he and Kalle Lasn, founder and editor of *Adbusters*, met Tibor Kalman in 1998 at AIGA's branding conference in New York. After glancing over a publication the pair had brought to show him (which contained the 1964 manifesto), Mr. Kalman suggested that perhaps the time was right to relaunch *First Things First*.

Joined by Rick Poynor, a design critic and former editor of *Eye* magazine, they redrafted the original manifesto, bringing the language "up-to-date while trying to retain the original spirit."[6] After being contacted by Poynor, Garland gave his approval to the revival of his thirty-five-year-old treatise. After drafting the 2000 version, Dixon, Poynor, and the current editor of *Eye* magazine, Nick Bell, began approaching designers to endorse the manifesto. In an interview, Poynor confirms: "*Adbusters* approached roughly half the names on the list. I approached most of the others. We contacted people we thought would be sympathetic. Even so, some said no."

When asked why not just publish the manifesto and allow an open signing as Garland did that December evening in 1963, Poynor answers: "The names were a way of helping to get the manifesto noticed in the countries where it was published—in America, Britain, and the Netherlands. An anonymous text is unlikely to have generated the same degree of attention. This is an issue of personal conviction, and it was important for readers to see the names of real people who believe these things. Also, the manifesto was published in the spirit of the original, and the original had named supporters, including Ken Garland."

While he did not help write the recent manifesto, Garland remains a signatory. He writes, "Looking back now, the *First Things First* manifesto I published in 1964 and cosigned with twenty-one other designers and photographers reads a little self-righteously, but I still stand by every single word of it, and I still say our priorities are completely crazy. Whether earnest manifestos are the way to tackle the problem is quite another matter; *First Things First* doesn't appear to have had much effect in spite of the stir it caused at the time, does it? . . . Ah no, it didn't get us very far, I admit. Not only are we no nearer our objectives today than we were in 1964, but we have actually moved backwards."[7]

Poynor echoed this sentiment, saying, "It was important to *Adbusters* and some of the signatories to reaffirm the continuing relevance of the original and the fact that its challenge has never been adequately addressed. If anything, the situation is much more serious now. We took strength from connecting the new manifesto to an explicit tradition of dissent."

A New Generation of Designers

Continuing in the spirit of dissent from the sixties, the publishers, while targeting a broad, international design audience, took extra care to reach design students by sending posters of the manifesto to design schools around the world. Coincidentally, many of the signatories are educators. Lasn confirms, "It's time to give students a new perspective on what they are doing. If we can communicate some of the excitement of working on something that actually means something beyond just marketing another product, if we can communicate that to the next generation of designers, then I think the whole industry will heave. Once the teachers and students in the design schools realize that, then they will change the world. That's how revolutions begin."[8]

Poynor supports this position: "Attitudes can change dramatically from one generation to the next. *Adbusters*'s initiative stands the most chance, perhaps, of influencing young designers. . . . I hope the manifesto will be used as a discussion point in design schools."

Poynor invited Kalle Lasn and Chris Dixon to speak at the Royal College of Art in 1999, where Dixon presented an early draft of the manifesto and a lively debate ensued. On the other side of the Atlantic, at schools such as the University of North Carolina and the California Institute of Arts, students are debating the issues and are even developing class projects around the manifesto. Some of these projects will be published in a future issue of *Adbusters*.

Culture Jamming with Adbusters

The *First Things First 2000* manifesto is merely one component of a larger campaign by *Adbusters* against the culture of consumerism and capitalism. *Adbusters* uses the tactics of advertising itself to create "uncommercials" and spoof ads. In addition to publishing its quarterly magazine that features these parodies, it promotes its cause by creating and advertising events such as "Buy Nothing Day," in which *Adbusters*'s staff and other advocates stood outside department stores on Black Friday, November 28, and advocated for shoppers to "go home." In an effort to recruit advocates to travel to Seattle and protest against the WTO meeting, *Adbusters* launched an extensive international campaign titled "The Big Question" that included print ads, billboards, radio ads, and television spots that aired on CNN. (The "Big Question" was "Is Economic 'Progress' Killing the Planet?")

Adbusters also posted a billboard in Las Vegas, timed to coincide with the annual AIGA design conference. Designed by Jonathan Barnbrook, the billboard featured a quote by Tibor Kalman: "Designers . . . Stay away from corporations that want you to lie for them."

A description of Lasn's book *Culture Jam: The Uncooling of America* reads, "The brands, products, fashions, and entertainments—the spectacles that surround the production of culture—are our culture now. Only by 'uncooling' these icons and symbols, by organizing resistance against the power trust that manages the brands, can America reassert itself." Enter designers and advertisers into Lasn's crusade. Who better to "uncool" the brands they create via design?

A Wide-Reaching Reaction

First Things First 2000 struck a chord among students and practicing designers alike in the United States, Canada, and Europe. To the surprise of some of the signatories, letters have been pouring in to the editors of all seven magazines. Some are passionately in favor of the manifesto and others are scathingly against it, calling it everything from "elitist" to "crap."

A small group of designers in England even went so far as to write a manifesto against all future manifestos in the field, titled *A Call to Arms Against Future Retro-Manifestos From the Disillusioned.*[9] They write, "Design is encased in capitalism, and even though there are many brownie points to be won for the individual through the creation of coffee-table books, high-brow exhibitions, and niche magazines, this link will persist." They remind us that ultimately, not much will be changed by the creative industry turning its back on advertising: "The omnipresence of design is not due to its inherent potential but rather lent it by the powerful machinations of advertising and marketing. The definition of design will never be changed by individuals turning away from the discipline but rather by the choices and negotiations they enter into when creating commercial art. It is our belief that only by injecting milligrams of what we hold at heart into the very mainstream of popular culture is there any real hope of changing it into something else."

Nancy Skolos, an educator at Rhode Island School of Design and a design principal of Skolos/Wedell, believes in including advertising and business courses in design programs so that designers can start assuming a greater leadership role in commerce: "I don't think we can change the world just by deciding that we're not going to design ads anymore. It's a mistake that design schools don't teach advertising, because maybe if we understood it better, we could participate in a more constructive way. The only way to have an effect is to somehow be part of the system rather than to say it's not working and we're not going to participate."

Some advertising creatives took offense at *First Things First 2000.* Stavros Cosmopulos, one of the founding partners of Hill, Holliday, Connors, Cosmopulos, Inc. in Boston, feels that his work contributes to the health of the American economy. In an interview, he stated, "Advertising is an essential element of commerce. Many people hate advertising because it's everywhere. Yet for many retailers, if they don't run an ad, there's no business that weekend. Besides, how would you restrict advertising? You could put whole companies, whole industries, whole towns out of business." He comments on *Adbusters*'s campaign strategy: "*Adbusters* wants to stop advertising, yet they're using advertising to announce their particular perspective and make fun of advertising. But advertising is strong enough to be ridiculed. Advertising will survive because it's an important element of our society."

John Calvelli, director of the department of graphic design at the Museum of Modern Art in New York, posted the manifesto for his staff. He acknowledges, however, that even in less commercial projects it is not always possible to ignore advertising and marketing: "I think the poster-size copy I made is a good reminder for the designers here of why some of them might have chosen to work here. However, I must also say that our work for the museum is hardly untouched by the need to use effective marketing tools, advertising, and business strategy to help achieve the museum's objectives."

Aside from economic issues and democratic rights, some responses are questioning the historical basis of the *First Things First 2000* manifesto. The group in England that issued the antimanifesto writes: "Back in 1964 when the original *First*

Things First manifesto was launched, the argument that the public was being fooled by the relatively new mass media of advertising had some merit. To make the same argument today implies a sadly low opinion of the public's intelligence and inflates the influence of designers by mystifying their power to beguile. Far from duping the public, the advertising industry is now paranoid about being ignored by media-savvy consumers."

Others question how updating a historical document reflects on the profession itself. Loretta Staples, a professor at University of Michigan's School of Art & Design, wrote to *Adbusters*: "Despite the earnest, well-intentioned renewal of the manifesto—an attempt to kick-start design in the new millennium—I remain skeptical. The redeclaration itself signifies how little design's self-image has changed." Staples also questioned the maturity of both the manifesto and ultimately the profession: "A significant portion of the design profession continues to prove, year-in and year-out, its apparent inability to engage in complex critical topics—an inability displayed in the lack of self-critique that characterizes the very profession and all its official organs. . . . For all the talk about design's ubiquitous power, design professionals remain strikingly uninformed and self-absorbed."[10]

DK Holland, a partner at the Pushpin Group and the editor of this column, agrees that the manifesto's position lacks maturity: "Branding bad; design good. This anti-marketing message is a very simplistic representation of a very complex subject, not a well-constructed thesis. For instance, this manifesto states that 'the profession's time and energy have been used up manufacturing demand for things that are inessential at best.' We need soap, toothpaste, detergent. We need choice. Branding is not the bad guy here, greed is."

Michael Bierut, a partner at Pentagram, adds, "I like that *First Things First 2000* encourages designers to think about why they do what they do. I dislike that it implies an artificial scale of clients from worthy to unworthy. Can't every one of our projects get our very best efforts? Don't purchasers of dog biscuits deserve wit, intelligence, and ingenuity in their lives?"

The Signatories

Holland wonders, "Did the designers ever get together and talk about the manifesto before they signed it? The flaws in the manifesto fly out at you when you start to analyze it. A very sharp editing pencil would have made a big difference to its credibility."

Conceding that there was no organized forum in which the signatories debated the issues before signing, some of them acknowledged the flaws in *First Things First 2000*.

Erik Spiekermann, founder of MetaDesign, comments, "I did write my reservations down, but I don't think they ever got published. I think the manifesto is a little bit naïve, because the world isn't as simple as that anymore. It's not a question of people like us refusing to work for 'evil advertising,' then everything will be better. There's another question here, the question of what we do with the people who look to us, the people who work with us, and how we provide them with a decent environment and make a living. But it's time we said some of this." He warns that there is not enough noncommercial work to go around: "We employ 250 people at Meta-Design worldwide. More than half of our work would fit into that category of not exactly advancing mankind. But we have to bring in the money to provide a paycheck and decent work environment for staff. If we only did those sort of jobs [noncommercial work], I wouldn't employ 250 people. I would employ maybe 10 people."

Sheila Levrant de Bretteville, professor and director of studies in graphic design at Yale University School of Art, adds her concerns: "I believe in a 'bottom-up' way of things happening. The 'top-down' way does not feel good to me, because it feels like this group of people is telling other people they should be doing something. And that's part of what's problematic about manifestos. They have a big 'should' about them. It feels authoritarian, which runs counter to the essential spirit of asking questions."

Despite their concerns over the flaws in the manifesto, signatories who were interviewed had the same objectives in signing it—to launch a long-overdue debate about ethics in design practice and to encourage new directions in the fields of graphic design and advertising.

De Bretteville states that she signed in the spirit of initiating the call to answer unmet needs in society that today's designers are no longer answering. "I heard in the manifesto an asking of people to think again about what they want to use their energy for, and that's what I got caught on. . . . The manifesto came at a time when it's almost a wake-up call. That's what I responded to, because there hasn't been a lot of political activity where people are paying attention to the [needs and problems] of society. What issues are not being addressed? What needs could design meet that haven't been met?"

Steven Heller, the art director of the *New York Times Book Review* and chairman of the School of Visual Arts's graduate design program, considers himself a supporter of the document even though he doesn't agree with every point: "There has been little discussed about the responsibility of designers to society, culture, and the world. Signing the manifesto didn't necessarily mean that I agreed with every point, but I agreed in principle that we, as designers, should be addressing these issues. This is not something that I feel one needs to take sides on. It's a piece of material that one can ponder on and debate over, and whether you come out on one side or the other, as far as I'm concerned, is not as important as the conversation that arises. So, my point of view is really that of a supporter, and one who wants to see the debate continue." He reminds us to consider the nature of manifestos. "All manifestos tend to be idealistic tracts. They tend to be things that are meant to incite and provoke, and they are not rational in presentation."

William Drenttel, a partner in the design consultancy Jessica Helfand/William Drenttel, echoes Heller's statement. "The manifesto, by definition, is about an idea," he says. "This is not some program where we can say these are ten things you shouldn't do as a designer. I don't think anyone signed it as some 'high-falutin' statement." For Mr. Drenttel, the question is not about the elimination of advertising but rather the degree to which it affects our culture. He acknowledges, "We live in a commercial world. Advertising is communication. It's unrealistic to think there will be no advertising. I think there should be limits, though. I'm opposed to there being so much marketing and advertising and design in every aspect of our life. The cumulative effect of that is you have stuff in your face all the time, and I think it's terrible. I don't think it treats people with respect." He asserts why he signed the manifesto: "I thought that the manifesto accurately raised the issue that, in fact, there is an awful lot of marketing and design and promotion that I don't know that any of us need."

Jessica Helfand states, "It is not only possible but imperative that designers start advising their clients when they're wrong and suggest changes, adjustments, and improvements—even ones that don't initially have to do with design." She challenges practicing designers to consider this question in their work: "How can you reconsider the roles and responsibilities of designers in light of the technological, cultural, and economic parameters of the way the world is working now?"

Jeffery Keedy, an educator at the California Institute of Arts, signed the manifesto to initiate a discussion about ethics, as he is concerned with the overall image the design profession projects. "I am concerned with a broader notion of values of the whole design field and how those come across; what the collective mentality is and how designers represent themselves. In my experience, commercial values have become more important to design practice, and of course that's concurrent with the economy being so good. As a teacher, I've noticed that students seem to be more plugged in to the commercial realities and are comfortable with the whole commercialized aspect of design practice. I think, 'What are the shared values of the profession, of this group of people who do graphic design?' It seems in the past decade that more and more of it is influenced by commercial aspects more than cultural aspects. So that's why I signed on to this—because I had been noticing that things seem to be getting very commercial."

Andrew Blauvelt, the design director at the Walker Art Center in Minneapolis, feels that the issue is bigger than ethical issues in design practice. "For me, it's not so much about specific moral issues in design ('Should I design for tobacco merchants?') as it is about the transformations in the larger world of communications and the rights of consumer-citizens. ('What happens to our ideas of privacy and public life when companies can track all of our preferences online or when our cities are reduced to gigantic corporate messages?') Of course, these are larger than design. However, design is central to how much of this debate will be played out in the future."

Milton Glaser, founder of Milton Glaser, Inc., strives to alter the status quo by raising a greater awareness of social issues and the fact that the practice of design has consequences that go beyond selling goods. "Design has a social role; it has an effect on people, and people in this practice should think seriously of the ideas that they are transmitting to others." He reminds us, "The reconciliation of the spiritual and the material is one of the great problems of life. It is a constant ethical dilemma: How do you do what you think is right and still put bread on the table? Every once in a while things get worse, where the overriding materialism of a moment produces terrible effects on people. So the problem is, what can you do? How can things change?" He asserts, "I'm very suspicious of all those who have easy formulas, who say you must do this, you must do that, because I don't think that's where answers reside. I think the first thing that happens is the consciousness of what it is that you are doing to maintain an existing condition."

The last word goes to *Emigré* editor Rudy VanderLans. He writes, "The manifesto's aim is not to hold designers culpable for the world's social and economic problems. On the contrary, it sees designers as having real potential to help cure its ills and make this world a better place. . . . You can ridicule the language of the manifesto or make yourself feel better by saying that design and advertising have limited powers and shift the responsibility to your marketing departments, or you can dismiss the whole effort simply as a cheap way for [magazines] to get some attention. But those tactics, it seems to me, evade the question at the heart of the manifesto: 'What are you doing, in your professional life, to make this world a better place for all?' Obviously, there are no simple answers. True, the manifesto only suggests in broad, ambiguous terms what can be done to put our talents to better use. But much can be done, there is ample room for improvement, and it's up to each of us to figure out how to best accomplish this."

Organizing the Debate

Both signatories and nonsignatories alike want to debate the issues *First Things First 2000* raises. Poynor challenges, "What would be interesting would be to engage the issues raised by *First Things First 2000*. What are the political, economic, and cultural realities? How does *First Things First 2000* relate to the emergence of a new protest movement against the dominance and values of global capitalism, as we saw so clearly in Seattle?"

Although *First Things First 2000* targets creative professionals in both the advertising and design fields, it is graphic designers and design educators who are advocating this debate—not professionals from advertising or marketing. Perhaps this is because the manifesto was printed only in design journals and not advertising or marketing publications.

Despite the interest in this debate among graphic design professionals, the commercial environment and the billboard promoting *First Things First 2000* at the AIGA design conference in Las Vegas did not generate discussion. Véronique Vienne wrote in a recent article, "No one talked about what was happening in Seattle. . . . There had been practically no references to the social or environmental responsibility of designers."[11] Michael Bierut, president of the AIGA, adds, "I was expecting more of an anticommercialism backlash at the conference, provoked by the excess of Vegas. It didn't materialize to the extent I secretly hoped."

While the *First Things First 2000* billboard was designed in the spirit and voice of Tibor Kalman and, in doing so, reflects a desire to carry on his memory and life's work, it is key to keep the debate focused. Without this focus, the manifesto will not effect any more change than it did in the sixties. DK Holland reminds us, "Tibor was a brilliant agitator. He loved to stir up trouble, get people thinking. But it was not his style to focus the debate. That was left to someone else. And, if no one takes on that role with the manifesto, then chaos is sure to continue to breed more chaos." If the graphic-design profession is to have this debate—and if *First Things First 2000* is to have any long-term effect—the debate must be an organized and informed one.

It is logical, therefore, to have this discussion in an organized forum, hosted by a national, professional organization. At the time this article went to press, the New

York chapter of the AIGA had plans for such a moderated debate in early April.

Along with organizing the debate *First Things First 2000* raises, designers should be aware of the economic, political, cultural, and social issues that affect advertising and design. This fundamental knowledge enables constructive debate. To promote understanding of these issues, the debate arena should be expanded to include representatives from advertising, marketing, business, cultural, and social institutions. Opening the forum to other professions ensures that alternative perspectives are heard and the debate does not become exclusive and partisan.

Even with the organization and expansion of this debate, an unanswered question remains: To what end? While debate is healthy and may be—as the signatories put it—"long overdue," the *First Things First 2000* manifesto and the subsequent debate will not "revolutionize" or "heave" the profession, as Kalle Lasn hopes. Criticizing and parodying advertising and marketing tactics is easy; implementing the ideas of *First Things First 2000* and affecting social change is not. At best, the debate may inform creative professionals of various economic and cultural issues and raise an individual's awareness of ethical and social issues in advertising and graphic design. Yet, maybe this is where change begins.

At the end of our interview, Bierut hinted, "Wouldn't our next [national] conference in Washington, DC be a good place to continue this debate?"

Notes:

1. David Postman, et al., "Why the WTO United So Many Foes," the *Seattle Times* (December 6, 1999), A1.

2. Allen Casey, "Tibor Kalman: An Interview by Allan Casey," *Adbusters*, No. 23 (Autumn 1998): 25.

3. Ken Garland, *A Word in Your Eye* (Reading, England: University of Reading, 1996).

4. Ken Garland, *Some Thoughts*, brochure, 1982.

5. Ken Garland, *A Word in Your Eye*, 1996.

6. Chris Dixon, *Adbusters*, No. 27 (Autumn 1999): 53.

7. Ken Garland, *Some Thoughts*.

8. "An Interview with *Adbusters*'s editor Kalle Lasn," *Emigré*, no. 49 (Winter 1999): 16.

9. Even Westvang; Medienoperatoere, Oslo; Tom Elsner & Hilla Neske, Artificial Environments, London, "The Readers Reply to First Things First Manifesto 2000," *Emigré*, No. 52 (Fall 1999): 3.

10. *www.adbusters.org*

11. Véronique Vienne, "Confessions of a Closet Situationist," *Communication Arts* (March/April 2000).

First published in *Communication Arts*, May/June 2000.

We, the undersigned, are graphic designers, art directors, and visual communicators who have been raised in a world in which the techniques and apparatus of advertising have persistently been presented to us as the most lucrative, effective, and desirable use of our talents. Many design teachers and mentors promote this belief; the market rewards it; a tide of books and publications reinforces it.

Encouraged in this direction, designers then apply their skill and imagination to sell dog biscuits, designer coffee, diamonds, detergents, hair gel, cigarettes, credit cards, sneakers, butt toners, light beer, and heavy-duty recreational vehicles. Commercial work has always paid the bills, but many graphic designers have now let it become, in large measure, what graphic designers do. This, in turn, is how the world perceives design. The profession's time and energy is used up manufacturing demand for things that are inessential at best.

Many of us have grown increasingly uncomfortable with this view of design. Designers who devote their efforts primarily to advertising, marketing, and brand development are supporting, and implicitly endorsing, a mental environment so saturated with commercial messages that it is changing the very way citizen-consumers speak, think, feel, respond, and interact. To some extent we are all helping draft a reductive and immeasurably harmful code of public discourse.

There are pursuits more worthy of our problem-solving skills. Unprecedented environmental, social, and cultural crises demand our attention. Many cultural interventions, social marketing campaigns, books, magazines, exhibitions, educational tools, television programs, films, charitable causes, and other information design projects urgently require our expertise and help.

We propose a reversal of priorities in favor of more useful, lasting, and democratic forms of communication—a mindshift away from product marketing and toward the exploration and production of a new kind of meaning. The scope of debate is shrinking; it must expand. Consumerism is running uncontested; it must be challenged by other perspectives expressed, in part, through the visual languages and resources of design.

In 1964, twenty-two visual communicators signed the original call for our skills to be put to worthwhile use. With the explosive growth of global commercial culture, their message has only grown more urgent. Today, we renew their manifesto in expectation that no more decades will pass before it is taken to heart.

Jonathan Barnbrook
Nick Bell
Andrew Blauvelt
Hans Bockting
Irma Boom
Sheila Levrant de Bretteville
Max Bruinsma
Siân Cook
Linda van Deursen

Chris Dixon
William Drenttel
Gert Dumbar
Simon Esterson
Vince Frost
Ken Garland
Milton Glaser
Jessica Helfand
Steven Heller
Andrew Howard
Tibor Kalman
Jeffery Keedy
Zuzana Licko
Ellen Lupton
Katherine McCoy
Armand Mevis
J. Abbott Miller
Rick Poynor
Lucienne Roberts
Erik Spiekermann
Jan van Toorn
Teal Triggs
Rudy VanderLans
Bob Wilkinson

For more information on the *First Things First Manifesto 2000*, go to *www.adbusters.org*.

Step One: Put Money
Where Mouth Is

David Sterling

Talk's cheap. Never have those words rung so true as in the
recently exhumed *First Things First Manifesto 2000*—a call-to-arms for designers to
stop pandering to greedy corporations, take the world by the axis, and steer it toward a
brighter tomorrow. The manifesto was signed by a handful of design "celebrities," pre-
sumably to alert the rest of us to the import of its message.

Graphic design is a process, but it is also a tool. You can use it to provide important information, to give directions, or to sell widgets. What graphic design is not,
however—which the FTF does not admit—is UNICEF (The United Nations Children's
Fund), the Red Cross, or the Peace Corps.

But, hey, it's a job—usually a fun one. And graphic design can help the world:
When we're providing information, we are hopefully enlightening others; when we are
providing directions, we are helping people find their way through the world; and even
when we're selling widgets, we're boosting the economy and providing jobs.
Furthermore, when created with the right heart, graphic design can have a powerful
social impact.

Still, why do we feel a need to make graphic design more important than it is? It's
a job. Perhaps every profession wrestles with ego issues, but it seems a particularly
exhausting struggle in our case. Let's face it: Graphic design as we know it is tightly
interwoven with free enterprise. You might say the two even grew up together. Most of
us work on a daily basis to help our clients sell stuff, whether it's something as earthly
as widgets or as heavenly as tickets to a church social. And even when we're designing
information or way-finding projects, we are still tied closely to our clients who, after
all, are paying us. To try to purify our work of the smell of money is both hypocritical
and in vain.

We are hypocritical in other ways, too, particularly about our profession's profound narcissism, which Freud would tell you is the flip side of idol worship. For one
thing, if we wanted to "help the world," we'd probably already be doing it. After all, the
ideas in FTF are nothing new. They've been around for at least forty years, and yet
we're still talking about them. For another, you have to admit that helping the world

just isn't very, well, sexy. But apparently—judging from the buzz it has created—circulating manifestos signed by leading stars in the design firmament is, and attending FTF roundtables featuring prominent names announced in edgy posters by hip designers is. If we get close enough to these stars, some of the magic dust from them just might rub off on us. And we won't really have to do anything. Ask yourself this question: If you were at a national design conference where Stefan Sagmeister was speaking in the same time slot as Sue Crolick—which would you attend?

What? You say you never heard of Sue Crolick? My point exactly. She just isn't box office. But her mentoring projects in Minneapolis have had a profound impact on the lives of hundreds of local youth over the past several years.

People, the problem is us. The design media feature too much about trends and not enough about work of real social substance; our professional conferences give too much air time to the same name-brand designers (over and over again) and not enough to content beyond the merely formalistic. And—worst of all—we designers, the audience for the magazines and the conferences, support the system with our dollars. In this tail-chase of idolatry and narcissism, we pay dearly to be close to the stardust in the hopes that one day it will work its magic on us, and we, too, might be—important. And popular. We invest so much of ourselves in aggrandizing our profession and its more colorful practitioners because they represent idealized visions of ourselves. The danger is that, like Narcissus, we become enchanted by our own reflection. We're not slaves to corporations, as the late Tibor Kalman once suggested. We're slaves to the stars, one of which Kalman succeeded brilliantly in fashioning himself into. No, if you want to change the world, come down to earth. You have to roll up your sleeves, pick up a shovel and dig in. Caution: You might get dirty. And very, very tired, as Crolick will tell you.

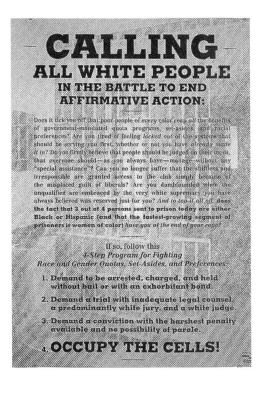

Perhaps the most glaring shortcoming about the *First Things First Manifesto* is that its very position assumes there are no designers working to help improve our lot. But then, I suppose such an assumption is like a ridiculously unbelievable plot point in a B-movie: If you take it away, there wouldn't be a story.

The good news is that there are people down here on earth who are already doing what *First Things First* urges us to do from on high. Plenty of them. Sue Crolick is one. These are the doers, as distinguished from the commentators (Kalman) and the critics (FTF). They are using their talents to strengthen community, to help survivors of disaster, and to share with children from marginal neighborhoods the healing power of creativity.

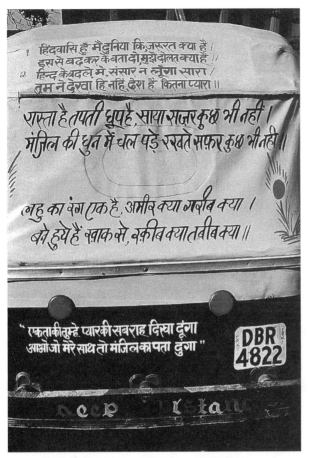

And yet, you probably haven't heard of most of them.

This, then, is your chance to meet a dozen inspiring people who are proving that the creative professions can make a difference. Most are graphic artists; some are from other creative fields. And although their work may not wind up in an annual or at the next design powwow, its sheer human content makes it very, very sexy. Most important, instead of signing a credo that is eerily symptomatic of that enchanting reflection, each of these people is putting their money where their mouth is.

David Thorne

Graphic designer, activist, and founding member of Resistant Strains, Thorne believes that art and design have a political responsibility to the public. He has organized and produced poster projects and public art works protesting economic inequalities, showing solidarity with the Zapatistas in Mexico, and most recently with the Maximum Security Democracy Project, which addresses the inequalities and injustices of the U.S. prison system. After printing, the posters are distributed to various activist groups and educational organizations and disseminated to the public.

Wendy Brawer

Graphic designer, biker, and environmental activist, Wendy Brawer is in the forefront of the environmental design movement. She developed the innovative Green Map system, which allows communities to take stock of and easily locate environmental resources and activities in their areas through an internationally recognized system of symbols. She is also an active member of O2, a global collective of designers interested in ecological concerns, which makes particular effort to use mechanisms of new technology such as the Web to disseminate information and coordinate their activities.

Tim Rollins/Kids of Survival

Artist Tim Rollins has had a long history of combining his craft with activism. In the 1980s, he was cofounder of Group Material, a political artists' collective active in the downtown arts scene. A few years later, while a special-education teacher in the

South Bronx, he formed his Kids of Survival. KOS seeks to harness the power of art to help kids from the most disadvantaged communities learn about their history, the systems of oppression that they experience on a daily basis, and how art can help them overcome these barriers. His collaborative projects with kids result in powerful art on such topics as Malcolm X and Martin Luther King, Jr. Rollins was also a participant in the many healing workshops for survivors that took place after the bombing in Oklahoma City. Since 1991, he has been working to found an institute of fine art in the South Bronx that would provide free schooling for artistically gifted high school students from the local community.

Sue Crolick/Creatives for Causes

Sue Crolick had a full career in advertising and design when a year of health problems forced her to slow down and reexamine her priorities. The result of this redirection was Creatives for Causes, a community-outreach program founded by Crolick in order to provide a much-needed resource for children in her area. The organization runs a program called "Art Buddies," which brings at-risk children from various after-school programs together with adult mentors. The pairs create portraits of themselves and explore various occupations to stimulate the children's imagination and belief in their own potential.

Ram Rahman/Sahmat

Yale-educated graphic designer Rahman is one of a group of some 4,000 artists, architects, and designers who form Sahmat, a political-activist group in India. Sahmat stages projects primarily to counter the intolerance and bigotry of the country's powerful, often violent, religious right. For one project, Rahman created posters and portable exhibits to protest a well-publicized Muslim bombing of a Hindu temple. Other productions of Sahmat have included everything from staging vast carnivals and performance pieces that condemn the religious right, to having protest poetry handwritten on thousands of the pedicabs that clog New Delhi streets.

Alfredo Jaar

Chilean-born artist Alfredo Jaar is a conceptual artist of wide international acclaim. Formerly an architect, his projects deal in direct graphic terms with issues of human rights and freedom. Now living in New York and working all over the world, Jaar often uses photography as a starting point for visual content but then constructs an extremely layered temporal and spatial experience for the full impact of the works' meaning. Projects include those surrounding the Rwanda crisis, political dictatorship, oppression, sociopolitical issues of first- and third-world countries, and, most of all, the surviving human spirit.

Bob Blackburn

African-American printmaker and artist Bob Blackburn started his nonprofit printmaking workshop in 1948. The studio is a community-based artist workshop where anyone is welcome and an atmosphere of support and community is encouraged. Of central importance to Blackburn is to make the tools of art accessible for any-

one who wants to use them and to create cross-cultural dialogue in an open and nurturing environment. Efforts are made to accommodate lower-income artists. He also has initiated an outreach project with third graders from New York's public schools, in which children create prints about poems they have written. His model of a community-based, nonprofit printmaking workshop has been the inspiration of a similar workshop begun in Namibia by a former student.

Judith Baca

Graphic muralist and activist Judith Baca has been creating murals in the urban landscape of Los Angeles for over twenty-five years. She organized her first mural project in predominantly Latino Eastern Los Angeles to help young people from warring gangs find a way to work together toward a collective positive goal. In 1974, she founded the Citywide Mural Project, which provided a means for a number of artists to produce murals in their communities, and then two years later she founded SPARC (Social and Public Art Resource Center), a multiethnic community-arts center that creates public art for the community. SPARC's ongoing youth workshops consist of having middle-school students conceptualize public banner projects addressing various social problems.

Jim Hubbard

Photographer Jim Hubbard has called himself an "advocacy journalist" and an "issue artist." Based in Minneapolis, his work is centered on documenting social issues. In the 1980s, he started photographing the homeless, portraying with humanity and compassion people and communities that national groups were trying their best to ignore. In 1989, he started the Shooting Back Education and Media Center in

Washington, DC to teach skills such as photography, writing, and media literacy to homeless and at-risk children. Nine years ago, Hubbard started the Native American Youth Project, emulating his DC model in Minneapolis. He is the author of *Shooting Back from the Reservation: A Photographic View of Life by Native American Youth* and *Lives Turned Upside Down: Homeless Children in Their Own Words and Photographs.*

REPO History

REPO History was formed in the late 1980s by a group of artists, educators, and writers who were interested in making public art projects based on the relationship of history to society and culture. Using the actual urban space as their canvas, their work aims to "reread" and "remap" spaces with an attention to issues of race, class, and sexuality. The first project in 1992 explored the history of Columbus's discovery of America; subsequent projects have addressed gay politics, women's rights, and gentrification. Often the work consists of signage projects and public installations. The current members are Neil Bogan, Jim Costanzo, Tom Klem, Janet Koenig, Lisa Maya Knauer, Cynthia Liesenfeld, Chris Neville, Jayne Pagnucco, Leela Ramotar, Greg Sholette, and George Spencer.

Pat and Greg Samata/Evan's Life Foundation

Following the tragic death of their two-year old son, the Samatas—established graphic designers in the Chicago area—turned their loss into a positive force by forming a foundation to help children in need across the country. The stories are heart wrenching: A young girl living on the streets of San Francisco wanted desperately to escape a life of prostitution and the shadow of her drug-addicted parents. The solutions are simple, yet brilliant: The foundation bought her a plane ticket to fly to another state to live with her grandmother. Many of the requests are just as compelling and direct. A young boy who wanted to go to after-school programs was afraid to walk across gang lines; so the foundation supplied him with tokens to bus there. Board members, a multidisciplinary group of designers, clergy, and legal experts, vote on grant distribution. Often, however, the stories are so gripping that they decide to fund the grants out of their own pockets.

Lily Yeh

Painter, muralist, sculptor, educator, and healer, Lily Yeh has virtually single-handedly restored to life a devastated quarter of Philadelphia's north side. Entering it in 1986, Yeh looked around, saw what needed to be done, and found close at hand the resources with which to do it. A notorious alleyway between two buildings—home of drug dealers and users—became "Angel Alley," as she called upon the neighborhood's jobless and children to help her clean it out. Lily decided that what the space needed more than anything else was protective angels, so together the group created on the walls African-inspired mosaic angels out of discarded bathroom tiles. The transformation was remarkable. No more a blight, the space is now a welcoming place to be walked through from one part of the neighborhood to another. From that point, her work was clear She decorated more walls with murals; she converted an abandoned building into a community center; she transformed bombed-out lots into vegetable gardens and a training area about nutrition for the neighborhood's impoverished and malnourished. And every summer now a harvest festival fills the streets with neighborhood children in costumes and masks as they carry the garden's bounty from home to home. Yeh's Village of the Arts and Humanities is no longer just a mosaic in an alley or a mural on an abandoned building; it is a five-square block neighborhood that is colorful, full of life, and home to the many families whose lives have been utterly turned around by her vision, vigilance, and love.

The people whose stories you have just read are really down in the trenches, working with children, working with the homeless, tackling social issues *mano a mano* with the most powerful tool they know—their art. While these represent only a handful of the many engaged in such projects, it remains a rare breed who has the luxury of time or money to commit themselves to this work full time—or who have somehow been lucky enough to figure out how to have it all. But if we were to include all the countless studios and individual artists and designers who make a practice of giving of themselves regularly through volunteerism, mentoring, or pro bono work, then collectively the number of these stars would crowd the others right out of the skies.

First published in *Communication Arts*, July 2000.

Crisis as Opportunity:
Creating Revolutionary
Thinking

Maggie Macnab

Several months ago, I was hired by a forty-year-old engi-
neering firm to redesign the company's corporate collateral materials. The firm wanted a "fresh look" but was resistant to the idea of creating a totally new identity. So its
old (and, in my opinion, staid and nondescript) logo remained. Still, I pushed myself
to think divergently and was pleased with the stationery applications I presented, all
of which were received favorably and one of which was selected. I was feeling secure
in my success when the designer's ultimate dread surfaced—the client wanted to help
direct the design process. "Let's put the logo in multiple sizes across the front of our
presentation folders!" offered one of the engineers.

"No. That won't work," I responded flatly.

This exchange is not uncommon between designers and clients. Many clients perceive cutting-edge design as being out of control. To designers, this reluctance seems
stodgy. But as in all yin-yang scenarios, we need each other to exist: Clients need the
edge that makes them appear different and better than their competition; we need
our design work to be recognized for its creative value. It keeps us both in business.

The silence and sharp eyes in the room forecasted the reaction I'd get to any
future suggestions. I spent a good deal of time over the following days considering
our exchange, very aware that my knee-jerk response didn't get me what I wanted—
creative license—and it also endangered the future designer-client relationship. Then
I took a true creative leap, and considered that perhaps I was the one unwilling to
take a risk by responding in a rigid way. What if what they suggested was valid? Not
perhaps in the verbatim translation, but in the translation of what they meant?

The following week we met again. I began like this: "Before we proceed today, I'd
like to apologize to the group for not hearing what you were saying. I responded defen-
sively to your suggestion because I was so wrapped up in being the expert. If I had
been listening, I would have heard you emphasizing what you've become known for—
your commitment to precision and quality—and that the priority was to demonstrate
that this commitment hasn't changed. You are also concerned that your image looks
up-to-date. My job is to define and relate both these messages graphically, satisfying

every criteria, from the practical to the aesthetic. So, I want you to know I'm here to do what you've hired me for—to listen to your needs and concerns, and combine that information with my skills to communicate your company's image effectively."

Please note that I said nothing about using their concept in a literal sense. But by altering my own perception there was a real shift of attitude in the room. The struggle of who got to be on top was transformed: We were then pulling together for a common cause.

I bring this up because it's a recurring situation—not exclusively between clients and designers but in almost all human relationships. Only when a shift occurs in relationship to the self can there be a shift in how we deal with others. But who wants to change? If we were asked to leap into a net that might not exist, we'd be, at best, hesitant. Consider that we ask our clients to do this each time we present a creative idea, pushing them ever closer to the edge. And they pay us for it! We human beings want assurances that our tangible investment will reap a tangible, positive result, and no amount of cajoling, convincing, or award-winning can create that comfort zone in our clients or in ourselves. Maybe the point isn't to accommodate another's comfort level. Maybe the point is to learn how to push our own comfort zone, first in relationship to ourselves, and then in relationship to others. And here is where the human creative process comes in.

Unconscious Evolution

One of the theories of human evolution holds that around 40,000 years ago, give or take a few millennia, our species had a global explosion of creativity that jump-started innovation. This theory proposes that more happened in the first five minutes of that period than in all of the millions of years of human existence preceding it. New tools were not only created, they were decorated as well for what appeared to be the sheer pleasure of it. An abundance of other forms of artwork evolved—clothing decoration, jewelry, cave paintings, sculpture, pictographs, hieroglyphics—an endless variety of symbolic representations of style conveying everything from social stature to interpretations of nature and how we fit into the universe.[1]

But this is only one theory. While many psychologists believe this evolutionary step was abrupt, most anthropologists believe our innovative process was more gradual. Dr. Jane Christian, Professor Emerita of Anthropological Linguistics from the University of Alabama, said in a recent interview, "Complicated and extensive creative thinking in social interaction, language development, and the invention of tools has been going on throughout human history. The Australian Aborigines evidently created their dreamtime myths around 40- to 60,000 years ago. You can look at the beauty and organization of Mousterian tools, from our Neanderthal cousins, which are not only suited perfectly for the jobs for which they were created but are very aesthetically pleasing. They also buried their dead in fetal positions covered with flowers. Just because we haven't found as much fossil evidence predating an approximate 40,000-year mark doesn't make the time frame conclusive. . . . It's quite likely nearly all of it disintegrated."

Christian acknowledges the human brain as "the most complex structure found in the universe," but also believes our creativity is much like that of other higher mammals, the difference being a matter of degrees. In her studies of human babies and language acquisition, she found the beginning steps to complex linguistic systems to be quite similar to that of chimpanzees, starting with gestures and closed call systems (a limited vocabulary of sounds associated with actions), but then finally diverging in a most human fashion to an open and arbitrary communication system that connects symbol with meaning. Even chimps trained in signing, when given a fruit never seen before, come up with new phrases to describe it; for example, "hurt fruit" for lemon. Wild and domestic elephants have been observed drawing, dancing, and weeping. And over the last thirty years of studying dolphins, we have discovered a very complex communication system.

For the human species, a creative system of communication has a critical survival value. There is much more survival potential in "A herd of eland over the next ridge!" than in "Hoot, hoot!" (or "Good eat!"). Evolution echoes existence by creating intricate and complex changes when the circumstances deem it worth the effort. Our ability to perceive and emulate our world in detail has provided humans with an unprecedented edge—if we pay attention long enough something new always emerges from the mundane. We possess the uncanny ability to translate that new information into understandable patterns that further our evolution. Life itself is revealed in a way that scientists call "self-similar." In other words, our DNA is programmed with an inherent design that unfolds in a fairly predictable linear pattern but responds to environmental randomness that stimulates unpredictable results.

Wei ji: The Chinese word for "crisis" is made up of two parts—danger and opportunity.

Danger was originally pictured as a man on the edge of a precipice.

Opportunity is a reminder of the seemingly small, but important, opportunity that can arise from danger.

Whatever the theory du jour, most everyone agrees that the crucial aspect of our creative evolution was the transformation of the very matrix in how we relate to one another. Our increasingly complex social structure produced civilization, providing us with such benefits as intricate spoken and recorded language (cross-generation communication), agriculture, invention of new tools that aid in both adaptation and alteration of our environmental circumstance, and art, through which we experiment with new and futuristic concepts that create a bridge to allow cultural evolution to occur. David Lance Goines states in his article "Why Art? Solving the Big Head Problem" that "the creation and savoring of art is a cultural preparation for the future by enabling people both individually and collectively to test many possible alternate realities. Through art, we look at the unimaginably complex future, and try to find a path, so that we may create order from the bewildering disorder that confronts us. It is a collective dreaming, wherein specialized members of the human organism dream for the entire organism. The translation of ideas into graphic language is the translation of an individual dream into a collective dream."[2]

Unlike modern times where we live with the prejudiced notion that only the gifted can create, in ancient times everyone was an artist. To create something unlike anything else is intimately tied to our survival and our need to push the species ahead. But the underlying duality of change and the individuals who represent it has historically—at least in Western culture—been met with strong, and sometimes brutal, disapproval. It doesn't take a university study to know how difficult it is to challenge the status quo with a new idea. Group approval is essential to our survival, just as is evolving to a new level of consciousness. We bump up against this regularly in business—a microcosm of a world controlled by linear thought.

Modern culture has used this successive thought process as a way to simplify complex ideas. A set of sequential events assigned to predict the outcome allows for organization and planning by narrowing the options, whether or not you are in truth predicting the future. It's just easier to keep a group going in the same direction when there's overall agreement of what that direction is. The very nature of being human is change. When differences begin to override the established direction by creating new options, we have to feel our way toward a new balance. It's chaotic, and that has a tendency to frighten us.

Man's circumvention of natural evolution has had a cost to our communities that has become too high to ignore. We have invented cumbersome and highly detailed structures, such as our current political systems, originally in an attempt to simplify the decision-making process. Unfortunately, this simplification appears to render us impotent in some crucial areas. Situations such as the welfare state and a consistently lethargic voter turnout seem to indicate that what worked well for a while no longer does the job. Although Dr. Christian will tell you that she believes unnecessary centralization is our downfall, perhaps even our primary defect, it is exactly the difficulties encountered by today's complexities that are presenting us with our most significant possibility yet: the next transformation of our species, which resides in accommodating the new challenges our world presents. New challenges are not the enemy—the rigor mortis that sets in from resisting them is. As designers, we have to think creatively to survive. We have an opportunity to apply this style of thinking to new ways of relating.

Conscious Evolution

I had a very interesting experience recently. I went to a fairly intensive seminar that asked the elemental questions "What is it to be human?" and "What is reality?" I went with the goals to learn to trust myself more and trust other people at least somewhat. We did an exercise I knew I wouldn't like: We had to be with other people. This exercise involved looking fully in the face of the person seated next to me for several minutes, not talking, not smiling, not averting eyes, just being. In the second part, we stood in front of a room of nearly 100 people doing the very same thing. This lasted nothing short of an eternity, but the results astonished me. I discovered I like people. I want to know people. I want them to know me. Beyond our unique qualities is a common longing: We need connection as much as we do autonomy.

Thinking about this later, I realized my overall experience of this culture is the avoidance of true relating, in both intimate and community interactions. Intimacy with others means exposure, vulnerability, the possibility of rejection. In my childhood, I experienced vulnerability as pain.

Without going into detail about my personal emotional traumas, I'll bet almost anyone can identify with what I'm talking about. In those early formative years, I equated events that hurt with having no control over the situation and therefore being unable to alter it. Because children's emotional skills are undeveloped, the response is often reactionary. Being young and impressionable, the child's response to strong experience becomes a permanent part of our survival kit, whether or not it serves us later. My response to crisis in those early years led to hiding my vulnerability behind a tough and competent appearance. Certainly being competent is a good thing; even toughness has its place at times. But dependence on old patterns as the only option prevents us from creatively addressing new situations. Simply put, we don't learn, and that is contrary to our nature. It's almost impossible to relate to others with a defensive attitude, as I described in the instance with my clients. I discovered that by consciously shifting my concept of vulnerability—that it might possibly be a good and valuable thing—I created a new perspective on who I am and how I relate with others. Oddly enough, when I changed, the people around me changed.

It is remarkable to consider that the entire population of our species has doubled on this earth since the 1940s. Due to our increasing "togetherness" over the last century, finding new ways of relating with one another is inevitable. One of the psychologies that has emerged out of this need is called Gestalt, an integrative therapy that takes into account the entire context of a person's life, not just the separate issues of events past. Its founder, Fritz Perls, interpreted the word "responsibility"

as "response-ability," or developing the skills necessary to get the job done. In this context, the phrase, "There is no freedom without responsibility," means freedom involves making choices. "Response-ability" requires matching skills to the task at hand. A shift in relationship with others can only happen on an individual basis, with each of us committing to individual responsibility. Implementation of that responsibility could create a very valuable new tool: a level of communication that could transform our entire species. If we are able to consciously respond to the issue at hand rather than resort to an automatic response that stems from an event thirty years ago, we might actually move forward in relationships instead of remaining stuck.

Most of us in the creative professions already appreciate the value of being able to use this more spontaneous, adaptable style of thinking. This appropriate response to circumstance is known as "flow" in studies of creativity, the "white moment" for athletes and performers, and "no-mindedness," a Zen concept in which self-consciousness and time disappear, allowing access to a universal creativity. If you have ever lost yourself in creating something that felt as though it was "through you" rather than "of you," you have experienced flow. Another clue is that your energy feels renewed rather than depleted. By only engaging the areas of the brain necessary, the rest is reserved for problem solving or other tasks.[3] Pushing ourselves to venture into new realms of ourselves is the true work of being human, and it is at once our difficulty and our grace. When we open to the possibilities within ourselves, we reveal a universe of possibility outside of ourselves.

We are all "men on the precipice" at this crucial point in time, and we have some choices to make—not only where do we go next but on which path and for how long? As visual designers of information, we have the advantage of placing one foot in both realms—information and invention, doing and being. It is our task to demonstrate creativity and intuition in the context of the logical and pragmatic business world. Our daily environment challenges us to be aware and awake human beings to accomplish this in a harmonious fashion. Expressing a broadened tolerance and becoming skillful in unexplored levels of communication is a tall order. We have been taught to discount some of our latent talents such as intuitive interconnectedness, and we're going to be needing all of our faculties for what's ahead. It is simply common sense to acknowledge and develop any and all of our innate interpretation and communication skills. To create a coexistence of cooperation through active participation in the world isn't a touchy-feely new-age thing. It's age-old survival.

I realize this is asking a lot. There is no doubt it is a lot easier to remain resigned. But I, for one, like the cosmologists' idea that has persisted for at least 2,000 years, which says that our existence is a way for the universe to reflect upon itself. I like the job of translating the information that comes my way, adding my spin to the curve ball, and tossing it back out again.

It was, and remains, no easy feat to admit shortcomings. The engineers' resistance to doing the job my way provided a communication opportunity that took me beyond where I'd traditionally gone with clients. They also made a leap—not only by describing themselves graphically but also in their flexibility to convey who they were. It wasn't easy for them to incorporate my suggestions, some of which have required significant effort at the grassroots level of implementation. Their willingness to try out some things with which they were not totally comfortable, and my ownership of the discord in the relationship, allowed for a much better result. Though no client-designer relationship is perfect, the point is to make the effort to communicate, realizing and accepting that something is often given up on a personal level for the gain of the greater good. Perhaps the distinction is what one gives up. A little piece of soul? I don't think anyone should be asked to do that. A little piece of ego? That's something we could all live with.

Carl Jung's idea of a collective unconscious says that we already have experience of one another, and always have. I recently spoke about human connectedness with David Ulansey, professor of philosophy and religion at the California Institute of Integral Studies in San Francisco and research associate in the Department of Near Eastern Studies at the University of California, Berkeley. He said, "The most apparent clues to our transformation are the cracks in the edifice of our reality. Life changed for all of us in the sixties when we saw ourselves from outer space. That image of a small blue planet in the infinite expanse of space showed without question how connected we truly are. It has forever affected our 'civilized' perception of the separation between cultures and peoples. The most ancient concepts of our interconnectedness to each other and the universe have lain dormant for millennia, like seeds stored in our unconscious waiting for the human climate to change, and now they are beginning to grow again."

Mathematics, chemistry, computer science, philosophy, physics, psychology, biology, the arts—all traditionally exclusive disciplines—now interweave to create information that holistically fills in more of our existential picture. Ilya Prigogine won the 1977 Nobel Prize in chemistry for his model of dissipative structures (a term he coined that means "self-organizing patterns"), which demonstrates large perturbations of energy that cause living systems to fall apart and then to fall together again in a more elegant order. Perhaps our fear of chaos is exaggerated. Prigogine writes, "Creativity becomes the ever-urging drive that pushes reality forward. . . . Giving up the ideal of certainty may appear to some a defeat of human reason; I don't believe so. We begin to be able to describe an evolutionary universe, in agreement with our present picture where evolution plays an essential role on all levels of description from cosmology to human history. Far from coming to the end of science, we are only at the very start . . . of being able to produce a coherent view of the universe. [We are] overcoming a type of rationality that is no longer appropriate to our time."[4]

We will need pattern-seers from all walks of life in order to decipher the complexities that face us and integrate them into the whole. We are all needed to interpret the puzzle because it is through our collective experience that the next solution will be uncovered. Suddenly, "we the people" is who we are once again.

As our next—and perhaps last—significant evolution, this time is fraught with danger and opportunity. The potential in what we have created is incredibly dangerous because it is so powerful. Technology threatens our existence with nuclear and biological weapons, poisons that are haphazardly released into our life support systems. We bear silent witness to a shocking extinction rate of plant and animal life in our own lifetime. But it also reveals previously invisible worlds of intricate beauty and is beginning to unveil the inherent inter-relatedness of existence at the most fundamental levels. The societal changes happening through human connection are turning the traditional hierarchical pyramid upside down. None of us has any idea what might replace it. But we are also evolving our communication skills exponentially via the Internet. We now have the ability to access others almost anywhere in the world to provide a tangible modern-day experience of our web of connection. Now we can actually transcend many of our traditional cultural, political, and economic boundaries.

In our brief period here, we have exclaimed ourselves in a most obtrusive way. Our in-your-face attitude has done exactly that—put us face to face, surrounded by a bewildering world we played a large part in creating. We can hold ourselves hostage, baffled by an overload of information and tormented by our ineffective response to it, or we can choose to take on our individual response-ability, making personal leaps that creatively address our predicament. At this juncture, the discomfort of risk is irrelevant. With so much potential contained within each of us, reinventing ourselves into a new reality is our first order of business.

Special thanks to Jane Christian, anthropologist and human rights activist; David Lance Goines, artist and designer; Jay Myers, psychobiologist and computer whiz; David Ulansey, philosopher and teacher; and Fred Yost, scientist and artist.

Notes

1. William Allman, *The Stone Age Present* (New York: Simon and Schuster, 1994), 186-219.

2. David Lance Goines, "Why Art? Solving the Big Head Problem," *Communication Arts* (January/February 1996).

3. Daniel Goleman, Paul Kaufman, and Michael Ray, *The Creative Spirit* (New York: Dutton, 1992), 47.

4. "Ilya Prigogine: Creativity in the Sciences and the Humanities: A Study in the Relation Between the Two Cultures" in *The Creative Process*, Lars Gustafsson, Susan Howard, and Lars Niklasson, editors (Stockholm: Swedish Ministry of Education and Science, 1993).

First published in *Communication Arts*, November 1997.

Fame, of course, is relative. Michael Jackson and OJ
Simpson are famous. Most people have never heard of Milton Glaser or Paul Rand. In the context of this little guide, fame refers to something very specific: A famous graphic designer is famous among other graphic designers. My mother, for instance, knows that I'm "famous" because my sister-in-law, who's a dental hygienist, used to clean the teeth of a graphic designer in my hometown back in Ohio. Nothing could have astonished my sister-in-law more than when her patient asked her if she was related to me.

Other than that, I can't say for sure that being famous counts for anything. I was asked once to prepare a presentation with the title "Lifestyles of the Rich and Famous Graphic Designers." Rich I know nothing about. It was surprisingly easy to calculate fame, however. I took out the Membership Directory of the American Institute of Graphic Arts. I went through the list and ticked off anyone who had a name I even vaguely recognized from awards books or the lecture circuit. The result was 185 or so names. With further thought, I could have even put them in order, from most famous to least famous.

That was in 1989. Five years later, there are even more famous graphic designers. Yet, I sense that most people feel there really aren't enough famous graphic designers. A lot of women designers don't feel there are enough famous women designers, a lot of African-American designers don't feel there are enough famous African-American designers, a lot of designers from Ohio don't feel there are enough famous Buckeye designers, and so forth. And, of course, a lot of individual designers don't feel that they themselves are sufficiently famous.

This is too bad, because I feel that becoming famous isn't really all that difficult. Most kinds of fame are based, to a certain extent, on individual merit. But there are a lot of trivial things involved as well. These have to do with things like speeches and competitions. You can only do so much with the talent you were born with. On the other hand, these trivial things are sometimes amusingly simple to manipulate. But remember, there's no guarantee that being famous counts for anything.

People who enter design competitions, particularly people who enter and lose design competitions, comfort themselves by imagining that something sinister goes on in the tomblike confines of the judges' chambers.

When you judge a competition yourself, you learn that nothing could be further from the truth. Behind the closed doors are table after table covered with pieces of graphic design. Like most things in life, only a few of these are really good. Each judge moves along the tables, looking at each piece just long enough to ascertain whether he or she likes it. It takes a long time and a lot of people to produce even a modest piece of graphic design. The judging process takes less than a second.

The predictability of this ritual, which has all the glamour and sinister aspects of digging a ditch, makes it easy to devise some simple rules that will increase your chances of winning:

- Don't enter things that rely on complicated unfolding or unwrapping operations. The first few judges won't bother opening it. The one that does won't bother putting it back together. Also, don't enter things that involve confetti or other supposedly festive materials spilling unexpectedly out of envelopes.
- Try to enter so your thing is the biggest one on the table. The pieces to be judged are almost always separated into categories so that like is judged with like. Having your piece be one of the largest in its category gives it a tremendous advantage. For instance, your 17" x 22" season-schedule poster for the local symphony orchestra that looks nice over your desk will look pathetic next to a gargantuan Ivan Chermayeff Masterpiece Theatre bus-shelter poster. Enter it as an "announcement" instead. It will compete much more successfully, trust me, against things like wedding invitations.
- Don't enter slides unless you're sure they're going to be projected. (See the previous bullet item.) Nothing is smaller than a 35mm slide with a big old entry form hanging off it.

How to Give a Speech

- Graphic designers are lucky in that when speaking before a group they can show slides almost the whole time. This obviates most of the advice on speechmaking you get in airport bookstores about eye contact and forceful gestures. The only thing left to remember is the reason that the audience is there—they want to see what you're like. The rules:
- When in doubt, show two trays of 80 slides each, first one, then the other. Dissolve units break down. Side-by-side images get out of sequence. More than 160 slides make peoples' butts hurt. Don't worry, plenty can still go wrong.
- Never describe the slide people are looking at. A slide presentation should follow the same dramatic rhythm of an Alfred Hitchcock movie: tension followed by release, tension followed by release. Describe the design problem you were asked to solve. Give the audience a moment to think what they would do. Then, show them what you did. Done properly, this acquires the cadence, and ultimately the effect, of telling a joke. It's boring to be told what you're looking at—you already know what you're looking at. Instead, try to make the audience

guess the next thing they're going to see.

- Never read your speech. It's tempting, but it tends to make an audience really, really dislike you. If you must, use really comprehensive notes instead.

- If possible, avoid showing slides of annual-report spreads or slides created with presentation software. It's very difficult to say anything funny or interesting about projected images of spreads from even well-designed annual reports. And presentation software slides—with all those gradated backgrounds and rules and bullets and Times Roman with crisp little drop shadows—will make your audience afraid you're going to bore them. At the very least, they will question your choice of typeface.

- Choose the last slide of the first tray with special care. It should be really great or really surprising or really funny. Why? To ensure a satisfied buzz in the audience during the endless amount of time it takes to change to the second tray. For that reason, never change trays in the middle of a thought; the sense of deflation in the audience is palpable when the second tray goes on and you're still talking about that same old damn project.

How to Do Great Design Work

It should be obvious by now that great work, in this context, is work that gets published and wins design awards. Work that communicates effectively and solves marketing problems for actual clients will make you rich, not famous, and consequently is not discussed here. Here's how to make great work:

- Do lots of work. You only need to do about three really great pieces a year to become famous. Depending on how much talent you have, you may have to design a lot of good things on the off chance that a few of them might turn out to be great. Design anything you can get your hands on. Stationery makes a nice gift; design some for every member of your family and all your friends, particularly those with funny names that permit visual puns. Brewing beer is complicated and messy, but it provides a pretext for designing beer labels. Avoid, however, designing clever wedding and birth announcements, which are sacred events that shouldn't be cheapened with clever design concepts unless the design concept is really, really clever.

- Do lots of posters. In America, posters are not as relevant a part of the cultural landscape as they are in Europe, but they look good reproduced at a fraction of their original size on the pages of a design annual.

- Do lots of freebies. It's a cliché, but it's easier to do great free work than great paying work. Be careful, however, about working for charitable causes or large cultural institutions, which can be even more cumbersome and bureaucratic than corporate clients. Also, even in the shallow, craven context of this article, there is something particularly distasteful about trying to leverage a worthy cause like fighting HIV or breast cancer in your own personal quest for fame. Do those projects for their own merits, not to win prizes. Instead, find a local theater group. This will permit you to solve easily understandable problems (see the first bullet item on how to win a design competition) with posters (see the previous bullet item).

- Make your paying work as good as it can be. While a lot of famous designers make compromises to pay the bills, I don't know any that actually do really bad work just for the money. It seems to be really bad for morale and consequently makes it harder to do great theater posters.
- Have something cool-looking you can always do when you can't come up with any other solutions. Every really famous designer I know has a visual strategy he or she can fall back on when all else fails. One makes lovely Matisse-like torn paper collages, another makes a complicated three-dimensional model and takes a picture of it, and still another puts big black horizontal stripes on everything. This fallback position, if chosen carefully enough, will eventually become identified as your signature style, another hallmark of a famous designer. Reluctance to develop a surefire fallback position will only mean that you will waste a lot of time trying to invent exciting new solutions that probably don't exist for problems that probably don't deserve them.
- When in doubt, make it big. If still in doubt, make it red. This rule of thumb, a slight but crucial improvement on "If it's big and ugly, it isn't big enough," is embraced by a surprisingly wide range of contemporary famous graphic designers. It appears to be, like the typeface Garamond, one of the few things that everybody agrees on.
- Finally, remember what my mom always says. She says, "It's nice to be important, but it's important to be nice." She's not just the smartest woman in the world but the mother of a famous graphic designer. Trust her.

First published in *Communication Arts*, May/June 1995.

IV | Design Looks At Itself

For graphic designers, good design is an end itself. And the best design emerges from a highly individualized, intuitive process. The tension created by the desire for both self-fulfillment and client satisfaction provides the fuel for this part of the book.

A Few Reasons
We're All Doing
Worse Work

Sean Kernan

The place where business and art meet is a chronically sore joint where the two collide in pursuit of their common goals. From my point of view—that of the creative—the demands that business makes at this juncture too often lead to work that is not creative at all, and time and again I find myself chasing weak ideas for perfectly sound business reasons. I have to say it bothers me more and more when clients seem genuinely pleased with the mediocre results.

I'd be so much happier if I could just shrug and say, "Listen, they got what they wanted, they paid the bill. Let it go." But no, off I go, muttering under my breath that the work could be better and the clients so much happier if they'd just leave me and the art director alone to call the shots.

When business looks at itself, it wants to take measurements. Businessmen tend to believe that what's useful is what's measurable, that what isn't is too woolly to mean much of anything. And the unit of measurement that works best for them is time, which as we all know is money.

And so the joint aches because so much creative activity takes place outside of time, while current management practice uses time as one whole side of the equation—time spent producing, and the value of that time. And these days most managers see it as a duty to stuff more work into whatever time is available in order to get more value out. They worship in the Church of Productivity.

There's no question that time/money works well indeed as a measure of a lot of things, but it works after the fact, when the numbers are in, using them to project an expectation for a similar process. But in the area of advertising and communications, one can measure the effectiveness of an ad after it has run, but one can never really measure why it was effective. The creative aspects of commercial work are ultimately only gauged by things as imprecise as a feeling in the gut, a glow, a sense that things just . . . work. And there's no way at all to predict how long it might take to get to that point. Someone can get the idea in the first meeting or after rounds of focus groups.

In short, creative work is really right and done when its makers—the designers, illustrators, writers, directors, editors—know it is. And that sense of done-ness doesn't happen on any schedule—by the end of the day of shooting, or by the investors' meeting, the media deadline, or any other time. We can recognize that something has come together and is good, but we can't say beforehand just when it will do so. Good commercial art, just like good fine art, is done when it's done.

But I'm describing a perfect world here. Let's be realistic. When one undertakes to produce something—a brochure, a website—one has to commit to someone's idea of a deadline. There's just no other way. The timeline is part of the plan from the beginning.

So imagine a project manager's face when one of the "creative suppliers" turns up empty-handed at deadline and explains, "I dunno, man, this just isn't happening for me yet." The reality is that when the deadline hits, the project is as done as it's going to be.

The trouble is that time has been nibbled away so severely in recent years that the quality of creative work is getting harder and harder to uphold. Efficiency and cost-cutting have become a near-religion in business. If you want to be a corporate hero, a sure way is to hammer costs down and make sure you're seen doing it. It's like telling prehistoric hunters to maintain their mastodon quota while cutting spear use by 20 percent.

Of course there really are lots and lots of good reasons for management to cut costs, but there are also reasons to know when to stop. In a business such as ours, where the immeasurable qualities really count, you can cut to the bone and into it before you know it. I think a lot of our clients don't understand where bone begins, at least not in the area of creativity. And a few think that bone doesn't matter.

The creative work that we do for business uses the processes of art and gets its particular magic from them, so it's worth our looking at art closely to get some idea of how it does what it does.

Basically, art uses illogical, idiosyncratic, and arcane approaches to manifest what can't be gotten at any other way. As this year's Pulitzer Prize–winning poet Charles Wright put it, "I write to find out what it is I have to say."

Fine artists start each session of work with an impulse and perhaps some notion of what they'd like to have happen, but with no idea of exactly what will come out, or when. They can plan, make notes and sketches, but when they begin, the big question in their minds is, "How will this play out, where will it go—and can I follow it there?" If they're really lucky the work that they do will take them past whatever they had in mind. At its worst it will just lie there.

So artists begin to slide around the paint or the words, or they make a string of notes just to see where the string will lead. They follow someone on the street and slip into his head, becoming him long enough to steal his consciousness for a character. Or they gaze into blank air and hope something will materialize. The writer Annie Proulx says she visualizes a landscape and then waits to see who walks out of it and follows him.

And in this great realm of imagination *there is no measurable time*. The clock just stops when the work begins.

So at last something might begin to happen, either in a hot burst or a slow incremental laying down of a line. And when enough of the line is laid down, the work of revision commences. Many say that this is where the real work is done, that the heart of writing, for example, is rewriting. One listens to the words and looks at the lines; at the colors; at the way the design jumps page to page, screen to screen; and at what is revealed and in what order. The work is manifested, reviewed, and refined until it is brought to its finish. It is a labor of finding the images and the rhythm— musical/visual/verbal—that picks the audience up and takes it away. As the poet Wallace Stevens said, "Music is feeling, not sound." That is, art is not its medium, it is what the medium carries.

In art that has meaning, the creative person takes what he is working on, breathes it deep into his own being, and then pours it out again in what is called the heuristic process.

"Heuristic" is a fantastic word. I first encountered it in a poetry class, and although the teacher didn't explain it, I knew it was important by the way she rolled it around in her mouth. So I ran off after class and looked it up. It comes from the same Greek root as the word eureka (I have found it), and it means finding the truth of a thing within one's self. Without this process, one merely quotes, the way a picture postcard does. With it, one's thoughts may become moving and true.

So this creative act is a complex process, and it takes place mostly out of sight. One thing that any artist will tell you is that there is absolutely no way to predict how long it might take to consummate it.

And anyone who has worked in an agency or design firm knows how dumb it would be to say so at an input session with a client.

But it is true. The process we use in the commercial arts is this same miraculous and inexact one used in the fine arts. It's central to all the creative work that we do in business. When it is followed and allowed to happen, people look at the results and say what we all long to hear: "Great work!"

Immediately a question pops up here: Does commercial work have to be great, or even good? Let's face it, if one looks outside the design magazines and awards shows, it becomes clear that good commercial work is very rare. There are ways to communicate that are not distinguished, and they work well enough. I heard of a manager who began a meeting about a new project by writing on a board the phrase, *Great is the enemy of Good.* What he meant was, let's get this one out the door quickly, it only has to be good, and any effort beyond that will not pay us back.

Surely he knew what he was talking about. But he was defaulting to the time/money measurement. Safe to say he got what he paid for. But what a contrast with a statement I read recently by the writer James Salter, who said, "The secret of making art is simple: eliminate anything that is good enough."

Still, I know what the man at the meeting meant, and I sometimes think this way myself, as we all do. But I hurry when I have to so I can get on to the good work, and I fear that the Great Time Squeeze of our productivity obsession will insinuate itself into every part of what I do, into its heart. But no matter what the time allows I always try to achieve what a scientist might call an elegant solution in all my projects. I do things that I know most people don't notice, particularly with light and the energy of the frame. I think of it as Quality, and I want it always to be part of my work, not an option to add if there's time.

Of course, some businesses treat customers in ways that have nothing to do with quality. I know a printer who set up a photography studio and operates it at a loss simply to channel work to his printing presses. How can I compete with that? Well, by doing good work, by taking the time to go through this artistic process with my projects.

Those of us who long ago caught a case of the Arts are compelled to find the life in things and express it, to put things through the heuristic process. To a client who doesn't believe in this kind of thing, it looks like we're juggling invisible balls. To one who does, he'll see what we're doing... and know it is for the good of the work.

But good work is important. It's certainly the kind of work I want to do. And there are enough clients who want it and enough of us who want to do it. Together we exert a defining influence on the field of communications.

A problem arises when people come to me to do work that is like other work of mine they've seen, and then don't understand what was involved in doing it. It is like looking at Fred Astaire dancing and not understanding how much work he put into it to make it look easy.

As a weird example, there's the time necessary to realize ideas that simply can't be done as they are proposed. I spend increasing amounts of time these days executing photos based on layouts that have been Photoshop-ed using elements gathered from here and there and kludged together. In a presentation comp there's no need to deal with how things might actually relate visually. Elements—say a pocket compass and a globe—are clipped from various sources and shown same size. It's useless to argue in the studio that globes are always bigger than compasses; in the comped collage they aren't, and the comp is what we have to do. So I have to spend my time getting as close as I can to that illusion because that's what was seen and approved—no substitutions, no material changes.

Being able to do this is a skill, I guess, but what I *should* be doing with my client's time is making a careful, balanced, thought-out piece of work using my ability to work with the artistic process. At a minimum I should be able to say, "Let's make the compass smaller" (or the classic "Why does it have to be a compass?"). But I can't change a thing. I'm obliged to express the idea that the direction of the company (the compass) is just as important as its international reach (the globe) by making them the same size. That's what we have to say and this is how we have to say it. (This is not a far-fetched example. But you know that.)

One mad day I spent six hours trying to match on film a color copy of a marker comp, simply because the client knew she could not go back to her office with anything that was in any way different from what her boss had seen. It was insane. The result in the end seemed a stunning accomplishment to me, not because it was any good at all but because the match was so exact—murky darks, acid highlights. The printed piece itself was so strange I couldn't possibly show it to anyone. A color copy of a marker comp!

Is this kind of thing new in our business? No, it's always been a little like this. But the drag on the creative process has been made more intrusive by new technologies. A presentation comp looks so finished, so smooth, that clients see executing it as just re-doing what's already been done. It's hard to explain why it's not.

But let's say we do explain it, and let's say that there is room to do a certain amount of exploration during the course of our work. If we're lucky we can do the kind of real exploration that takes ideas further and refined them. If we're not we can do a kind of phony exploration, just generating variations in the blind hope that whoever makes the final decision will at least like one of them. There's a lot of this. I recently did a project in which I had a few hours in a facility to come up with an image that suggested an ability to safeguard large amounts of crucial data. The facility was cramped and not very visual, but I knew that with some lighting work I could come up with a strong, dynamic image.

And I did. But rather than consider that a beginning and then working to take the shot further, I had to make two other completely different images. The only reason was that we were in that common position of not having a good insight into the mind of our corporate client. So the solution was to make several different images in the hope that he'd like one. If we had come back with a single image and he just didn't like it at all, we would have failed, no matter how well we had refined the image. But if we had a few cards to deal him, even if he didn't like any of them all that much, he would still like one more than the others, and we'd be able to steal home.

So we shot several setups, with multiple versions of each—one with this person, one with that person, one with both. It worked out fine, in the sense that there was one that the client liked. Still, on the plane flying home I mentally ran through possibilities that we hadn't had time to try for the first shot, that I hadn't even had the time to think of, and I wished we'd just been able to let the creative process run and take us to a single stronger image instead of dividing what time we had to make multiple solutions.

Of course, it is true that at an early stage of any project one should look at possibilities for a while, just to give things a chance to emerge. But eventually one needs to commit to an approach that seems promising and give it enough energy to take it all the way through. I'm convinced that the very act of focusing on something actually draws energy to the event and makes things happen. Why can't one just see the final form right away? I don't know. I just know that the working through is necessary, along with the time to stand back from it.

But the time! Where is the time for this? The productivity paradigm so beloved of contemporary management has come to overwhelm the way we work in creative fields, and it doesn't allow time for the percolation that is so crucial. (And, unfortunately, sitting and thinking looks pretty much like doing nothing.) You can measure time, but you can't quantify thought and you can't measure good.

Some people blame the computer for this problem, but computers are just tools— great ones at that. The problem is that clients know we have them. That secret is out. If you recall, the early promise of the computer in design was that it would shorten some tasks and leave more time for creative speculation. Hah! We all know how that has worked out. I recently watched as an agency created four different layouts, fully comped with swipe art and kerned type, and then made big color outputs to present to a client for what was really a very preliminary discussion of a project. They weren't even trying to sell the client, just determining some general directions for a campaign. I mean, fussing the type on a preliminary comp! And where did the time to do this come from? You can be sure it was subtracted from later on in the process where it could have done some real good.

One might argue that some tasks had been shifted forward in this case, and that the chosen layout had a shorter path to production because of the work done up front. But I think that the comps were just bait for an approval. They weren't the result of the real focused, purposeful work that makes things really good. I think that in this case all that doing ate the contemplation time that the computer freed up. It cut the creatives off from the exploration of the complexity and feel of life, and it led to work that referred chiefly to other ads—all rather incestuous.

It occurs to me that, although it takes time to make tight computer comps, it is in fact easier than doing the real creative heavy-lifting. I mean, you start playing around on a screen, and almost at once a dull headline looks kind of finished. Then you throw in some art work lifted from somewhere, and then, wow, you can pop the colors in Photoshop, do some texture thing with Painter. And hey! Looks kind of like an ad!

Brenna Garratt, managing director of corporate marketing and branding at Belk Mignona in New York, whose experience extends across the computer transition, says that only for a brief period did computers buy creative time. "Clients found out how fast it was, and then they started demanding variations and revisions at four o'clock meetings and expecting them the next morning or over the weekend. The practical effect is that you have to think much faster, think on your feet, do concept work on the phone. It's not at all contemplative, and in the end no one thinking too quickly thinks as well as they should.

"Maybe advertising is different. My image is of someone getting that brilliant headline idea in a taxi and scribbling it down. But at my office we do complex corporate projects, and evolving one of those isn't a matter of a quick flash. An annual report is highly strategic, and it takes lots and lots of time to get it right. And time is what's disappearing.

"Listen, there's even this new FedEx Sunday service. Sunday is the last big chunk of time left to raid. When are we supposed to think? Or are we not?"

(Author's note: I'm writing this on a Sunday. The editor is e-mailing me comments on a Sunday!)

I don't want to make the mistake of letting this discussion become a damn-the-computers rant—I'm kind of tired of those, and I use and like computers. The real issue is this compression of work to fit into less time. I don't know of anyone who says it's not a problem. So is there a solution?

Well, there's no magic bullet. As I said earlier, our work is finished when the time runs out. We're not, after all, prima donnas. We will deliver, and on time; if we have to work Sundays, we do it.

But we really need to lobby for what we need to do good work. And to do that we have to understand the part time plays and respect that. If we don't who will? Part of what we need to do is state the problem in forums like this that are read by that segment of management that works in communications.

On my worst days, when I see something of mine that I know could have been better, I am tempted to throw up my hands and go see if the Muse will still have me. But the fact is that when I'm not kvetching about it, I like what I do. Having deadlines and the restrictions has taught me to do things I don't think I'd have learned any other way. It has taught me discipline. And the reality is that I wasn't kidnapped by gypsies and sold to an agency.

In truth, we're hybrids, and our real work is to balance and reconcile our own artistic impulses with the needs of our business clients and make it all work—for them and for us. Understanding that and embracing it is another part of the solution, maybe the biggest part, and it's the part that we control. Even if it is hard sometimes, that's the deal.

And occasionally, against all odds, the artistic process finds the room to breathe. I initiated a project with an agency, a kind of self-assigned promotion for them and for me. We began a few years ago, but it kept getting stalled. The design firm would get a "real" job, and our work would go straight to the back burner. Then when time allowed, we'd pull it out and work on it some more. But then we ran into annual-report season, and everything ground to a halt again.

So it went, more off than on. But each time we resumed work we did so with new eyes for what we had done to that point, and we were able to give up some things that weren't really working and to come up with some new things that did. As of this writing it is about to go on press, and it has, in its frustrating way, found the time to be treated as an artistic undertaking. I'm sure it will come out better and more satisfying and will last longer than any of the projects that kept displacing it.

So we can simply ask for the time we know we need to do something well, demand it if need be. And if it's not forthcoming . . . well, we can always decline the project. I know this seems so drastic. I mentioned doing this to a designer friend. She said that she wasn't far enough along in her career to turn things down, and I knew what she meant. But if you are ambitious for your work, sooner or later the question of whether you should accept an assignment will come up. And saying no to one kind of work could just be a big step toward another, better kind.

First published in *Communication Arts*, Illustration Annual 1998.

Two Scripts

Sean Kernan

I never asked for a creative mind. It just came with the pack- age. And, when I had to use it to figure out how to make a living, the business of being a photographer in advertising and communications seemed perfect. By then I was taking photographs for fun anyway. If they'd pay me to do it, fine. So I started to apply my creativity and intuition in service to the world of business, making images that would help fulfill the hopes of my clients. Much of the time this arrangement has worked smoothly, but sometimes vaguely abrasive incidents seem to arise like bubbles from within the process itself. And because I love looking at the phenomenon of creativity in all kinds of circumstances, I spend a lot of time thinking about these edgy events.

Why is it that artists and businesspeople working toward the same end get into difficulties with each other at all? (By artists, I mean, in this case, people in the creative professions—designers, art directors, illustrators, photographers, writers—us! By businesspeople, I mean our clients.)

There is an explanation, and when I saw it demonstrated, it was as though a key were sliding into a lock. Pins dropped into place one after another, and the door to understanding opened.

I came across the answer while reading a piece by the writer Sol Stein about an improvisation exercise that was used in classes at the Actor's Studio. Here's the way it works. A director sets up a defined situation with two actors, say a man and a woman. He takes the man aside and tells him, "You run into this person. Your immediate objective for this scene is to tell her that you got her message. That's all. (And, incidentally, she is rather taken with you)."

Then the director whispers to the other actor, the woman, "This man you're meeting is rather obnoxious and he has owed you money for a long time. What I want you to play is, 'Where's the money?' He owes you, you want it, and that's it."

Now, the idea in an improvisation is for the actors to take a simple starting point, commit to the situation, and bring all of his own experience and feeling to the work to explore what a character would do if the situation were real. It's a way of bringing the truth of the actor's experience to life.

So, there you have the setup. The rest of the class watches as the two actors approach each other and meet at center stage. The man calls out enthusiastically, even warmly, "There you are! Listen, I got your message."

"That's good," says the woman—no greeting, no enthusiasm. She gets right to the point, "Where's the money?"

And bang, there's a conflict under way, just like that. Each actor sticks to the attitude he's been given to play. They hear each other well enough, they even respond, but each returns to his objective and works it. The annoyance grows, the conflict escalates, the tensions crackle. There is life, drama!

Why? Because, as the director explains after the scene, dramatic tension arises when people who are sure they're talking about the same thing are not, not quite or not at all. It is as though they were on the same stage with scripts that are slightly—or very—different. Polonius plays the wit and liveliness of a Noel Coward character, and it is particularly awkward and foolish because Hamlet is playing. . .Hamlet.

This kind of tension doesn't come from art, of course. It is from life and is reflected in art. For years, ever since I decided I would earn my living doing commercial photography, I have found odd moments of difference cropping up with clients as we worked. This made no sense. After all, we'd come together to produce a piece that would sell the client's product or service. But sometimes I'd have different ideas of how to go about it. I would want to take an image in a new direction, and the client would want to do just what we'd said we'd do. Or the client would want to do a picture that I thought borrowed too much from another image he'd seen, while I wanted to find something more original. Or there might be any number of other disconnects.

When I heard about the Actor's Studio exercise, the reason for the small abrasions became clear. The problems came from different understandings of the same situation. It was built into the foundation of what we were doing, and it would always be there.

Artists and businesspeople play from different scripts. They appear on the same stage, but they are in slightly different plays with different endings. And most of them have no clue at all that each other person is heading for something quite different.

Now are things a little clearer? They were for me, and the demonstration of how the problem worked has helped me deal with these things before they go too far wrong.

To be sure, it seems like artists and businesspeople are in the same play. Both want to do a good job and get a good result. The difference lies in their ideas of what constitutes a "good job" and the reasons they want to do it.

Take the businessperson. I have a client who has a very successful business. He is savvy, entrepreneurial, and educated—M.B.A. and all that. He's worked extensively in advertising and is now in mail order. He understands merchandising and marketing very well.

During the course of our relationship, his designer and I have spent considerable time working on his projects. Naturally, we keep wanting to try new approaches. And while the client is excited by new approaches and want's us to come up with them, he doesn't really trust what he hasn't seen somewhere else. So, he frequently reins us in at the last minute. Or he hedges by executing in both new and old ways.

What does he want? Overall, his objective in business is to find products to offer, buy them at the lowest price he can, produce his offering (a catalog, in this case), have the designer make the book appealing, have me photograph the objects attractively, then find a price point for is products that is as much above his cost for all this as he can get it. He has to set the price just at the point before people say, "Nah, too much."

So, he's playing with an equation. When the differential is favorable and he makes a profit, he's happy. Each little thing that he can do to get costs down—less expensive paper, more product density on the page, cheaper manufacturing of product—while elevating what he charges extends the differential. This whittling and shaping of merchandise, cost, presentation and price is what he does. As the differential increases, he becomes happier. It is his form of expression, his Way, and as such it's very deep.

I think fulfilling this form is a big part of what moves businesspeople. It's a deep feeling, and it must be a lot like the one that a scientist gets when an elegant solution carries him over an impasse, or that fills the heart of an artist when the separate energies of color and line add up to an energy that is stronger than both together. And when it's put this way, most creatives at least understand it. They may feel a little something of this sense of rightness when they price their own work. But it's not quite the same gut response.

Artists get feelings from something entirely different, even when they are working with a commercial purpose. Their work makes them feel alive and worthy, and it drives them just as strongly.

Rather than describe how it works, I want to show you. I got a call about a year ago from someone at a design firm who had seen some personal work of mine, a series of still lifes. She wanted me to create some more in a similar vein to use in a brochure for a landscape architect. I was pleased that this strong work I'd done from my own impulses might find such a use. I even convinced the designer to let me do the garden photos that would run opposite the still lifes.

This was as good as it gets. I'd found a project that grew out of my own artistic work. I'd met a designer who was giving me the freedom to dream up the imagery, and I had subject matter that was beautiful to begin with (I didn't have to make things look better than they were, for a change). And on top of all that, they'd pay me!

There wasn't endless money in it, but I knew it could be one of the nicest projects, commercial or not, that I'd ever done, so we came up with a budget that was fair, if not munificent. I'm sure that for the landscape architect, it was more than he thought he'd ever spend on promotion. I began in the studio on the still lifes, and almost at once I did something unbusinesslike. I used some expensive props I'd already bought, but I didn't charge anything to the project. There was value for the client in their use and some cost should have been figured in, but I knew the budget wouldn't bear it. Still, the props were just what was needed. Oh well, big deal.

Then I made a worse business decision. I looked at a print I was about to send off to the designer and promptly had a better idea. Doing the shot had revealed a further, deeper possibility. So I set the whole thing up and shot again.

The budget was set and agreed upon, so I couldn't charge for the second shoot, but I knew that if I hadn't shot it again, I'd have looked at the finished piece and always known that it could have been better.

This was the point at which the artist in me asserted itself and overruled my business instincts. It was the exact point of balance. The whole project tipped over toward artistic exploration and was never businesslike again.

Here's the point. If the businessperson's satisfaction comes from increasing the cost/price differential, satisfaction for the artist—even the commercial artist—lies in doing something as beautifully, and as well, as it can be done. Cost can be a worry, time can be a concern, but these things don't stop us from doing what we have to do to make the final result stunning. In the end, we want to stand before the world in joyful silence with this perfectly crafted expression in my hands while people say, "How beautiful . . . how perfectly expressive . . . how moving!" It's kind of a dopey image, but it's true. Perhaps someone will say, "How much did that cost?" It's a point, but it's not the point.

Well, my project went on. I flew south to photograph the gardens. The landscape architect met me and took me around to his garden projects, and they were just remarkable—rich, varied, inventive, serene. We covered five gardens in two days, sometimes chasing the light frantically, sometimes waiting for it to be just right. It was exhilarating.

I had already done all the still lifes we'd need, but when I got back and saw my garden film, several new images suggested themselves to me. For example, I had brought back a picture of a beautiful stone staircase with plants weeping over its edges, all bathed in the light of evening, so I did a new still life of a hand holding a polygonal stone to run opposite it. Doing the new still life meant I had to switch out an earlier photo, but the juxtaposition was so perfect that there was clearly no choice. The extra work eroded my differential further. But the artist won.

In the end, I shot twenty still lifes to get the nine that ran. I was the one who pushed on, improving and exploring. When I got stuck, the designer would give me valuable input and suggestions. Her enthusiasm was as great as mine. I spent time and money, knowing that it was my time and my money. That didn't really matter to me. At a certain point I stopped worrying and told myself that this would be a beautiful piece, and that was what this project had to be in the end. I felt a deeper and deeper satisfaction.

The piece has just been printed. When the first press sheets arrived, I held them in my hands and felt the glow spread. Only 500 copies were printed. Perhaps a few thousand people at most will ever sit quietly with it and see it in its entirety, the way it was meant to be seen. The essayist George Trow pointed out that in our media culture, when ten million people see something it begins—just begins—to be considerable. So this piece won't even appear on the cultural radar. But the chance to work on it has been something rare, a chance to do something as well as I can do it.

And everyone who has worked on it feels the same way. The people at the design firm have given it time and attention that can never be compensated. I don't know for sure, but I suspect that everyone who worked on the piece throughout ignored the bottom line just to do it as it should have been done. Now, I'm sure my client, the catalog owner, would understand my happiness, but the way that I got happy would make no sense at all to him. Here I was spending time—not hours, but days and days—and I could never bill it or get it back. How could I make it up?

Well, really it wasn't all that hard. Other projects came in, things that weren't so entrancing. I did them, did them well, on time, on budget, and to everyone's satisfaction, including my own, and I was paid. So it's not as though I was setting other assignments aside to do the garden piece. I just worked on it on weekends. I was cutting down the differential and doing it willingly, and if I wasn't making it up completely elsewhere, at least I was cutting my losses. After all, I have been doing this kind of thing for years and I'm still in business.

The best explanation I can make for my behavior is that I was acting out my script, and it is different from my clients'. And we're playing with deep conviction. Because I have such conviction, I sometimes get exasperated that others won't do what my script indicates they should. I want to bang heads just to help clear their minds so they'll see what I see. The fact that good work, mutual respect, and profit come as a result of this process seems nearly a miracle.

The conflict that arises from this opposition has been eased somewhat since I had its workings demonstrated to me by the Actor's Studio exercise. When someone says something that sounds different from what I'd mean if I said it, I think, "Two scripts!" and things make sense. I understand what is driving the other person. If I can understand that their motivation is different and see what it is, I can at least find a way to talk with them.

Take the word "creative." When an artist—a painter or writer or composer, people I think of as real artists—sets out to do something creative, he or she seeks to discover something and let it manifest. It may draw on what is familiar, but its power comes from the fact that it has, at its center, something seen in a new way, and the newness makes it clearer.

But I find that when my clients say, "Let's do something creative," they at once pull out examples of other work, "creative" work. It's like watching a bunch of legal researchers digging through case law looking for precedents. They may find something they like and then depart from that, sometimes transcending it, sometimes just tricking it up in new clothes, but always starting with a past execution. The reason is simple: They have to be as sure as they can that this approach might work.

The reason for taking a creative approach in the commercial world is to capture the attention of jaded eyes with a fresh treatment, but business wants the assurance of precedent at the same time. One result is that visual effects have a way of becoming "looks." A few years ago, shadows started to creep into commercial photographs, offering a hint of mystery, of otherness. Perhaps they implied something unknown, something larger, taking place beyond the frame.

Quickly, it became a look. A wily old-line rep said to me, "Ya notice all those shadows everywhere now? Y'ever wonder where those shadows are coming from? They didn't usta be there." Well, they came from the same place that all those floating clock faces come from, or those swooshing delivery men, or glowing computers and floating globes, or those selective focus moves that point strongly to something that turns out to be nothing much. (As Spike Milligan once said, "Look! . . . A direction.")

It's a whole stockpot filled with things that look as though they just might mean something, and our business draws on it constantly to make soup. By contrast, art, the real thing, seeks to express things that really mean something but that are ineffable, that can't really be expressed any other way. Its process starts without a defined goal, and when it gets to the end of its journey, one just knows it. The work doesn't state its premise, it finds and reveals it, not just to the audience but to the artist, too.

Unlike art, commercial communications start with a given that must be expressed. It is a huge difference. Sometimes it's even a relief to have limits like that. I was working on a self-assigned project recently in which I wanted to explore how the visual rhythm of trees made an effect like music. I spent weeks in the woods of New England and the West Coast with no idea of exactly what I was looking for. I could only go out and hope that when the light was right, I'd be someplace where this effect might manifest and that I'd recognize it was happening. I'd call my wife late at night from some woodsy motel after I'd come in from shooting and express my anxiety over whether I was getting anything.

I kept thinking, I wish someone had just said, "A single gnarled cypress, ocean in the background, nice light. Has to say strength, integrity." An assignment, a clear objective. Precedent! It would have been so much easier. But in the end it would have lacked the resonance and contradiction that difficulty and grit bring to art.

It would be a mistake to think that artists and business people necessarily oppose each other, but they are different, and that becomes obvious when they're playing on the same stage. We face this in dealing with our clients and have to do some pretty smart reconciling to get things done. And so do they. It must be frustrating for them, too.

It's the process of reconciling that often leads to the best commercial work. The businesspeople on the job determine the goal and keep things on point, the artists explore complexity around what seems to be a simple goal.

At its absolute best, each player gives up a little space for the other's point of view, and the results can be amazing.

For example, at a photo shoot a few years ago a number of models were seated at a table in a modern, loftlike setting. Their work was to look young and trendy (and, I think, to smoke). Suddenly a young man with a towel around his waist and nothing else wandered through the back of the set. The photographer caught it. I don't know why the man was there, but he was definitely not part of the shoot plan. The models reacted hilariously, the artist had the sense to grab it, and the client had the wisdom to run it.

The moment was alive, even though it had nothing to do with what they'd set out to do.

For the sake of this discussion, I have set the poles of art and commerce farther apart than they necessarily appear. Of course people with an artistic basis concern themselves with costs, process, and outcomes. And of course businesspeople make intuitive leaps that can lead to unexpected results and satisfaction.

And, of course, the need to reconcile creative adventuring with reliable outcome can precipitate solutions that transcend the best hopes of both sides. That's where our business is fun, when its fun.

But it doesn't work when one mentality scorns the other. Then the real opportunity for creative symbiosis can be lost. I heard a colleague, a photographer-turned-businessperson, say that it was time for photographers to grow up and become businesspeople. Becoming businesspeople (or at least more businesslike) would be okay, but "grow up"?

Respect also has to work in the other direction. A client tells us what he wants, and he has the right to get just that. Imagine going to a restaurant and ordering roast beef and having the waiter say, "Look, I brought you something much better—goat-cheese pizza with watercress chutney! You'll love it!" And then insisting, and sulking when you continue to want what you want.

Still, there has to be a way for the group working on a project to get to a strong image, one with some texture and rasp that can actually catch and hold attention more fully than one that is so smooth that the mind just slides over it. I've had clients look at an idea and say, "People won't understand that." But, if people get a little bit snagged and intrigued by something that doesn't reveal itself entirely at first, they will be more likely to hold it. All the great campaigns seem to have that aspect to them. Those that don't are like cheese food.

Dr. Gail Brauning, a psychologist who runs a seminar on harmonizing left-and right-brained people in work settings, did a study of business organizations that showed that groups made up of like-minded people tended to decline because they didn't have people who would tell them things they didn't like but needed to know. The most effective businesses combined creative and analytical people. And, very interestingly, the most effective people in these businesses, the CEOs, tended to combine both creative and analytical capacities within themselves.

I know that the disconnect between the artistic and business mentalities is not news to anyone who is likely to be reading this magazine. But the next time you are annoyed by it, try just thinking to yourself, "Different scripts!" Don't say it out loud. Try not to laugh. And get a peek at the other person's script if you can. It always helps to resolve a situation if you know what is really happening.

First published in *Communication Arts*, September/October 1997.

Designers and Visibility:
Design—Not Biology—
Is Destiny

Véronique Vienne

Last year, in this column, Moira Cullen wrote a piece on gender and design in which she proposed Hillary Rodham Clinton as a role model—a risk taker willing to spark controversy in order to cut across gender, class, culture, and party lines. Today, in spite of her high visibility (or maybe because of it), the wife of the president is fighting an image battle she apparently cannot win. An exemplary woman by all accounts, she is treated by the media like just another celebrity, not like the hard-working public advocate she is.

In contrast—and in retrospect—Jackie Onassis could do no wrong. When she died, she seemed to have only admirers, no detractors. Unlike Hillary, who is a powerful player, a savvy communicator, and an accomplished speaker, the former Mrs. Kennedy had no political voice, was obsessed with privacy, and spoke softly, almost inaudibly. So why did the popular press lionize her to the point of idolatry?

Jackie seemed to have a natural affinity with the printed page. Paper was her natural element; ink was her true medium. She was simply a living icon. While her consistent two-dimensional image was a visual treat, Hillary's ever-changing hair, make-up, and wardrobe style has become a press joke. Every new attempt at defining her image only adds to the confusion. Ubiquity is not synonymous with visibility. The eye is an editing device: We only see what we recognize, and we only recognize what we already know. Design—not biology—is destiny.

Ellen Shapiro, a New York graphic designer who makes her high-profile clients even more visible (American Express, Goldman Sachs, Paine Webber, just to name a few), once tried to challenge the known content of a universal image. "The baby was dressed in pink, with matching ruffles, bonnet, socks, and booties," she tells. "On impulse, I wondered what it would be like to ask the mother if her baby was a boy or a girl." She never found out—questioning some of our shared assumptions is simply unthinkable. Confounded by the irrevocable character of her perception, she realized that gender is first and foremost a powerful optical illusion.

Right from the start, little girls are imprinted with the concept of "femininity"—and with the color pink—in the same way young birds are imprinted at birth with the sight of their mothers. Gender is so confusing it must be color-coded. In our Western culture, the female of the species learns at an early age to associate pastel colors with infantile helplessness and its maternal response. Did you ever wonder why the sight of a baby in pink prompts adults to make cooing sounds? Eye-catching pink, still the best-selling color for doll packaging, magazine covers, ice creams, and lipsticks, triggers in most teenage girls a sense of utter vulnerability combined with a vague anxiety regarding their sex. Later, remembering that they must be seen but not heard, women will dutifully seal their lips in shades of coral, mauve, rosebud, and peach.

You never forget that first pink dress. My mother wrapped mine in tissue and gave it to me. I just have to look at its faded silk, hand-sewn smock embroidery, puffed sleeves, and apron ties to remember what it was like to wear it. I must have been eighteen months old. That's the tallest I ever felt. By the time I had outgrown the dress, I was on the road to becoming a woman—someone who associates pleasant visual clues with a need for approval, protection, and love.

No wonder female designers later in life have trouble sorting out their feelings about colors, patterns, shapes, and textures. The blank page reminds them of the pristine dress they cannot soil; bright colors suggest forbidden toys; sharp angles signal the edge of the comfort zone. The visual world is charged with potential transgressions, and personal visibility is fraught with dangers.

"I didn't want to become a woman, I wanted to be a boy," says Rebeca Mendez. "At first, designing made me feel dead inside. I couldn't find the person behind the design." Like so many other designers, she hates being objectified, or rather adjectified, as a "woman" designer. She says she was reconciled with her gender—and with her professional choice—when she realized that design had little to do with "visibility," and everything to do with what's below the surface. A rather shy Art Center College of Design graduate student with a slight Mexican accent, she is today considered one of the newest and freshest voices of her generation. Her approach to design is internal, not external. "Paper represents the skin," she says. "I am interested in what we can see beneath—veins, tendons, skeletal structure." Her work shows intricate layers of translucent surfaces that overlap and intersect, revealing delicate emotional and physical connections between graphic elements.

For many designers born with XX chromosomes, coming out as a woman designer seems to be a critical step in the creative process. "It's important to realize that women have very different lives from men," says Ellen Lupton, curator of contemporary design at Cooper Hewitt, a writer-designer who became a household name when her book and exhibition *Mechanical Brides: Women and Machines from the Home to Office* won national acclaim. "We are tempted to reject the term 'woman' because it is disenabling and we don't want to be perceived as victims. But we won't be truly successful until we accept the fact that, as women, we can gain ground and lose ground, all at the same time."

Neither victims nor goddesses, women are in possession of one of the most powerful forces of nature: They can create new life. The "fe" in "female" is derived from "dhe," an ancient Indo-European prefix that replicates the sound of sucking. Also found in fecund, fertile, fetus, feed and feel, "fe" suggests a movement inward, into the body. For a woman, the act of creation is preceded by the act of gestation. While the idea of visibility is, for male designers, obvious and primary, for female designers it is only secondary. Birth is what happens "after."

With a massive injection of estrogen, the field of visual communication is undergoing a major transformation. The design process is fe-minized—literally "sucked" inside. The structural grid is slowly sinking below the surface. The division between image and type is being blurred. The page is acquiring more depth. The text, this symbol of male authority according to deconstructivist theories, is progressively losing its readability. References to the body abound. Hands, eyes, lips, organs, x-rays, footprints, and human shadows are turning up as icons. No longer a reflecting mirror, the graphic surface is now a threshold. Instead of looking at, readers are invited to look in.

April Greiman was one of the first designers to freely incorporate images of her own body in her work. "The personal and the professional agenda should be integrated," she says. "I am interested in the metaphorical properties of femaleness and look for kindred clients to match my own needs." Resolutely feminine, she is not a feminist but a universal female role model for both men and women designers. "Fame and visibility came only recently," she notes, "thanks to the support of the men who, I am proud to say, have been inspired by my work." Neville Brody, Rick Valicenti, Scott Makela, David Carson, and Rudy VanderLans are some of her champions. Still, she is weary of the limelight. "I respond visually, not verbally to praise," she says. "When people ask me to talk about my work, I look at my watch and mutter something about having to go back to work."

Less ego-directed than men, women are more self-involved; they unbashfully bring a personal dimension to their work. Margo Chase, a former medical illustrator who is known for her trend-defining album covers, masterfully handles the most intricate designs with the dexterity of a surgeon. She has been accused of being "feminine, ornate, and decorative" because she always incorporates elegant and lyrical semiorganic forms in her work. Instead of becoming defensive, she turned her biology degree into a unique trademark. Chase's typographical approach to problem-solving is zooidal—the result of a progressive cellular division of simple design elements. "I used to be invited to lecture because I was a woman designer, but now people call me because they are intrigued by my slide show on the subject of design germs," she says. If you don't want to be treated like a token, try impersonating a female bacteria.

Personal commitments are often an integral part of the creative process—but sometimes they coexist without mixing. Pat Gorman, who with her partner Frank Olinsky, came up in 1981 with the original MTV logo, now prides herself on being both a discreet designer and a good acupuncturist. She is known for her refreshingly primitive graphic approach and for her caring concern with AIDS, cancer, and heart-disease patients. "Problem-solving means helping people solve real problems, not trumped-up ones," she says. "I'll turn down a lucrative album cover for a rock group in order to design an unglamorous poster for the rain forest." The music business seems to foster nonconformity. "I have grown used to living in terror of making a fool of myself and being found out," she adds candidly, verbalizing what many women designers secretly fear the most. "I guess I am not a big supporter of the good-taste mentality," she concludes.

Sylvia Woodard, who teaches graphic design at Yale Graduate School of

Architecture, remarks that more and more of her female students are "interested in issues and learning to communicate them—not in serving corporate America and being members in good standing in men's institutions." The real story—the late breaking news, she says—is that more and more designers are opting out, not opting in. "They want to find new ways of working with each other—be inventive and stay on the edge."

Male or female, the next generation of graphic designers will be entrepreneurs, not managers. As the economy slows down and the technology speeds ahead, they can look forward to being thrown into the vortex. Less time and fewer dollars will be left to enter competitions, attend conferences, and network over lunch. People will have to opt out just to stay in the game. "I am starting to say no to things that don't contribute to my well-being," says designer-writer Fo Wilson. "One of the most important skills I have learned is not to be concerned with success." This sentiment is expressed by women coast-to-coast.

"I learned from Chuck Anderson and Joe Duffy to promote myself," says Sharon Werner in Minneapolis, "but I am not quite as aggressive as they are. I do not try to put on airs. What works for me is to be up front and honest." She speaks plainly, and her typographical style is unceremonious, candid, and surprisingly witty. She is representative of a rare breed of talented designers who know how to deliver the message and throw it away. The woman behind Werner Design Werks, Inc. makes the work of Duffy and Anderson look overworked, fussy, and almost "feminine" in comparison.

In Chicago, Jilly Simons keeps Concrete, her design office, purposely small. "I do very little marketing and never look for new business—I just design promo pieces from time to time." She wants every project to have a one-of-a-kind feeling, and, as a result, her work looks crafted rather than designed. "I don't think that I could achieve the same level of quality and the same level of pleasure if I let it get blotted," she says of her four-and-a-half-person operation.

In San Francisco, Linda Hinrichs, who left Pentagram after being for years its first and only female partner, now has her own design office, Powell Street Studio. "I admire women designers who manage to be successful in a city where, unlike New York, Los Angeles, or San Francisco, the cost of living is not exorbitant. These small-city pioneers are redefining success for all of us and making it possible for other women to think of design as a profession where one can keep a balance between business and personal life."

Women's genuine lack of interest for traditional ego perks—or at least their genuine unwillingness to pay the price for it—could turn out to be a major cultural influence. Already the emotional gap between mothers and nonmothers is slowly closing. "It's not easier, but at least it's okay to have a family now," says Hinrichs, who has a teenage son. "You don't have to be a closet mother anymore, you can even turn dropping out into an opportunity."

Karin Hibma, married to Michael Cronan, worked for years as his business partner. A couple of years ago she started a direct-mail sportswear operation, The Walking Man, in order to juggle her creative talent and her personal ambition with her two kids' schedules. "As a creative director, Michael reports to me for the clothing business," she explains, "and I report to him as business manager of Cronan Design."

"Maternity" is no longer a dirty word. "I love the design business," she says, "because it's a midwiving process."

For her new book, *Silenced Partners: Women of Modern Design*, Virginia Smith, author of *The Funny Little Man*, is exploring the complex relationship between men and women partners in the design profession by researching early modernists like Varvara Stepanova, who was married to Alexander Rodchenko, and Lilly Reich, who was an early collaborator of Ludwig Mies van der Rohe. "Traditionally, women were perceived as bringing a sense of domesticity to the workplace," she says. "Femininity used to equate babies, home, decoration—not design." Women will be the first to admit that it is still the case. The truth be told, diapers and design deadlines don't mix. Terrible twos and clients' tantrums don't mesh. School schedules and airlines schedules don't coordinate well. Giovanna Di Paola, who started, with her husband, Michael Jager, a prolific Vermont design office that produces some of the most serendipitous graphics, brochures, and catalogs for the snowboarding industry, says, "My three-year-old child is a new focus in my life, and I had to reduce my involvement with clients. There is a price tag to pay for being a mother. Although I am still growing as a designer, I had to give up my visibility. Forget judging shows or attending conventions . . . I am maxed out."

For many women, graphic communication represents a chance to develop a powerful voice without having to speak up in public. Hillary Rodham Clinton would not make a good graphic designer. Edison, not Gutenberg, is her patron saint. She does not "read" well in the press because she's more interested in the context than the text, the substance than the form, the message than the print media. Hillary does not need another makeover—just a small injection of ink in her bloodstream.

"Behind the veil of the printed word, women can find their voice," says Cindy Jennings, a corporate communication designer who recently moved her practice from Kansas City to Raleigh to work on a master's degree at North Carolina University. "The graphic expression is less demeaning than standing on a podium, taking everybody's time."

And making everyone yawn! The main criticism women had of the Miami AIGA design biennial last fall, besides that it was male-dominated, was that it was excruciatingly boring. "We talk to each other at conferences as if we were each other's clients," remarks Jennifer Morla, a leading San Francisco graphic designer whose intensely personal work has broad universal appeal. "We are locked into a trade mentality and fail to share our real experience."

Access to the printed word gives graphic designers an aura of authority. While men in the communication field are quite comfortable with this state of affairs, women tend to be critical of speakers who do not take advantage of this fortuitous situation to address important environmental, social, or community issues. In Los Angeles, Lorraine Wild, founder of the award-winning firm ReVerb, a four-women-one-man "consensus," wonders if getting recognition from peers means anything anymore. "The system is designed to support one particular version of the history of graphic design. Just like everything else attached to design, 'seeing' and 'being seen' has become more sweaty and obvious, more competitive, too time consuming—and somehow less fabulous," she remarks. "Our goal is not to win more awards but keep growing without stagnating."

San Francisco graphic designer Lucille Tenazas, a meticulous and articulate speaker and one of the most visible new leaders, has given a lot of thought to the responsibility of the designer-as-spokesperson. "I never repeat myself and never give the same lecture twice," she says. "I dissect my subject matter into fragments to encourage the process of questions and answers. I empathize with my audience—what they think and feel is not different from what I feel and think." For her, a speaking engagement is a chance to articulate her guests' concerns as much as her own.

Well-known women designers—Paula Scher, Sheila Levrant de Bretteville, Nancye Green—are living legends but not role models to a new generation. Today, less visible contributors to the communication field—teachers, department heads, art directors, writers, artists, curators, or clients—are more likely to inspire awe. People like Ruth Ansel, with her long list of art directing prestigious magazines, from *Harper's Bazaar* to *Vanity Fair*, says, "I never thought of myself as having a career." Or Michelle Barnes, a Denver-based illustrator who organized WIG (Women Illustrators Group), a networking salon for isolated artists who make a living meeting publishing deadlines but seldom get a chance to actually meet and share ideas; or Jeri Heiden, vice president of creative services and chief art director at Warner Bros. Records in Los Angeles, who consistently supports the work of women designers without ever ghettoizing their contribution. Or editorial design consultant Mary K. Baumann, who is exploring, with her husband Will Hopkins, the fuzzy frontier between printed matter and virtual design and who remarks: "I am getting progressively less visible as I go deeper into cyberspace, but it does not bother me." Or Kati Korpisaakko, a magazine art director at Condé Nast who has given many now-famous fashion photographers their first assignments but says, "I would feel very silly to be written about." The list of female mentors is long, and drawing it is a thankless task: You cannot give credit to people who don't want credit for themselves. Susan Slover, principal of Susan Slover Design, Inc. in New York, says it best: "Individually, we're all good at what we do. But together, we're even better."

Looking back at the last decade, Laurie Haycock, design director at the Minneapolis Walker Art Center, noticed that the greatest influence in graphic design were the silent brokers who "created a scenario for others to make permissive design." She mentions Sheila Levrant de Bretteville, Katherine McCoy, April Greiman, Lorraine Wild, Lucille Tenazas, Zuzana Licko, just to name a few. But she goes further. "We should also include the people who organized the lectures, wrote the comments on the entry forms, and edited the articles," she says. "Focusing on the text is a masculine thing. There is a new underground matriarchy in graphic design; its mandate is interactivity, not authority."

"It all starts with
   the way you feel
   about
   yourself.
Don't go into
   situations where
   you are
   reduced
   to less
   than what you are."

   –Maruchi Santana

"I have
   more problems
   being short
   than
   being
   female."

   –Jennifer Morla

"You are a designer
   at your desk
   but you
   become a
   'woman' designer
   as soon as
   you step out
   in the world."

   –Fo Wilson

"As soon as
   you write about
   not being
   visible enough,
   it becomes
   an issue."

   –Diana Graham

"When asked
   to give a talk,
   say 'Yes'–then worry
   about it."

–Sue Llewellyn

"When giving a speech,
   be prepared–be prepared
                     to be
   spontaneous."

–Mary K. Baumann

"When a
   woman takes a risk,
   everyone
benefits
   from it."
   –Moira Cullen

First published in *Communication Arts*, September/October 1994.

(Thinking About
Communication)

John Bielenberg

There was something about having my name on the door of a studio that changed the responsibility I felt to really understand the profession of graphic design.

It started in 1991, after I bought out my former partner. Intense and debilitating fear set in upon finalizing the buyout, followed closely by a liberating sense of freedom. First, the fear of the obligation of generating the commissions necessary to fuel the studio and then the freedom of finally being able to begin to define for myself what this business is actually about. Until this point, I was so preoccupied with the struggle of establishing a career and doing the work that I was unable to gain any perspective or insight into the truth of graphic design.

A primary catalyst in the search for understanding came indirectly from a client. While working on a project for an investment firm run by a brilliant man named Harold Arbit, I became acquainted with a human behavioral concept called heuristic bias. Simply stated, heuristics are preset patterns of thinking that enable us to make quick shortcut decisions. There are thousands of examples of heuristic bias, but one of my favorites is called overweighing information. An illustration of this is when people read in the newspaper about a shark attack and then steer clear of the beach, even though the actual probability of being harmed by a shark is infinitesimal. They have altered their behavior based on an inaccurate conclusion drawn from an overweighed bias.

Judgment and choice are pervasive activities that affect every aspect of our lives, including the design process. For the most part, judgments are made intuitively without apparent reasoning and sometimes almost instinctively. This results in a relatively useful decision that allows us to function in a very complex environment. One can imagine the gross inefficiency if everyone had to completely analyze every decision before any action was taken. Thus, heuristic biases are a necessary part of our brain function. However, as the illustration [this refers to the diagram called Core for a Mass Audience] shows, people can make illogical decisions that seem rational and thoughtful.

CORE FOR A MASS AUDIENCE

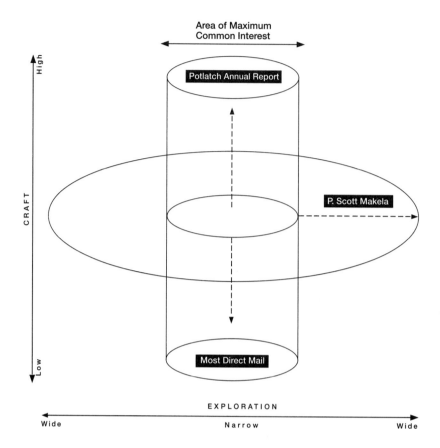

I realized that graphic designers, like all human beings, are subject to these same principles. Although graphic design is generally thought of as a creative profession, graphic designers are sometimes victims of preset patterns of thinking that inhibit them from free creativity and from truly understanding the essential nature of what they do.

Very Cool, So What?–The Intoxication of Craft

Just like an addict creates a lust for drugs or alcohol, the designer develops a craving for the new, the visually compelling, and the beautiful. The image becomes an end in itself. The graphic language sometimes takes a dominant role over the message being communicated. Small capitalized type letterspaced and reversed out of a dense black background looks cool because of the dynamic tension of scale and mass, even if you can't read the type. Sometimes the graphic language is the message. Not every document needs to be read to understand the meaning or essence of the communication. The fact remains that the reversed type would be visually interesting regardless of whether it is communicating the proper message.

Why are we interested in viewing small 2-D reproductions of layouts in design annuals without much, if any, sense of the context, message, goals, or audience for these pieces? Because graphic designers have developed a hyperliterate visual sense and a highly refined appreciation for the craft of graphic design. I call it the intoxication of craft. Within any field the quest for, and celebration of, high craft is admirable, but the responsible creation of graphic design involves more than the skillful manipulation of elements on a page or surface.

I concluded that the intoxicating power of the design solutions we see in design shows, and around us daily, interfere with our ability to clearly understand the role of the designer in the communication of a message. Designers overweigh the craft component of visual solutions much like people overweigh the possibility of a shark attack.

Designer as Engineer

The profession of graphic design is principally about engineering a connection between a message and an audience. I use the word "engineering" to define a rational and thoughtful problem-solving approach that also accommodates a creative and intuitive phase. In graphic design, the message and the intended audience are usually generated or dictated by the needs of a client rather than those of the designer. Addressing this issue, *ID* magazine quotes Tibor Kalman as saying, "Graphic design is a language, not a message." The responsibility of the graphic designer involves crafting the most appropriate and effective visual language given the defined objectives of the assignment.

This relationship between engineering and graphic design should be obvious to anyone practicing in this field. However, discussion about design often addresses the tools and craft rather than the appropriateness of the solution for the specific audience. During 1993's AIGA Conference in Miami, I was perplexed by the debate between Roger Black and David Carson. Although played for laughs and quite entertaining, the discussion revolved around their vastly different typographic approaches to editorial design. The truth, of course, is that each approach can be effective

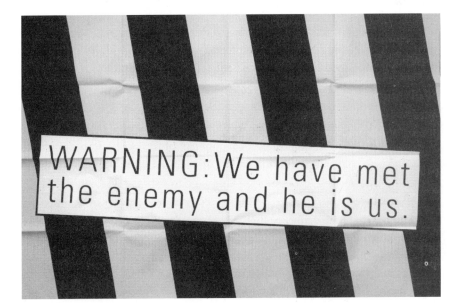

Warning Poster. 4' x 6' poster silk-screened in two colors onto billboard paper.

depending upon the criteria of the design objectives. The formal structure and elegance of Roger Black's *Esquire* layout is as successful and appropriate to its audience as the unstructured and informal chaos of David Carson's *Ray Gun* design. "I like it" or "I don't like it" should not be part of a serious debate about the profession of graphic design.

The Core of Maximum Common Interest

I developed the diagram pictured here to try and depict the relationship between the design of a graphic language, a message, and an audience. I call it The Core of Maximum Common Interest. It shows that you can define a core of common attributes within any given audience. The wider or more mass the audience, the more general the attributes must be. For example, if you are trying to reach a mass audience like *Time* magazine, Carson's design for *Ray Gun* would probably hit outside the densest part of the core on the outer perimeter of the disk. Also note that within a given core the graphic-design solution can be created with either high or low craft. The annual reports that Kit Hinrichs of Pentagram has created over the years for Potlatch Paper are firmly entrenched within the appropriate core but at a very high craft level. Unfortunately, a design can also be effective at a low craft level. Almost all direct mail would fall into this area of the core.

Above: *?!Book.* 5 1/2" x 8 1/2" hardbound book printed in one color on recycled paper with foil-stamped covers.

It's not coincidental that most cutting-edge design today is created for niche audiences. The youth market is especially ripe for experimental solutions, as it is more accepting of change and less prone to the shock of the new. However, if a new design style is powerful and timely, it can pull or expand the mass core over so that that style is assimilated into the popular vocabulary. A recent example of this phenomena is the work of P. Scott Makela in Minneapolis. He originally developed his unique densely layered approach within the experimental laboratory of the graduate program at Cranbrook. I expect that this style evolved out of both the emerging computer technologies and his ability to freely explore a language to express his own messages. Although originally reaching a narrow audience, I suspect that we will witness a gradual widening of the core to embrace this new visual language.

The Conflict

Conflict often exists when you combine the intoxication of craft, exposure to and interest in cutting-edge design, with the engineering of a client-driven message to a client-defined audience. Graphic designers are generally drawn to the profession for reasons that have little to do with engineering process and lots to do with creativity and self-expression. Whenever I ask my design students at California College of Arts and Crafts why they want to be graphic designers, nobody ever mentions client objectives in their answer. I believe that this conflict between the needs of a creative professional and the needs of a commissioning client has always existed to some degree in the field of graphic design and other creative professions. An understanding of the process does not necessarily equal harmony.

There is a principle in physics that states that *systems tend to attain a state of minimum energy and maximum disorder.* The energy and motivation of the designer to explore new solutions is required to propel the process of an evolving visual vocabulary forward. It is this very conflict that forces the core to widen and move. Without conflicting agendas, it is possible that the tendency of a system to maintain a state of minimum energy would result in a stagnation or cessation of visual exploration in the field of graphic design.

The Conclusion

I have embarked on a continuing series of self-initiated and funded projects that address issues related to the practice of graphic design. In this case I am the commissioning client, and this allows me to craft both the graphic language and the message.

The first piece I produced was the Warning Poster. Intended primarily as a teaser to the other projects to come, this poster addressed the need for introspection by the design profession. A subtheme was the designer's role in wasting paper to communicate a message in an inefficient way that could have been done more simply. The poster was four by six feet in size. I also realized that although I could only produce a

Above: Virtual Telemetrix Annual Report. 11" x 17" brochure printed in black and pearlescent varnish on recycled Kromekote paper.

limited number of posters, if it were featured in design magazines or annuals, the message would reach thousands of designers. The design of the piece thus had to be direct enough to communicate a message, rather than just a style, when it was reproduced at a small size. In essence, I was using the publication as my production. The actual printed poster functioned as mechanical art.

The second piece was the red *?!Book*. This was a 100-page hardbound book, and the only message was that it had been printed on recycled paper—a bizarre example of waste and lack of content. Like the Warning Poster, the easiest way for me to communicate with a wide audience of designers was to use the design annuals as production. It didn't matter which spread was featured, because each page says essentially the same thing. I now know that in my attempt to whittle the visual language down to its most primary form, I ignored some of the elements of current styling and craft that determine whether a piece will be selected in a design competition.

The most current project was an annual report for the fictitious company Virtual Telemetrix, Inc. This was originally intended as an attempt to trick designers and competition judges by producing a visually compelling document that communicated absolutely nothing. I decided that this joke was too self-serving and one-dimensional, and the report evolved into more of a parody that pokes fun at the designer, the annual report, and corporate America. This time I made sure that I included enough visible craft and production finesse to ensure that competition judges would take it seriously. I needed to engineer the solution to hit within the overlap of my core and that of a wider audience of designers.

I will continue to produce these projects in an attempt to further my understanding of the profession of graphic design. Although understanding will not completely eliminate the frustration and conflict inherent in the designer/client relationship, it can help direct that energy into a more productive mode. The struggle to clearly view this relationship and its value is the challenge that differentiates the designer from the decorator. We have the potential to wield great power if we understand that our true value is in communication.

The principles of heuristic bias, the intoxication of craft, the core diagram, and the concept of the designer as engineer are tools that help me maintain a perspective on the process we must go through to produce graphic design that functions on the highest levels of both communication and craft. Ralph Caplan has used the term "exotic menials" to describe the general perception of graphic designers. I believe that understanding the role of visual language in communication of messages, in combination with our skill at crafting appropriate solutions, is what can elevate us to a position above this perception.

First published in *Communication Arts*, March/April 1995.

V | Design in Context

Good graphic design is a mirror of the world. This part of the book looks into the mirror to show the reader the vast opportunity design has—to illuminate and inspire.

Blowing Up
the Museum

Cecilia Holland

I know nothing about design, but I have strong opinions
about it anyway, and I had a very strong opinion about the jacket of my novel *Pillar Of
The Sky*: I hated it.

The irony was that I had requested that Knopf hire Braldt Bralds to do this jacket.
For a previous novel of mine, *The Sea Beggars*, he had designed an award-winning

jacket I loved. The story of *The Sea
Beggars* took place during the Dutch
revolt against Spain in the sixteenth
century, and the jacket featured a pretty
girl in full Dutch costume, leaning
invitingly toward the reader, an orange
in one hand, a ship in the other. Bralds
was of Dutch heritage, and his design
captured the zest and excitement of the
history.

The jacket for *Pillar* seemed to me
a disaster. *Pillar* was set in the Bronze
Age, at Stonehenge, for which Bralds
obviously had no personal frame of reference. It was all abstract and distant to
him, and he made Stonehenge look
like a Neolithic Disneyland. I knew
from my editor at Knopf that they had
sent the design back twice for revisions, and the biggest and worst revision was right there in the middle of
the jacket, a weird human figure, dwarfed by the enormous stones, dressed in a
diaphanous gown á la Frederick's of Hollywood. It looked like Tinkerbell visits the
Dawn of Time.

On the other hand, the first jacket had been sublime. I brooded on this until my sister, who is a designer, suggested I call Bralds and ask him what had gone wrong.

"You never know," she said. "You might learn something."

I called Braldt, who remembered the project very well and was as unhappy with the result as I was. Knopf had rejected all his designs, in the end forcing Tinkerbell on him, or out of him, and he had resolved to stop doing book jackets as a consequence.

I could understand this. The next time I spoke to my sister, I waxed righteously indignant about the suborning of artist impulse, the evil taint of commerce, etc.

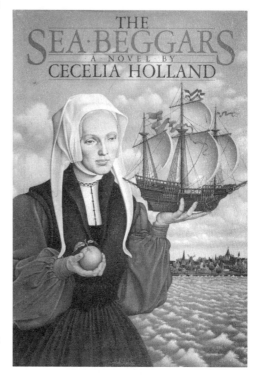

She said, "You don't know what you're talking about. There's a whole layer of this process that is invisible to you, which is the book designer at Knopf. That's where you ought to go asking questions."

Then she said, "One of the designers at Knopf now is Chip Kidd. He's very con-troversial, a lot of people really like his work, and a lot of people don't. Why don't you call him?"

Which I did and got through immedi-ately, which surprised me; nobody at Knopf is ever at the phone. Chip Kidd was young, intense, curious, articulate. I had no idea what to ask him; as I talked to him I was looking at a collection of his work, very intrigued and mystified. There was something barbaric about all of these pieces, like an explosion in a museum, Christ's head stuck on a clown, chunks of odd type, decapitated photographs. The jackets looked to me like puzzles, secret messages—a characterization Kidd himself rather genially agreed with but which satisfied nothing. The jacket is supposed to present an idea of the book; what these jackets presented was enigma.

After I had hung up, swarms of questions came to me, and the primary one was, who the devil do you think is looking at all this?

I asked my sister, "Who the devil does he think is looking at all that?"

My sister said, "That's the real issue. There are a lot of people who think design has gotten too self-involved, too self-referential, that designers are making work pri-marily for other designers to look at. There's a certain amount of worry that design is misleading people—providing false information, maybe. Dysinformation."

What a great word. Enchanted, I called another designer, Bill Drenttel, whose arti-cle in *Communication Arts* on the importance of the written word had struck me as subtle and intelligent.

Now I had a question to ask, and proudly enough I trotted it out. "Do you think design has become too self-referential?" And I mentioned Chip Kidd's jackets and their beguiling inscrutability.

Even over the phone I could sense Drenttel recoiling. Clearly I had stumbled in at the beginning of an argument in which he was very far advanced. He had heard all this "self-referential, inside-information, elitist codes" stuff before and he wasn't buying any of it. He poured forth with a flood of opinion: As for New York dominating design, people always said things like that about interesting and successful trends; people said the same things about San Francisco. And anyhow elitism is good; elitism means high standards and good taste. Look how the Knopf revolution in book packaging has drawn so much imitation. Chip Kidd's designs have brought many more people in to read books that otherwise wouldn't have, and damn it, I ought to be grateful.

I enjoyed this conversation very much, one-sided though it was, and ran it through my mind all the next few days. Drenttel made excellent sense to me. Publishing is still solidly based in New York; therefore it would be odd if New York designers did not dominate book design. Obviously the Big Apple has not lost its sense of mission. The mention of San Francisco rang bells with me: another city that prides itself on leading the heathen out of the wilderness. I don't care if they're wrong, so long as they're vigorous, and I was hitting a real vein of vigor here.

The use of the word "revolution" delighted me. American publishing has been staggering along under a burden of nineteenth-century techniques and concepts, and a revolution would come in handy. A few days after I talked to Drenttel and Chip Kidd, I went into a bookstore and picked out all the Knopf books on the shelves strictly by their covers.

Is that a sign of revolution? Or just somebody holding on for dear life while everything else is swept away? I talked to a friend of mine at Knopf, who is not entirely pleased with Chip Kidd's work or the larger event that is Knopf under Sonny Mehta, who replaced Robert Gottlieb as editor-in-chief there in 1985. "It's all just marketing," this person said. "All the focus is on the packaging of the book, rather than the content." The revolution may be mere glitz, a superficial and misleading coherence masking the widening chaos: dysinformation.

There was something I was missing here. I went into another bookstore and looked at all the covers, getting very frustrated. Then, a few days later, muddling in my own library, I happened on one of my early novels, and everything suddenly crystallized.

Harry Ford was the book designer at Atheneum in the sixties, when I began publishing. His jackets for my first five novels all followed the same form: a tall slim book, with the cover wrapped around, the top half a black background for the title, the bottom half chosen from an artwork contemporary with the period of the novel. The jacket for *The Firedrake*, which ends with the Battle of Hastings, used a section from the Bayeux Tapestry. For a novel about the Mongols, Harry found a Persian illumination of a Mongol siege.

To me, all these designs were magic. In a single stroke they placed the book not only in its historical setting but also in a wider intellectual context. The jackets made the book important because they made even the remote historical past seem real and immediate. They made the book a sort of core sample of the culture.

Harry Ford's jackets were extraordinary even for their time; he possessed unique qualities of knowledge and craft. But they were also typical of literary design from that period, in that they sprang from and tapped into a sense of a common American cultural base. Their references, like the Bayeux Tapestry, were historical, European, public, open, and the materials of a common past.

Contrast that with Chip Kidd's design for Cormac McCarthy's prize-winning novel *All The Pretty Horses.* In this brilliant jacket the image is a photograph cropped so severely that it takes you a minute to see that you are looking over a horse's neck at the distant horizon—a perfect emblem for the book. And by its requirement that you stay with it a while and make yourself see what you are looking at, the jacket also conveys something of the book's theme, of putting things together, of making sense out of confusion and chaos.

I realized now what so intrigues me about Chip Kidd's designs: They are stripped, cleansed of meaning. What is recognizable, Christ and clown both, has been broken up so that assigning it a traditional meaning is impossible. These designs reflect what has happened in American society as a whole in the past thirty years. We have deconstructed ourselves.

Somewhere in there, maybe about the time Tinkerbell invaded Stonehenge, Americans stopped knowing and believing in a single idea of ourselves and where we came from and what we're supposed to be doing. We no longer share an intellectual context. It's politically incorrect (and inadequate) to be Western and European, but we're really not equipped to be anything else. Harry Ford could reach back a thousand years to the Battle of Hastings and pull up something instantly recognizable as an emblem of that moment, but I wonder how many people today know or even care what happened in 1066; in some important respects 1966 is closer to 1066 than 1966 is to 1993. Between 1993 and that time a mere thirty years ago lies a chasm of destroyed values.

Common values are the connective tissues of a culture. Having boiled away the values of our past, we're left with nothing but a jumble of bones and teeth. Now here are designers like Chip Kidd trying to stick these fossils back together. Small wonder that, like the first dinosaur hunters, he comes up with some pretty fabulous beasts.

Is this the revolution? Is Chip Kidd reorienting book design the way Alvin Lustig did at the avant-garde New York publisher *New Directions* in the thirties? Maybe it's just that it takes a decapitated Christ to get my attention, because all this going into bookstores and staring at book jackets has finally brought something home to me.

There's a lot of interesting stuff going on here. In among the predictable and commercial lie true marvels. For one, there is Louise Fili's cover for *Bridges Of Madison County,* which held me for a long time. Fili of course is a woman, with a woman's drive to integrate and to complete. With its packed postcard image jammed into the middle of a blank brown screen, her work seems like a tunnel into the past, a reach backward, a conscious effort to recover something gone. Right in the middle is a big blob of dark red like a heart.

The contrast with Chip Kidd is tonic. Blowing up things is fun, but putting them together lasts longer. We've all had a great time, disassembling the universe, and where has it gotten us? We trashed the museum, and what we've wound up with is junk.

As Neil Postman says, symbols are magical and require respect. They derive their power from their connectedness with inflexible truth. Break them, disconnect them, and their power is gone—both the power to reassure and the power to shock. Without reverence, there's no blasphemy. Maybe that's why, now, so much art (and certainly so much advertising) seems to be struggling for shock value. "Young, hip, noir," is the way my anonymous friend at Knopf put it; to me it looks more like "Pinch me and see if I'm dead."

In this sense, then, a lot of contemporary image-mongering is indeed deliberately dysinformational. To maul and break symbols until their meaning is debased or gone utterly is to lie about meaning and about symbols. Also the audience is smarter than that. They see the trick, they stop responding. There's something naïve now even in trying to shock people, because nobody's shocked anymore. So what's to do? Maybe it's time for the tough stuff, recovering standards, reconnecting with the past, and seeing the whole world again.

First published in *Communication Arts*, September/October 1994.

Postindustrial
Postliteracy: Thoughts Inspired
by an Evening of Conversation

David Lance Goines

When writing was invented, it provided people with the
ability to transcend their own limited lives and pass on knowledge to generations yet
unborn. The first literature, *The Epic of Gilgamish*, concerns itself with the concept
of death, and writing indeed confers a sort of immortality on the author. The skill of
writing was difficult to acquire, and only a small portion of society needed or wanted
it: the priestly, administrative, legal, and religious classes and merchants, traders,
and the odd poet. That was about it. Despite an increase in the accessibility of writing tools and skills, literacy—however defined—probably hovered around 20 percent
of society until the beginning of the Industrial Revolution.

The great push to universalize literacy, which in the industrialized West has
resulted in near 100 percent literacy, is now undergoing a curious erosion. Inner-city
schools, such as those in Oakland, California, report a frustrating 75 percent D and F
average for black and Hispanic students. Though schools with high white and Asian
enrollment report high average grade points, the grades of their black and Hispanic
students are just as poor as in those schools where blacks and Hispanics are in the
majority.[1]

One conclusion is that black and Hispanic students are so disenfranchised, so
divorced from the dominant society, that they see no point whatsoever in participat-
ing in the educational process. This may be part of the story, but there may be more
to it.

In the film *Star Wars*, a comprehensive vision of a vast intergalactic culture presents highly intelligent robots, star ships, an intensely trained priest-warrior class,
and trade and commerce of every kind. What it also shows, upon careful examination, is a society that is apparently illiterate. Princess Leia Organa does not write a
letter to Obi-Wan Kenobi, she makes a short video recording and transports it via
robot. Luke Skywalker is a frustrated water farmer, stuck on a backwater planet.
Apparently, his education has been confined to robot maintenance, marksmanship,
and hair-raising aerobatics. In his uncle's home, there is no sign of literature or
writing. Trade is done in hard cash, and credit—if there is such a thing—is at best a

local affair. With the exception of cryptic identifying marks on military battleships, the film contains no writing of any kind.

The reason is not hard to find: Literacy, as we use it, was developed for the transfer and preservation of knowledge. If some other means is developed, one more in line with the way humans ordinarily communicate, this might be what the future holds.

Let us suppose for a moment that you were prevented from reading or writing anything. That you instantly became functionally illiterate. What would happen? Not much, if you think about it. You could get all your news over the radio and television via speech and sight. Traffic lights are red, yellow, and green, and traffic signs are different shapes and colors. If the words "stop" or "yield" were removed, it wouldn't make too much difference. If you want to communicate with someone far away, just pick up the telephone. If you want to leave a message, the telephone answering machine will record it. You can pay your bills with cash or with a credit card. You may identify yourself thoroughly with fingerprint, iris print, voice print, and photograph. Signatures may be forged, but not these. If you need to add, subtract, multiply, or divide, a pocket calculator does all the work. You do not need to learn long division any more than you need to learn to make fire with flint and steel or hunt through the veld for food. If you want to preserve a thought, speak into a recording device. If you want to preserve an image, take a photograph. If you want to preserve both image and words, take a video. If you are bored, go to the movies, watch TV, listen to music, or play video games, chess, or cards.

Complex thought develops during expression. How often do we have no idea what we are arguing until it is actually coming out of our mouths? How often have you watched your thought develop as you work it out on paper or, more recently, a monitor? The direction and content of Western thought has been guided and formed by the tools we've used to express ourselves. By extension, electronic media are necessarily going to change the course of thought. I believe this is already happening in graphic design and pop culture.

I have no idea what many billboards are saying about their product, and with some I don't even know what product they are advertising. This is neither good nor bad, it just is.

We have proven to be an extremely successful species. Evolution happens because something first works and then everything else shuffles into alignment. I expect there will be a long-enough period of coexistence of literate and illiterate for the shakedown to reveal the best survival strategy.

When in the course of evolution it is time to bridge the technologies, or to make adaptations in an evolutionary sense, the adaptive strategy is always flexibility. The animals that can do both what has been and what is coming are most likely to survive. It is true that some technologies are all but forgotten, and usually this is because better ways have been found to do the same things or because what was done in the first place is now no longer needed. Literacy is not necessarily the best way to do anything; it's just a tool that we're using right now until something better comes along.

The usefulness of reading and writing won't utterly disappear, but the goal of universal literacy is clearly a thing of the past and is becoming more circumscribed by the day. What is already happening is that a substantial segment of society cannot be addressed by literate means, and we can either adapt to this or blind ourselves to what may (or may not) be a bridge to an unimaginable—but inevitable—future. If you restrict yourself to the literate, you are at the very least cutting yourself out of some important lines of communication. Prediction is notoriously wrong because we are limited by what we know. What usually happens is that the real future—the one that actually happens—contains both possibility and impossibility that will only seem inevitable after it's already here.

Just like people, every technology has its birth, infancy, vibrant youth, maturity, decline, doddering old age, and death. Some hold long leases, others, mayflylike, come and go in the twinkling of an eye. Letterpress printing's last hundred years reached a zenith of perfection. The finest sailing ships were built after the nasty, grimy steamer was regularly plying the seas and frightening the fish. The most perfect mechanical watch postdates the plain, cheap, ultra-accurate electronic digital.

In each case, the thing that makes a technology perfect is the thing that replaces it. But in the swan song of a technology is more beauty than was ever in its vigorous growth and maturity. The giveaway for impending obsolescence is that the technology finally works right, it's finally almost perfect. That's the sign that it's actually dying. The clipper ship was made possible by steam power and industrial progress; the mechanical watch reached perfection through computer and laser technology that made an accurate watch so cheap that a mechanical watch became no more than jewelry, with accurate time-telling not much more than a bragging point.

Photography, sound recording, movies, radio, telephones, television, electronic media of all kinds, and latterly the Internet—with its chat rooms, enforcement of typing skills, and near or potential replacement of reference books, printed journals, newspapers, magazines, and libraries—are literacy's children and heirs.

The Industrial Revolution has been building a world that no longer needs writing or books. Sheet music was commonplace until recorded music became even more commonplace. I knew a fellow in the 1960s whose job it was to reverse-compose rock 'n' roll—fulfilling some sort of anachronistic copyright requirement, he wrote the lyrics and music by listening to the recording. Who learns jazz and rock by studying sheet music? A substantial percentage of professional musicians can't read music and don't care to learn, because they don't need to; and besides, the kind of music they're composing and performing is not particularly susceptible to musical notation.

Writing is not frozen speech, and musical notation is not frozen music. These are stopgap measures that were invented because the tape recorder wasn't invented first.

People are not getting dumber. Literate snobbery would like you to "kill your television," but administrators of standardized intelligence tests can find only one explanation for the across-the-board increase in intelligence test scores: the five to seven hours a day young people spend with the television set. The rapidly shifting quick scene changes, the necessity of holding three seven-minute segments of plot interspersed with many super-quick little stories and appeals, the frenetic demands made on the viewer all add up to getting smarter in an equally frantic world that demands smartness as a survival strategy. This is a postliterate medium if ever there was one, and it makes your brain different, and it's not bad.

The middle class is, has always been, and may continue to be, the literate class. It is the class of traders, merchants, and artisans, all of whom need to communicate over time and distance. Until writing was invented, this communication was uncertain, difficult, and transient. During the Industrial Revolution, the needs and desires of the middle class expanded to include both high and low, until all Industrial citizens took it for granted that "Reading is Fundamental."

As members of the middle class, graphic designers appear to share this notion, but a careful look will reveal that while we render lip service to literacy, an increasing percentage of our activity is focused on nonliterate communication. Signs, symbols, emblems, color, shape, motion, sound, and image are far more important tools than alphabetized words themselves.

A look around will show that the Industrial Revolution is emphatically over, that there are no "preindustrial" or "emerging" peoples or nations, and that you're either already a member of the rapidly shrinking middle class or your chances of joining it are shrinking even more rapidly. And if you're not a member of the middle class, then ipso facto presto chango you don't need reading and writing anymore, so why kid yourself?

Graphic designers—consciously or otherwise—are increasingly catering to preliterate, a-literate, subliterate, or illiterate consumers. You do not, after all, have to be well educated in order to spend money, and graphic designers most certainly go where the money is. It's our job to sell, not to educate or judge.

Perhaps the admittedly marginalized members of society are, in a sense, more in the vanguard than in the baggage train. Why learn to read and write and figure if you don't actually need any of these skills in your day-to-day life? Perhaps we are moving through literacy into a world in which literacy is no longer important or useful. Like an old tractor abandoned in the fields, perhaps literacy is a tool that we don't need any longer. So, we just walk away and leave it to rust.

Notes

1. Hank Resnik, editor, "A Roundtable Discussion: Race and Social Class in the Berkeley Schools 25 Years after Integration," *The Berkeley Insider* (June 1993): 14–15.

First published in *Communication Arts*, January/February 1999.

Where Ideas
Come From

David Lance Goines

You have to kiss a lot of frogs in order to find a prince.
–American Folk Saying

Ideas seem to come from a number of sources. A big one is
stimulus diffusion, which is roughly described as the transfer of ideas and technologies via cross-cultural influence. The interesting thing about stimulus diffusion is
that the most important ideas seem to be the result of poor communication, misun-
derstandings, and the rough tailoring of somebody else's notions to a new and different milieu. A good illustration of this is the introduction of vowels by the Greeks to
the Phoenician alphabet. So far as can be determined, the vowels result from a simple misunderstanding of the sounds and functions of several unpronounceable (to
the Greeks) Semitic consonants. Half-seeing or half-hearing something can lead to a
completely different interpretation than if you had been paying full attention.
Sometimes you can't pay full attention because you can't understand what's going
on; this is what leads children to their often bizarre interpretations of ordinary
things. It's no accident that most innovations are made by young people, to whom
new ways of looking at things are a normal part of daily life.

A second place where ideas come from is in response to the demands of the
marketplace. The Kremer prize is a prize that was offered to the first man-powered
flight that fulfilled certain rigid requirements. The Kremer prize, therefore, can be
said to have created the demand that led to a technological breakthrough. On August
23, 1977, Paul MacCready, an aeronautical engineer from Pasadena, California, and
one of many contestants who responded to the challenge, was awarded the Kremer
prize for creating the first successful human-powered aircraft. The Gossamer Condor
was flown over the required three-mile, figure-eight course by Brian Allen. The
Gossamer Albatross (created by the same team as the Condor) crossed the Dover
Channel in 1979.

Not to be discounted is pleasure in introducing change for its own sake. Change,
per se, is highly valued in the world of pure ideas. Advertising, for example, is in
constant flux. First, there is the perception that people get bored with the same old
ads and need a constant barrage of new ones to stimulate their jaded perceptions.
Second, and probably more significant, is that designers and art directors themselves

value innovation and change.

Deliberate or accidental misuse of an idea or technology can also lead to something new:

- Avon's Skin-So-Soft moisturizer has been discovered by consumers to be a really good insect repellent.
- Peanut butter is effective for removing bubble gum from hair.
- Dawn dishwashing detergent is good for degreasing animals that have been harmed in oil spills.
- In these cases, though the product itself is not new, the application to which consumers have put it is new; thus, the product becomes, in effect, a new product.

It might seem that the task of thinking is to find new solutions to old problems. The history of intellectual and technological progress, however, inclines me to think that once a question is asked, a solution will arise, sooner or later. Therefore the ability to ask questions is of more value than an ability to provide answers.

The Big Ideas

The first big idea was agriculture. This is the one that moved humanity from tiny groups of hunter-gatherers into large concentrations of highly interdependent, social creatures. Agriculture was invented, on and off, more than once in human history but basically caught on permanently about eleven thousand years ago. The consequences of agriculture were: cities and civilization[1], slavery, war, taxes, and record keeping.[2]

Out of these five, which seem to have developed as the result of the population explosion that followed the abundance and regular supply of food that agriculture promoted, record-keeping evolved by around the year 3000 B.C. into writing. The alphabet and metallurgy arose around the second millennium B.C. The alphabet was invented in Palestine or Syria, probably between 1800 and 1650 B.C. Monotheism, too, arose with or at about the time of the water-empire pharaoh Akhenaten[3] (c. 1375 B.C.), finds its champion in the Old Testament Moses, and takes root with the Near-Eastern nomadic peoples after being violently rejected by the Egyptians.

Of the institutions resulting from the invention of agriculture, at least two of them can be classed as negative. That is, they provide an impediment to the development of further ideas. These two offenders are slavery and war.

As the Roman Empire waned, and with it certain formal aspects of slavery, there began a flowering of technological development, particularly in the Near East, the results of which were transmitted to Europe through trade and the Crusades. The three most significant developments were alchemy, later developing into chemistry; medicine, the apotheosis of which is drugs and antibiotics; and the eventual invention in the West of printing by moveable type.

Alchemy, chemistry, and medicine are all related, and all owe a great debt to the Indian concept of zero as a placeholder (458 A.D.), without which numbers are useful only as simple counting devices. The scientific method, which is prediction instead of explanation, depends on numbers as an abstract system of thought.

The idea of romantic love, the roots of which lie in chivalry, is entwined in the development of medieval feudalism.[4] The fullest expression of romantic love—pure adoration unsullied by physical consummation—is found in the High Middle Ages. It may stem from Maryology, which is in turn the worship of the Universal Mother, which is in turn the worship and love for one's own mother. Perhaps the most abstract of all pure ideas, it rivals the concept of one God.

The latter half of the nineteenth century is distinguished by the development of ideas concerned with "the proper study of mankind." They are forms of history, concerning themselves with the long view, as with the work of Charles Darwin (evolution), Heinrich Schliemann (archaeology), and Sir James G. Frazier (anthropology), as well as the big view: Karl Marx (Communism) and, in the twentieth century, Einstein's Theory of Relativity. Around the turn of the century, we got the small view: Sigmund Freud developed psychoanalysis, and his disciple Carl Jung followed with psychotherapy.

Thoughtful Ideas

Broadly speaking, thinking can be divided into two classes: thinking and non-thinking. Thinking can be considered a positive act, as it makes further thinking or actions easier. Nonthinking can be considered a negative act, as it inhibits thought and action.

Ideas can be considered within the context of recurrence within a temporal and geographical frame. The alphabet, for example, could have been invented any time after the invention of agriculture, anywhere in the world. The McCormick reaper, which is an invention dependent on much narrower criteria such as adequate metallurgy, population pressure, and a high order of manufacturing, could have been invented anytime between, say, 1825 and 1900. For the sake of this argument, ideas will be ranked in order of frequency, from most common to rarest—that is, by how often they have been invented:

1. Making obvious what was previously invisible. The discovery of penicillin by Alexander Fleming (1881-1955) is a good example.
2. Minimalism: paring away inessentials to arrive at some sort of center.
3. Tricks, twists, and angles. Examples can be found in competent clothing and fashion design, applied design, and advertising.
4. Putting together two ideas to make a third; making a useful improvement on an already existing idea. Examples abound: The Colt revolver gathers many pre-existing concepts into a new device.
5. An idea which, although good, either requires a significant further development or is not suited to the needs or capacity of the culture in which it is produced. Examples of this are the piston and cylinder, invented by Ctesibius of Alexandria in circa the third century B.C., which he put to use pumping water; and the inventions of his compatriot Hero, who harnessed steam power to produce mechanical motion. Another is the digital computer, the principles of which were developed by Charles Babbage and Lady Ada Lovelace c. 1833.
6. An idea that is produced complete and intact, upon which no substantial improvement is necessary for a long time, despite the changes which it generates within the culture. Examples are the invention of perspective in c. 1425 by Filippo di Ser Brunelleschi (1377-1446), improved upon by Leon Battista

Alberti (1404-1472) in 1435; printing by moveable type (Johan Gutenberg, c. 1450) and the invention of lithography by Alois Senefelder in 1798. The alphabet and monotheism are outstanding examples of this class, having endured essentially unchanged since their invention.

7. Ideas that are seminal, though they have been invented repeatedly. The best illustration is the invention of writing: Mesopotamian, c. 3100 B.C. and Mayan, c. 600 B.C. and perhaps three times if the Chinese system (c. 2200-1400 B.C.) proves original. Counting time from a fixed point (calendars) is another. Monotheism, invented perhaps by the Pharaoh Akhenaten and popularized by Moses (c. 1450-1275 B.C.) may be another. Both these ideas are so simple that they can be explained quickly and easily to almost anyone. This does not, of course, mean that they caught on immediately.

Change in any one area stimulates change in all areas.[5] The Copernican revolution will serve to illustrate. When society is in turmoil, the individuals within it also experience unrest and disorientation. If they accept change in one area, they become able to accept change in any other area, as well. Conversely, a static situation promotes a conservative resistance to change, which, in turn, makes people less likely to look for different ways of doing things. Complacency and satisfaction with the way things are seem to be the enemy of creative thinking. As people and cultures grow older, they keep on doing things the way they have always done them, no matter how cumbersome or inconvenient. They vigorously resist any kind of change at all, no matter how much better it might be. Change entails risk, and risk implies the chance of loss. Loss is not what old people, who have little to gain and a lot to lose, are interested in. Fortunately, in each generation of people there is always a new group of people who have not much stake in the system, not much to lose, and not much sympathy with those who are afraid of change. Thus, it is usually left to the young and disenfranchised to introduce change.

There is also another class of human activity that can be called thoughtless ideas or the class of negative ideas. By frequency, they are:

1. Inattention, not learning from experience.
2. Carelessness, laziness, not doing a good job. (The Hubble Telescope embarrassment will stand as a prime illustration of this for some time to come.)
3. Not thinking something out all the way; not foreseeing the result of an action (rent control, the welfare system). Negative ideas 1 through 3 are generally accompanied by pride (hubris) and arrogance, which blind people to their errors, stop up their ears, and turn off their brains.
4. Letting someone else do the thinking for you; accepting received wisdom (women's social inequality in a postindustrial environment is a good illustration; religious tenets are a prime class of received wisdom that is not to be questioned).
5. Cultural immaturity, manifested in such things as racial prejudice, slavery, and war. Cultural immaturity is a kind of big-time bad manners. A nice phrase for it would be "cultural blind spots."

Applying the Big Idea

Hieroglyphics and ideograms take decades to learn. Using the acrophonic alphabet, an intelligent person can be taught principles in a few hours enabling him to read and write his own language.

In 1821, we were provided with an incontrovertible instance of what we suppose happened around the year 2000 B.C. It further provides us with a striking instance of stimulus diffusion. The American Indian, Sequoia, known as George Guess, served as a volunteer in the United States Army during the Creek Wars of 1813-14. He understood some English, but he did not speak it. Although illiterate, he recognized that the white man communicated silently over distance and time by means of writing. He reasoned that this powerful tool would be of use to his people. Since he had no idea how the white man's writing worked, except that it represented sounds in some way, he had to invent a principle for his new system. The one that occurred to him was the syllabic principle. Randomly picking 85 characters from a child's primer, which Sequoia owned but could not read, and assigning to them basic sounds in his own tongue, he contrived an acrophonic syllabary. For example, the value of H is "mi" and the value of S is "du." Sequoia found that he could teach any Cherokee to read and write in a few days, and within a few months the Cherokee people were writing letters to one another. The present day Cherokee syllabary is based on the original Caslon types that were then current.

All great ideas have been obvious to the prepared mind, and utterly invisible, though perfectly comprehensible after the fact, to the unprepared recipient. How long did people gripe and joke about standing in lines in banks before some unsung genius eliminated the problem by consolidating the lines into one, feeding people in an orderly, fair manner to the next available teller? In 1968, the Chemical Bank of

New York introduced a single queue winding back and forth between stanchions, delivering customers first-come-first-serve to the next available teller. In that same year, Halyville, Alabama, population 5,000, was the first community to designate the telephone numbers 9-1-1 for all emergency calls. Why did it take so long?

By what means can the mind be prepared to see that which is immediately under its nose? By learning to see, of course, but to see what is really there rather than what we think is there, would rather was there, or have been told is there.

Corporate Cowardice—CYA (Cover Your Ass)—stifles creative thought. An example of decision-making by corporate cowardice is the position enjoyed by IBM computers within the business community. International Business Machines made its reputation by providing well-made, dependable business machines. Its excellent service and innovative design made it the best choice for typewriters, which was the contact that most business people had with the company. When computers hit the market, IBM chose to go with big mainframes, neglecting the burgeoning PC until market forces compelled participation. Despite major contributions, by 1980 the IBM PC was no better than any other PC system, and for many applications, worse than quite a few. Customer service was average, and the machines were built neither better nor worse than the others. They did, however, cost about three times as much. IBM's reputation was still strong, and despite the realities, the only safe corporate choice was IBM. All systems have flaws, go down, and create problems but, if the buyer has bought IBM, he can at least say, "I bought the best." If he has bought a less well-known brand, and it has problems, he has no excuse and may be penalized. IBM thus, despite its mediocre performance and high price, is still the safe choice in a large business environment. What takes the place of genuine creativity within a corporate environment is often no more than meaningless action.

I am surprised at the frequency with which a new CEO begins his reign by commanding a redesign of the corporate-identity program, eradicating in the manner of the despotic Pharaohs all traces of his predecessor, and, as a byproduct, dynamiting generations of corporate identity and public recognition. Thus, the flying-horse trademark was replaced by a soulless red-and-blue Mobil "O"; the calligraphic "Ford" became a tiresome Helvetica monolith (and back again when the party-in-power was again replaced).

An exception to the general rule of corporate stifling of creativity may be when a powerful, creative individual forges and retains an influential position within a corporation, keeping the trust and confidence of his superiors. The best example I know of is that of Charles "Boss" Kettering of General Motors, whose design group kept GM far in front of domestic and international competition throughout his long tenure. In 1912, he developed the electric starter for Cadillac, and in 1949 the V-8 engine design made its appearance in the Cadillac and Oldsmobile 88. In 1950, Cadillac placed tenth and eleventh in the 24-hour Le Mans auto race. With the loss of Kettering and others like him, in the ensuing years GM pissed away its lead and in the 1970s surrendered its preeminence to foreign competition.

The Japanese Nintendo Corporation, which in the early 1980s entered a moribund industry only to attain complete domination by the early nineties, counters corporate mediocrity by an oddly revolutionary method. The R&D groups are given complete freedom, and the marketing department has no communication with R&D. The president, Mr. Yamauchi, said, "The marketing department would look at what is popular and tell the designers to make more of the same. If you work that way, nothing new and fresh comes out."

Becoming physically strong is done by physical exercise; learning to think is done by thinking; learning to be creative is done by creating; you start out slow and work up to whatever potential you have. There is no royal road, no shortcut, no trick. The longer you have gone without exercise, thinking, creating, the harder it is to start and the longer it will take to get good at it.

A Gymnasium For The Mind

What can you do to keep your brain working? Here are a few suggestions:

Foster your curiosity: Keep a dictionary close at hand. If you don't understand a word, look it up. Ask questions and research the answers: Why is the sky blue? Why is the letter A shaped like that? Why can you see through glass? Why is your reflection in a mirror reversed left for right but not top for bottom?

Practice being creative: write, paint, draw, play a musical instrument, sing. It doesn't matter how good you are. You'll get better, and you'll exercise your brain and body and make them stronger.

Question received wisdom. If something seems wrong to you, or even a bit odd, don't just accept it. When in the mid-1960s women tried to get jobs as toll-takers on the Golden Gate Bridge, they were told that the work was not open to women. When they asked why, it immediately became obvious that there was no reason on God's green earth why a woman couldn't stick her hand out and get money put into it, same as a man. The restriction disappeared the very instant someone questioned it.

Do things that are unaccustomed and difficult. Learn to type on a rational keyboard system (Dvorak), learn a new language, and listen to and try to enjoy music that you don't like and don't understand, such as jazz. (If you already appreciate jazz, try classical; if you already like classical, try punk, concrete music, or R&B.) It doesn't matter what you do as long as you're doing something. If you were to exercise your body by lifting weights, or running, or doing aerobics, it is not because in real life you will be called upon to run, lift barbells, or jump around like a lunatic, it is because you are making yourself more capable of performing other tasks entirely, or merely more likely to live longer and get sick less frequently. The exercise is the immediate, but not the long-term, goal.

Remember the dreamers and visionaries. Do not make fun of things that are strange and weird to you. Mockery is a way of isolating yourself from the new, the strange, and the potentially fruitful. Not all dreamers and crazies are valid; in fact, most of them are simply nuts. But, by rejecting all eccentricity, all oddity, you also reject the very thing you're looking for.

Notes:

1. Early in the Bronze Age, between 3500 B.C. and 3100 B.C., cities emerged in Sumeria and large-scale trade flourished.

2. The earliest known records date from 8500 B.C. They take the form of small,

clay tokens, some clearly representational and others abstract. Considered overall, the system had some fifteen major classes of tokens, further divided into some 200 subclasses on the basis of size, markings or shape. Each had a meaning of its own.

3. Husband of Nefertete, father of Tutankhamen. Akhenaten's new religion barely survived his death.

4. The roots of feudalism are, in turn, in the breakdown of the Roman bureaucratic structure and decay of slavery. Feudalism is dependent on the clear relationship between superior and inferior; that relationship being one of duty, both to specific although often abstract or idealized individuals as well as to oneself—also in an abstract sense. The concepts of chivalry, central to which is an ideal of duty regardless of reward, communicate well into romance and romantic attachments. An early illustration of the ideal of feudal duty is to be found in *The Song of Roland*.

5. "Change in one field decreases the hold of stereotypes in others. Stereotypes are most readily discarded during periods of general ferment." Thomas S. Kuhn, *The Copernican Revolution: Planetary Astronomy in the Development of Western Thought* (Harvard: Cambridge University Press, 1957).

First published in Communication Arts, Advertising Annual 1997.

I'm eating PEZ candies at my drafting table—pull the rabbit head back by the ears and it ejects a tiny pink brick from its throat—when I start to look around the house. Lucian Bernhard's cat is waving its paw at me from a box of rubber heels on the bookshelf; the Virgin Mary prays nonstop from her candle on the mantle; a Mexican Day of the Dead skull smokes a cigarette atop my computer monitor. Everywhere I look there are packages with images of animals and people, symbols really, engaged in the business of storytelling.

Of course the primary story these images tell is a plug for their respective products: "Buy me." But commerce is only one of their narratives, and, as some of these products are no longer made or sold, it may not even be a relevant one. The stories that interest me are those that resonate apart from consumerism: folk tales, religious or cultural myth, and fantasy.

But how is Lucian Bernhard's cat a narrative? It tells a story insofar as it triggers my imagination. I want to know: Does it have a name? Does it have any friends? What do they do on weekends?

Shape as Symbol: Giving the Package Life

Packaging at its most basic should contain and identify its contents. Beyond this, however, are limitless possibilities for embellishment and narrative. One possibility is the shape of the package itself.

Two packages that amuse me to no end are the honey bear from E. F. Lane & Son and the soap bubble bear (Pustefix Zauberbär) from Germany. These squeezable plastic figures are not just receptacles for honey and soap but also are personalities in their own right; one fully expects these two to serve honey and blow their own soap bubbles, as well as gossip after hours. These packages are not examples of anthropomorphism—attributing human characteristics to animals—but rather of a kind of animism, in which a life force is infused into an inanimate object. (This echoes the Native American practice of carving or painting effigies of animals on every-day, utilitarian objects to imbue them with the powers and attributes of the animal.)

Simple, jarlike containers function as well as bear-shaped ones in terms of holding honey and soap, but inanimate objects do not engage the mind like the animate, and my four-year-old neighbor Thomas will tell you as much. When I showed him the bears he uttered a "Hey cool!" several times, and then proceeded to make them talk and, to some degree, live. "I'm the honey man!" said one bear; "I'm the bubble man!" said the other. Meanwhile, Thomas completely ignored the more typical jar of honey sitting on the table.

A surprisingly animate package is the six-and-one-half ounce Coca-Cola bottle introduced in 1916. This bottle design is so distinctive that in 1960 the U.S. Patent Office recognized it as a trademark in and of itself, separate from the name and logotype. But what is the significance of its form? What is the narrative implied in its unusual shape? In his book, *Symbols of America*, Hal Morgan reports that "the fluted sides and bulging middle [of the bottle] were intended to suggest the shape of a cola nut." This is an interesting idea but a laughable one; the walnut-like shell of the kola nut looks nothing like the bottle. Whether intentional or not, the shape actually evokes a human form and, more specifically, a female form; the undulating shape of the Coke bottle is similar to the highly stylized statuettes of female deities produced by Greek and Cycladic artists in the period between 2500 and 2000 B.C. Thought to be fertility fetishes, these statuettes gracefully accentuate the upper body and hips, thereby creating a silhouette

not unlike the soda bottle. Further feminine associations come from the Coca-Cola company itself. It refers to the bottle shape as the "hobble skirt" design; moreover, an earlier prototype of 1915 was nicknamed the "Mae West" due to its exaggerated curves. The next time you grasp that bottle around the waist and hoist it to your lips, ask yourself if what comes to mind is a kola nut.

A fine anthropomorphic design is the Old Crow whiskey bottle (c. 1930), which animates the distiller's trademark. The advantage of this limited-edition ceramic is evident in its very existence six decades after its contents were joyfully consumed. It will never be discarded and, as a result, will advertise Old Crow whiskey with humor and style 'til kingdom come.

Humanizing the nonhuman satisfies our desire to reconnect with nature—a nature we lost somewhere between Eden and Poughkeepsie. Rather than attempt a return to nature, anthropomorphism brings nature to humanity by making it one of us—almost. This allows us a sense of camaraderie with our four-footed friends while nonetheless letting us feel superior to them. It also renders the unknowable and complex accessible. Is it any wonder that the user-friendly image of Apple Computers is due partly to its reliance on nonthreatening metaphors? I don't own an impersonal computer but a "Mac"; I don't type commands on a keyboard but rather select options with the help of a "mouse."

Can You Read Me? Image as Text

Images are more immediate than words; we respond to the shape and color of a stop sign faster than we can decipher its text. As John Berger observed in his classic book, *Ways of Seeing*, "Seeing comes before words. The child recognizes before it can speak." The primacy of images continues even after we can speak and read; unlike words, symbols do not need to be fully understood to evoke a strong emotional response.

An image that communicates quickly and efficiently can be found on the package for Death cigarettes from Holland. The icon of the skull and crossbones is so well known that a product name is unnecessary. In fact, the package is more striking for its lack of text; too often words are used to define an image that would be better left to speak for itself. (Consider the typical description mounted adjacent to a painting in a museum and you'll know what I'm talking about.) Perhaps this package's most stunning aspect, however, is the unadorned veracity of its symbolism—cigarettes will kill you.

A more abstract but equally powerful symbol identifies Lucky Strike cigarettes. With its four concentric circles isolated on a white field, Raymond Loewy's 1942 redesign of the classic 1917 label created a mandala for twentieth-century Western culture. The circle (or sphere) is an ancient and universal symbol, and its meanings are many: the Self, wholeness (hence "holiness"), perfection, eternity (no beginning or end), the sun, the eye, and God. The package's strength stems from the hovering bull's eye and the tightly controlled use of color: red and white, with accents of green-gray (formerly gold) and black.[1] This design forces the eye to repeatedly confront the name Lucky Strike and its associations with the Gold Rush, wealth, good fortune, and success.

In his book *Cigarette Pack Art*, Chris Mullen gives one possible interpretation of the use of a "good luck" narrative in the tobacco industry: "The idea of 'Lucky' tobacco is one that crops up over and over again. In a primitive way, the pack of cigarettes is a talisman against fate. It is an old French superstition that, in the face of the incomprehensible or threatening, the man with his hand in his pocket touches his left testicle for luck. Perhaps the pack is meant to provide alternative consolation." Mullen's hypothesis gives new meaning to the Lucky Strike slogan, "When tempted, reach for a Lucky."

The Power of Myth

Design that references religious or cultural myth can be especially effective because it associates the product with the power and history of the myth. An interesting example of this is the Lux Perpetua (Perpetual Light) prayer candle from Peru that features a portrait of the Virgin Mary. Like the burning of incense in other religious traditions, the burning of a prayer candle symbolizes one's prayers ascending heavenward to God. What is unusual about this label, however, is that Mary is pictured without her typical nimbus. It is only when one lights the candle that she finally receives her halo—in the form of the flame hovering overhead. By linking the appearance of Mary's nimbus with the acts of praying and lighting the candle, the design symbolically connects one's religious devotion to Mary's holiness.

The image for the Spanish Celestial razor blades (c. 1930) propels a mundane object of daily use into numinous realms. This is clearly not a literal representation of the product; the disembodied hand and blade reside in a flame without being consumed. Although on one level this merely suggests that the blades are durable and long lasting, on another it links the product with the divine by evoking such biblical traditions as Moses and the burning bush, and the fiery furnace of the Book of Daniel into which Shadrach, Meshach, and Abednego were thrown. In addition, the flame itself forms a mandola, the almond-shaped aureole enveloping representations of Our Lady of Guadalupe. Who wouldn't want to shave with such mythic blades?

For those of you amused by such a seemingly anachronistic marketing concept, consider these contemporary American products: Ajax cleanser, which seeks to associate the product's cleaning ability with the power of the legendary Greek warrior; the Eveready battery, which depicts a cat with a bolt tail leaping through a numeral nine to suggest that the batteries have "nine lives"; or Jolly Green Giant vegetables, a pairing which presents an even greater leap of logic than a Greek warrior scouring your toilet.

Narrative as Teacher

As Paul Rand has noted, the use of humor in design has the advantage of disarming and amusing an audience while simultaneously persuading and educating it. Although one might think that condoms are inherently funny, most condom packages seem to be designed with the comedic and aesthetic sensibilities of Jesse Helms. A happy exception is the condoms distributed by the San Francisco AIDS Foundation. Rather than sidestep the delicate subject of sex, this design embraces it, promoting safe sex with humor by juxtaposing a rubber-sporting banana with a chocolate doughnut. (The multi-colored jimmies evoke the rainbow flag of Gay Pride, a symbol of diversity and tolerance.) This narrative is continued on the inside of the package, where only the banana peel, the discarded condom, and a few jimmies are left; the banana and doughnut having been consumed by their passion. With a subject as serious as AIDS, a light approach is something of a relief.

A different but no less effective approach was taken by Bureau in its design for the compilation compact disc "No Alternative," conceived as a project for AIDS awareness and fundraising by the Red Hot Organization. The title "No Alternative" refers to the music, of course—it features "alternative" artists like Nirvana, the Beastie Boys, and Patti Smith—but it also emphasizes that we have no alternative but to respond to the crisis of AIDS.

The "Jane, Dick, and Spot" images of the girl (or boy; there are two versions of the cover) were chosen because, in the words of Bureau partner Marlene McCarty, "The idea of children automatically infers the idea of future. AIDS is going to be a part of the future of regular American kids." (This idea is further reinforced by the repeated use of a target.) Bureau superimposed typography across the child's eyes to de-emphasize her identity and thus allow her to symbolize all children, thereby negating the argument that AIDS can't happen to us. The design is remarkable in that it effectively sells the product and delivers a strong social message to a traditionally unreceptive audience: disenfranchised middle-class youth. McCarty describes this effort to market products whose sales benefit nonprofit causes as "grown-up activism."

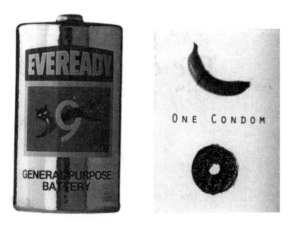

PEZ Anyone?

Narrative interests me because, quite simply, it gives my life meaning. Neil Postman, in his address to the AIGA conference last October, asserted that narrative "gives meaning to the past, explains the present, and provides guidance for the future." But Postman's concept of meaningful narrative is more grand (and more narrowly defined) than my own. His idea of meaningful narrative—"stories of human history"—revolves around religion, politics, and ideology. Mine is as simple as the Bon Ami cleanser chick that "hasn't scratched yet." This particular narrative (and countless others like it) is meaningful to me because it is imaginative and playful. It creates an improbable association between a product and natural history that I find surprising, amusing, and even—in an odd way—comforting.

I reload my rabbit. This time with purple PEZ.

First published in *Communication Arts*, Illustration Annual 1994.

Beauty

David Lance Goines

Beauty is truth, truth beauty;
that is all
Ye know on earth, and all ye need to know.
   –John Keats (1795-1821)
   Ode on a Grecian Urn[1]

And the true order of going, or being led by another,
to the things of love is to begin from the beauties of
earth and mount upwards for the sake of that other
beauty, using these steps only, and from one going
on to two, and from two to all fair forms to fair prac-
tices, and from fair practices to fair notions, until
from fair notions he arrives at the notion of absolute
beauty, and at last knows what the essence of beauty
is.
   –Plato (c. 428-348 B.C.)[2]

Maybe this is just a bad translation. Though the impenetrable load of double-talk that Plato has here shoveled out sounds nice, it isn't good for much. When you try to figure out how you can actually use Plato's ideas to make something beautiful or evaluate something to discover whether it is beautiful or not, you find that this sort of philosophical lumber lets you down rather badly.

So to begin with, let's just forget about totalitarian, anti-art Plato and his incomprehensible ideal forms and the other-worldly mystic Saint Thomas Aquinas, nasty lunatic John Ruskin, and all those old frauds and their transcendent hogwash.

Beauty is real. Beauty is the expression through art of wealth and power. The vehicle by which beauty comes into the world is art; anticipating the ideal of wealth and power, art gives form to the standards by which society judges itself.

Art creates beauty. Art is the vanguard of taste, trumpeting fashion before it actually exists.

Art, like science, goes where the money is. If you follow the history of art, you also follow the history of political power. Where is the nexus of culture? Why, it is always where the most impressive military and economic society of the day holds sway. Babylonia, Egypt, Athens, Rome, Florence, London, Paris, New York, Los Angeles, Tokyo—these are, or have been, centers of beauty, taste, and art. Not coincidentally, these also are or were centers of political and financial power. Artists are paid to tell everybody what beauty is and to display that beauty for the glorification of their patrons.

Beauty is an index of leisure, which is itself an index of wealth, which is an index of power. Flower arranging, for example, takes a long time to learn and a long time to learn to appreciate. Poor people do not acquire these refined tastes. For the poor, these tastes *do not exist*. The subtleties of such things are totally lost on them. The poor do not much like the art of Rauschenberg, Oldenberg, Klee, Arp, or Pollock. If they think of them at all, they think they're silly. Let's face it: Only the rich can afford aesthetics. When the poor want to become like the rich they emulate the tastes of the rich.

About the only thing that is constant in beauty is that is the opposite of ugly.[3] Ugly, too, is a constant. It is whatever the rich, healthy, youthful, strong, and powerful are *not* doing.

Beauty is constantly changing and culture-bound. What one person at one time finds beautiful, another person from another culture will often find ludicrous, incomprehensible, and ugly. So few of our young women wear brass hoops that stretch the neck, plates in their lips, and heavy facial or body tattooing. Hardly any men on the streets of New York sport a penis sheath. We do not dye ourselves blue.

> *"Clothes maketh the man."*
> *–Mark Twain (attributed)*

As an example of beauty in small, let us examine the infinitely fascinating arena of clothing fashions. First, what was fashionable (beautiful) yesterday is absurdly unfashionable (ugly) today. We can tolerate outdated fashion in specific contexts, such as a period costume in a play or film (though indeed it is usually heavily modified to suit the modern aesthetic), but in real life outdated fashion is not attractive. The more outdated it gets, the more ugly it becomes.

Clothing fashion before the twentieth century makes much of the conspicuous, even lavishly wasteful, use of fabric. Fabric, especially fancy fabric, was expensive, and clothing was even more so. Common people had few clothes. Rich people had many clothes of relatively sumptuous make. Rich people kept up with fashion, and poor people mostly did not. What rich people wore was, by definition, beautiful. What poor people wore was, by definition, not. Rich people had window curtains, and the poor who emulated them, such as my "lace-curtain Irish" forbearers, strove to work the sympathetic magic and get rich by copying the rich.

In the latter part of our own dangerous century, we see little in the way of obvious contrast between the clothing of the rich and poor. We have adopted as our models the class of performing artists (rock stars, movie stars), whose clothing is more a product of the imagination than a concession to either the elements or outward signs of wealth. We have put most of our effort into the body itself, neglecting the outer integument. The poor have as little ability to be "body fashionable" now as they did to be "clothing fashionable" in the nineteenth century. Rich people jog and have memberships to gyms; they watch their diets and are concerned with cholesterol; they do not smoke; they do not drink to excess ("Just Perrier, please"); they do not take drugs; they practice safe sex; they wear their seatbelts. Poor people don't do any of this stuff.

Throughout most of the world's history, fatness was admired as a sign of wealth, health, and fertility; thinness was a sign of poverty, disease, and barrenness. In the case of fatness in the time of general food shortage, the wealthy person is beautiful because he doesn't look poor. In the case of thinness in a time of plenty, the wealthy person is slender and athletic by way of contrast to those who have little leisure time for sport and health maintenance.

Fashion, created by art and adopted by the wealthiest strata of society, began in the late nineteenth and early twentieth centuries to model itself not after the old gougers of wealth but after the leisured, athletic, youthful figure.

> "Gather ye rosebuds while ye may,
> Old Time is still a-flying,
> And this same flower that smiles today
> Tomorrow will be dying."
> –Robert Herrick (1591-1674)
> "To the Virgins to Make Much of Time"

Beauty is evanescent and reminds us of our own mortality. A beautiful young person will be neither beautiful nor young for very long; that youth is fleeting makes the youthful beauty all the more valuable.

Coarsely put, youth is beautiful because it is healthy, fecund, strong, and rare. Age is ugly because it is moribund, infertile, weak, and common. Much of fashion is an attempt to look powerful (rich), youthful (fertile or virile), and healthy (leisured). Though the outward expressions of these attributes may change dramatically, beauty in fashion is always aimed at these things and flees from their opposites. Fashion is always as much the product of fleeing from ugliness or those things that indicate ugliness (poverty, age, weakness) as striving toward beauty. Its protean nature keeps everybody on the hop, inevitably leaving behind those who are unable to keep up—the old, the poor, the weak.

The pallid complexion that indicated that one was not a "horny-handed son of toil,"[1] suffering Apollo's furnace in rude agrarian pursuit, gave way to the healthy tan that indicated that one was not a member of the laboring industrial and mercantile class shut away from the light, unable to winter in sunny climes. The tan became popular shortly after WWI along with the rise of the twin sports of the leisure class: tennis and golf. Pale is back now, just as the rest of the world has figured out how to tan. Tough to keep up with the ruling class!

The much-admired ivory complexion of the nineteenth century bespoke the most powerful stratum of society, as well as being a direct, intentional contrast to the "lesser breeds without the law,"[2] whose skins were dark. Even freckles were déclassé as a sign of exposure to the sun, Irish ancestry, or mixed blood.

After the battle of Waterloo, the conquering English Duke of Wellington, coming upon a troop of his Irish foot soldiers bathing in a creek, is reputed to have expressed amazement that they were white. This betrays not only a wealth of class prejudice but also an indication that their sunburned faces and hands were in some contrast to those of their superior officers.

Commodore Perry's black ships sailed into the Bay of Yedo on July 14, 1853, and he and his officers walked ashore to negotiate a treaty with the shogun. The Japanese were completely unable to prevent them from sailing where and as they pleased and were immediately forced to accept a treaty opening Japan to Western trade. There was nothing the Japanese could do about it except try to catch up, which they rapidly did to our envy and their own perfect satisfaction. In the process, they were transformed in Western eyes from ugly to beautiful.

If a race of technologically and politically superior aliens, to us as we are to the naked savage, were to land on the Earth, our first, xenophobic reaction would be fear and loathing. They would initially appear to us to be ugly. But, as we grew convinced of their superiority, they would become the model of beauty, and we would lose favor in our own eyes.

Just as Saint Paul tells us that faith without work is dead, so is power without beauty. Beauty is the outward evidence of power. The Pyramids are beautiful. They indicate immense power. They always have, and they always will. Unless we reject power and wealth as desirable attributes, we will forever admire Stonehenge, the Pyramids, the Parthenon, the Coliseum, and Notre Dame Cathedral. All are symbols of power. Beauty is enduring, to show that even though the individual dies the works of his hands will serve to remind generations yet unborn that he was powerful, that he may be dead but his power lives on.

The fashions of the powerful displace those of inferior, subject, or provincial peoples. Note how the puissant dictator gauds his glittering, overstuffed military uniform with spurious medals and decoration, plumes his hat, surrounds himself with the outward trappings of power. We despise his two-bit effort, his sedulous overstatement, because compared to those he apes, he is not actually powerful.

Even the formerly revered gods of the weak become ugly and foolish when they come up against the gods of the strong and lose their worshipers to the gods of power. Hepheastus limps into oblivion faced down by the conquering resurrected Christ. Who worships Baal? Who worships Mithra, Isis, Zoroaster, Ra?

The powerful, the socially and culturally advantaged, can of course afford to admire the works of the past and of other cultures. They have nothing to lose by it. Not too long ago, the idea of archaeology and indeed, of cultural history, was unheard of. The dead were weak, the past was dross. Rich people, such as nineteenth-century Europeans, became interested in the past and treasured the works of the ancients for more than they would fetch melted down into ingots of gold and silver. That's more than the ancient grave robbers ever did. Or the Spaniards, looting the conquered peoples of the New World. Except for their value in metal, they had no use at all for the artifacts of the Americas. Conquered = Ugly. Weak = Ugly. Old = Ugly. Dead = Ugly. Beauty is power, power is beauty.

We admire the works of our ancestors of primitive peoples, of the weak and powerless, in direct proportion to our own strength. We can afford to find them beautiful. Nobody else has ever been as rich as we are and, in consequence, as benevolent, leisured, and tolerant. It is only in the last few decades that the dream paintings of the Australian Bushmen have found favor in the eyes of their Western conquerors. We are no longer arm-wrestling them for their land; we've got it—they are no threat. We are so rich that we can even afford to give some of it back. Having nearly exterminated these people and their culture, we can now afford to look at what they might, in their quaint and backward way, have to offer us. In the 1930s, American Indian women sold their silver jewelry, blankets, and basketry by the side of the road to get money for ammunition and food. Not many people wanted the stuff. We were all too broke to value the works of a down-and-out conquered people.

You will find, among other historical peoples, neither an interest in foreign culture nor an interest in the past that is in any way comparable to our fanatical pursuit of the antique, strange, or primitive. The city of Cairo is built of the facings of the Great Pyramid, which was generally perceived as a convenient quarry. Napoleon's artillerymen used the Sphinx to sight their guns, blowing of its nose. The Parthenon was exploded by accident when it was used as a powder magazine. Peasants farmed in the Coliseum. The Ukiyo-e woodcut prints of Utamaro and Hiroshige came to the attention of the West as wrapping paper for commercially valuable ceramics.

Rich people have big houses. They have more rooms than they absolutely need in which to do things they do not absolutely need to do. They don't so much have big houses because they like them as to show that they are not poor. Powerful corporations and governments erect big buildings made of expensive materials as outward indications of power.

An ugly building is one that is occupied by the poor and built to indicate power-lessness. A beautiful building, ipso facto, is one that indicates power and wealth. Fashions change, and now we do not much admire the architecture of Nazi Germany (what's left of it); but then again, they did lose the war.

To be sure, "there is no excellent beauty that hath not some strangeness in the proportion." Beauty needs to be balanced, to contain a hint of imperfection. As demonstrated by the hubristic intentional error woven into the Persian carpet, we mistrust anything too perfect as a temptation to the Fates to squash us for our presumption.

Beauty is rare and scarce. A diamond is beautiful because it is costly. We bought Manhattan Island with the equivalent of diamonds—a chest of glass beads, paste, and copper wire. Tawdry baubles to us, the conquerors, they were precious jewels beyond imagining to the autochthons. Gold is beautiful because it is enduring, incorruptible, and rare. If you really could transmute lead into gold, gold would be used for wires in high-fidelity sound equipment and to line pots and pans. Beauty belongs to wealth and power. That's what makes it beautiful. Likewise, the artifacts of the past are valued in direct proportion to their rarity.

> *"Power is the ultimate aphrodisiac."*
> –Henry Kissinger (attributed)

Beauty attracts beauty. A Rolls Royce has a magnificent paint job because the car is so valuable that anything less would be silly. What's a $5,000 paint job on a $150,000 automobile? Gold, so valuable in itself, demands fine workmanship. Diamonds are agonized over to discover the best cut to bring out their hidden fires. Rich, famous, and powerful men are often seen in the company of beautiful women. The women are beautiful because they are with the rich men as much as the rich men select them for their beauty. In the nineteenth century, they would have been well-upholstered with small, regular features, deep dimples, good teeth, small hands and feet, smooth white shoulders and dark, flashing eyes, i.e., a cultural paradigm of wealth. Now, they are tall and leggy, full-bosomed, and slender waisted, with blond hair, blue eyes, and aerobically toned muscles. It goes without saying that they have dazzling smiles. Each is an exemplar, a rub-your-nose-in-it of the ruling class. Each is an expensive ornamental object. Each is, in the main, what most of the people in the world aren't.

Things can become beautiful that didn't start out that way. Things can acquire a wealth of symbolism and association, can start out in Nowheresville and end up in the nexus of power. Marie Antoinette's facial mole becomes a beauty mark, copied in court plaster even unto this day.

When our ancestors beheld the forests and prairies of the Americas, the limitless steppes of Central Asia, and the vast, briny deep, you may be sure that they did not see beauty. What they saw was a hostile wilderness to be conquered. The noble red man, of course—despite the long-standing and somewhat offensive and condescending fashion of portraying him as living in childlike harmony with nature—enslaved his fellow man, polluted the environment as much as he was able, carelessly destroyed natural resources, and wiped out twenty-three species of American mega fauna (mostly by eating them) well before the white man came to help him out.

It is only in the nineteenth century, when we got a handle on the workaday business of subduing nature, that protoecological types like Henry David Thoreau (1817-1862) started talking about the unpleasantness of human society and the beauty of wilderness and so on and so forth. Now that we have won the war and nature bows her trembling head beneath our iron heel, we think that she's beautiful. Now that we have despoiled her, we too late discover that we want her virgin again. The only nineteenth century people interested in saving the whale were those who worried that next year's catch would be diminished if a too-efficient means of converting them into "oil for the lamps of China" depleted the pods below replacement levels. Gee, I sure miss the passenger pigeon, don't you? Talk to the folks in Brazil about the beauties of the rain forest. They don't think it's beautiful because they haven't gotten their money out of it yet. As soon as they have done so, they will revere the source of it, just as do we. If there's any of it left.

In conclusion, beauty is what we, as people on the long end of the leer of social decision-making, say is beautiful. We cast our eyes over past and present and pick and choose what is to be called beautiful, usually selecting things that are the product of dominant civilizations, cultures, and individuals. What they evaluate as beautiful remains cross-culturally and cross-temporally beautiful because both they and we are looking at things from the same perspectives of wealth and power.

The birds, my friends, sing only for the rich.

Notes

1. Denis Kearney, from a speech given in San Francisco c. 1878. See *The Oxford Dictionary of Quotations* (Oxford: Oxford University Press, 1955), 284.

2. Rudyard Kipling, *Recessional*.

First published in *Communications Arts*, March/April 1996.

Designers who know it tend to love D'Arcy Thompson's book *Growth and Form*, an extraordinary scientific treatise on how animal shapes change at varying stages in life. Thompson makes the point that creatures tend to be roundish and lovable when young, becoming more angular as they age. There is even a logic to the exceptions: Baby alligators are not nurtured while young, and they are fierce looking from birth.

Consider a parallel. Imagine being able to draw forms that capture the nature of the times we live in and show how they might change with age. You might draw shapes that are simple forms to represent the early years; the forms would get more complex and wild by the close of each century (and truly weird by the end of each millennium). In fact, though the reasons are not well understood, it is customary for societies to experience big and often disconcerting changes at the end of each century—often with some attendant social upheaval.

Because human lives only average about eighty years, we miss out on a personal connection to our ancestors several generations removed, and the advice and stories such a connection would involve. The lack of connection can often lead to the assumption that our time is somehow unique and unprecedented. In being mostly unable to truly discern long wave patterns, we can easily miss the tectonic shifts taking place today. For most people, the more natural and ready focus is on the more superficial aspects of change.

There are several important challenges for designers that matter deeply now and will grow in importance as we go forward. A thin attempt will be mounted here to identify them, though such a grandiose ambition for a short essay is preposterous.

Issue 1

Few designers understand the sheer scale of modern business transformation. The corollary here is important too: Few designers think it matters to them. But what separates design from fine art is its interdependence with commerce, so it's actually vital that designers both understand and care about these shifts.

Designers should be conversant with at least two sweeping themes. One is the shift to a networked economy. This term describes how once separate and distinct business-es have suddenly become interdependent in ways that few truly understand. It's as if businesses are suddenly attached to one another with rubber bands. Sometimes they cooperate, often they compete; occasionally it's planned, more often it's accidental, but now the actions that one firm takes may ripple through other firms. Very often these interactions create new businesses and industries along the way.

An illustration from close to home may help clarify how networked economies work. Consider how completely the design field has been transformed by the arrival of WYSIWYG displays, page-description languages, low-cost laser-printer engines, and Macintosh computers. These innovations all emerged at roughly the same time, yet were hardly coordinated with one another. Moreover, when they were developed, they each sought their own destinies, at the hands of firms like Apple, Canon, Aldus, and Radius, none of which was particularly focused on graphic design at the outset. Yet these innovations combined to create the fields of desktop publishing and computer-aided design, permanently altering the economics of the graphic-design and architec-tural fields, with ramifications for designers around the world.

A second major shift has occurred in innovation velocity. Caused in part by the networked economy and the use of digital systems and telecommunications as accel-erants, we are experiencing a time when new ideas spawn others at remarkable speed. What's more, these derivative innovations occur in ways that are unknown and unknowable, no matter how much market-research firms might throw at unclear issues and markets.

It's possible to illustrate innovation velocity as a trend, too. Toll-free 800 numbers were first launched in the mid-1960s. It took nearly thirty years for demand to exhaust the supply of these numbers. Recently, the 888 toll-free exchange has debuted, and telephony experts estimate that it will take only five years to exhaust the supply of these. Businesses everywhere have first become accustomed to the concepts, then learned to create more and more applications for them. Toll-free numbers are a soft indication of innovation velocity. A more fundamental and direct illustration might be found in the remarkable growth of semiconductors and sensors. Today we think little of placing more raw computer power into a disposable greeting card than the world had at its disposal only about thirty years ago.

These trends help show the true scale and permanence of business transforma-tion. Times like these, with their attendant radical shifts, usually make switched-on designers highly valuable. Among other sources of value, helping business under-stand and cater to end users is a key. By acting as an advocate for end users, designers can make innovations easy to understand, delightful to experience, and culturally con-nected. In any combination, these advances help to make novel things important, grounded, and hip, so they do much to help people embrace new artifacts and wel-come them into their everyday lives.

Issue 2

We need to understand what it means to live and work in revolutionary times.
During revolutionary times, there are always conflicts at the core. We are witnessing conflicts between large, established companies and small start-ups, between corpora-

tions as shapers of society and other institutions like church, school, or government, and between governments and the people they govern. New technologies come faster and faster, adding to the tension, separating the "digerati" from those who haven't the money or inclination to participate, and further fueling these revolutions.

Revolutions are exciting for some people. Researchers immersed in the Human Genome Project, or people at the center of, say, Netscape, are having the time of their lives, and every moment matters. Others find themselves thrown out of work, perhaps after decades of loyal service to a major company. Still others become extremists, producing cults, unabombers, neo-Nazis, and arsonists.

Some of the extremism of our time stems directly from this period of upheaval. There are distant echoes to the time of the Luddites in England, and to the Industrial Revolution, of course. Schumpeter termed this upheaval the "creative destruction of capitalism," and it has historically been an amazingly healthy phenomenon in shaping the wealth of nations and creating jobs for people. What may be new for the human species is the fact that our current revolution is made so public, so shareable, and so amplified by communications technologies, including the Internet.

At their best, our communications advances provide comfort and companionship for lonely hearts everywhere, a clear plus. At their worst, they allow people with extreme views to amplify one another's sense of disaffection, perhaps permitting kooks to share tips on terrorism with one another. Like it or not, we all have a ringside seat for the greatest experiment in human freedom ever conducted. Both bad and good results are to be expected, each in extremes and in abundance.

Here again, there's a special place for design and designers. In particular, designers are more comfortable with change than most people and typically share a deep value to continually make the world a better place. These positive traits can find voice and impact through the vital design skill of prototyping. Prototypes help make something that isn't real seem very tangible and believable. When several prototypes are strung together, they can combine nicely with great storytelling to become especially powerful, thereby helping to make the future easier to understand and accept. At its best, prototyping can help the future show up somewhat ahead of its regularly scheduled arrival.

Issue 3

Designers can play a pivotal role in resolving the contradictions between business and societal needs. It is a sad fact that corporations today are the most vital force for societal change. Corporations have become the educators of the last resort, they play crucial roles in the support of communities and the arts, and they pay to manage the health of their workers and retirees. Virtually everywhere, people are seeing that government is an ineffectual force for a time of revolutionary change, while churches and schools are less effective, as well.

Yet in a global, networked economy, few people can expect corporations to do everything needed for the success and well being of individuals. Corporations need continuous innovation; society needs stability. Corporations need global competitiveness, and societies need a common good. In the zeal to be efficient, agile, and flexible, corporations are not always willing and able to support local communities and maintain loyalties to them. Meanwhile, individuals are taking on increased personal responsibility for managing everything from health to finance and investment, to education, family care, and career planning.

These conflicts are huge and, candidly, often bigger than design's view of itself. Nonetheless, thoughtful designers can help corporations understand how valuable it is to motivate people, to support their needs in balanced ways, and to access what they need to know to make effective personal decisions. In this way, designers can help corporations understand the value beyond money in creating healthy cultures inside an enterprise and healthy communities outside of them.

On Building an Adequate Design Response

This essay calls for designers to understand the tectonic shifts of business, help constructively guide the energies associated with revolutions, and help act as a positive social force. The sensible designer will reject this instantly, while muttering about it being a bunch of goody-two-shoes nonsense. Meanwhile some confused readers may actually think it sounds reasonable and achievable. To discourage this handful of idealists, let's examine what it would take for designers to act on these suggestions.

Designers need to work in teams. Most design schools are built around assigning tasks that can be done by an individual designer acting alone. Most designers love the notion of personally authoring a solution and creating an artifact that they themselves love. This is fundamental to the training and temperament of artists, and the honest truth is that much of the act of creation must be done solo. But where designers are goofy enough to tackle some of the large-scale challenges that we now face as a society, others must round out the designer's knowledge and skills in multidisciplinary teams.

This is not some fancy-pants way of saying designers are dummies; instead, it acknowledges that all tough problems get solved in part through the judicious application of specialized expertise. It takes many kinds of talent to make a great movie, operate a particle accelerator, write a constitution, design a fiber-optic system for a populace, or any other important task. It only takes one person to write, say, the copy for a cornflakes ad. That's why society neither prizes nor highly rewards cornflakes advertisements. Of course, society does value and revere the sonnets of Elizabeth Barrett Browning or old Willy Shakespeare, which were singly authored. But these noble singular achievements are prized by individuals whose lives they touch—sonnets may help describe the societal-level challenges that are upon us now, but they do not fix them, and fixing them is where the action is for designers.

Designers need to combine their talents with unfamiliar expertise from other fields. Given their druthers, designers tend to hang with other designers. This is because other designers know what's hot and what's not and help one another decode the trends that sweep through the popular culture worldwide. This form of shoptalk is vital of course, lots of fun besides, and an irreplaceable way of building on one another's insights and ideas. But designers must also come to welcome the expertise that exists among, say, social scientists and strategists, engineers and materials scientists.

Every basic problem society faces today can benefit from the judicious use of cultural anthropology, cultural sociology, and cognitive psychology, yet few designers know how to describe the essential differences between these branches of social science, let alone bring some of these cats to bear on a pressing problem they're trying to crack. Cultural anthropologists can help figure out what artifacts mean in our times and how they are used; cultural sociologists can help puzzle through the new ways we deal with one another in our lives and interactions; cognitive psychologists can help figure out what confuses us or interferes with our tasks. Such plain-spoken terms help designers to immediately grasp how valuable these specialists can be in a time when technology makes everything subject to change. The good news is that more and more designers and design firms are starting to realize this, and smart designers should only hang out in firms where such talent is on tap.

Design teams not only need to accept but actually embrace the notion of accountability. A vanishingly small number of designers would be willing to put their own money behind the items they invent for clients. Yet that is precisely what we all expect clients to do in our wake. A reasonable test of both the teams you assemble and the ideas they produce is thus: Are you willing to quit your job and go into business making and selling the stuff you recommend? If the answer is no, then you should more readily understand why clients fail to implement the items you so lovingly craft.

By the way, the answer is usually no for any number of reasonable reasons. Perhaps you just did the graphics, not everything else. Maybe there's a jerk on the client side who has cut too many corners and the result is compromised. Maybe you're just not really that interested in the product category. Yet, examined deeply, each of these reflects on the team, its skill deficits, and limitations. It is unreasonable to expect clients to implement well those ideas that we would ourselves reject.

Designers need to invent and use a series of methods that bring rigor and robustness to the field. Designers generally loathe the data and directives brought to them by marketers and researchers. Meanwhile, clients too often hide behind it, because it is somehow "scientific," real, and verifiable. So here's the critical fact that they never taught you in design school: You are absolutely right to reject this nonsense. In almost all particulars, it fails to inform the design process in a way that will lead to breakthroughs. But the corollary is important too: Just because the client brought you drivel masquerading as research doesn't mean that you can simply make up any answer that suits you. Part of the reason why design is among the Rodney Dangerfield of professions that "don't get no respect" has to do with the fact that it has not yet evolved to the point where we can articulate why we believe what we believe. This is not because what we believe is silly or naïve but rather because it is vexingly complex, layered, and hard to fully understand.

It is essential to the future of the design field that we make it a more complete profession. When people go into an emergency room with, say, an arterial geyser, they don't expect doctors to stand around giving various personal interpretations of what might be done. Purposeful, clear, pointed actions are called for: actions that improve vital signs and save lives. Designers have been forced to act as the poor stepchild of marketers. But, despite the representations that most marketers make for their methods, they are devoted to selling what already exists, not helping to invent what doesn't yet exist. The wise design team will be able to point this out in a thoughtful, constructive way, while substituting methods, like video ethnography as one example, that are extremely credible for clients and incredibly useful for inventing the new.

Designers must come to understand that making something hip and culturally connected is only one dimension of being strategic. Designers who achieve pop-star status, like Calvin Klein, Philippe Starck, and Frank Gehry, tend to shape the cultural expectations of our field and perhaps even influence our own ambitions. The truth is that it is an amazing achievement to make something hip and hot. It's amazingly valuable too; just ask Nike. But designers need to be conversant with a broad range of generic strategies that are valuable and know the methods needed to deliver these benefits. We can design things to be more cost-effective, more operable, more understandable, more accessible, more maintainable, more endearing, more recyclable, more engaging, more participative, more attractive, more manufacturable, more adaptable, on and on. What we often need are clear reasons why one or more of these strategies are preferable to others in certain situations. We need to help our clients reason their way through an infinity of possible alternative actions.

Close attention to these five points can help designers be more valuable to those who employ them and more effective in addressing the issues that shape our lives and our times. Moreover, these five design responses are all practical, achievable, and actionable. Indeed, all of them are in evidence somewhere in the world. As futurists are fond of noting, the future is already here, it's just not evenly distributed. If the approaches described here seem interesting to you but are not in evidence where you study or work, consider looking around. For a small number of designers in a growing number of places, capabilities like these open the door to bigger projects with greater impact on our (astonishing) life and times.

The French term *fin de siècle* captures the notion that the end of the century is typically a strange period that departs from conventional morals or social traditions. At this particular one, designers can step up to some crucial challenges, more interesting than any seen since at least the Industrial Revolution and arguably the most interesting ever. Grappling with these challenges demands more than a sense of cultural hipness and style, though these are neither trivial nor unimportant. Switched-on designers who partner with and leverage specialties like strategy, anthropology, sociology, and psychology will be increasingly rewarded. When these combinations are forged, designers can help make the breakthroughs that change our world.

First published in *Communication Arts*, Design Annual 1996.

None of
My Business

Michael Cronan

When graphic designers create brochures for themselves, they grapple with describing what graphic design is and what it does. It's a daunting task because it requires us to examine our fundamental beliefs about our function as designers and what part we play in the mechanism of our society and our culture.

Over the past few years, scientists have put forward a number of interesting theories about the ways ideas move through cultures. One, by biologist Richard Dawkins, draws a parallel with the spread of ideas and how DNA functions.

The gist of the theory goes like this: Just as genes can be considered information packets that replicate as a way of extending their existence, so too ideas can be considered packets of information that reproduce as they are transmitted from one person to another.

Dawkins calls these idea packets "memes." "Examples of memes are tunes, ideas, catch-phrases, clothing styles, or ways of making pots or of building arches. Just as genes propagate themselves in the gene pool by leaping from body to body via sperms or eggs, so memes propagate themselves in the meme pool by leaping from brain to brain via a process which, in the broad sense, can be called imitation. If a scientist hears, or reads about, a good idea, he passes it on to his colleagues and students. He mentions it in his articles and his lectures. If the idea catches on, it can be said to propagate itself, spreading from brain to brain."[1] In fact, a meme has just replicated itself in your mind as you read this paragraph.

How are memes aided in their existence? Dawkins maintains that art and music, the written word, books, television, even posters, exhibits, and packages, all qualify as transmission devices. As it turns out, many of these devices are the creative domain of the graphic designer.

Wild stuff? Not really. Dawkins is able to draw rational comparisons between genes and memes, and some have a disquieting ring of truth. Just as genes promote themselves into a wider existence in animal populations, a meme in the form of a tune, for example, will more likely be copied if it's "catchy." One of our main functions as graphic designers is to make things "catchy." As Dawkins points out, "Some memes, like some genes, achieve brilliant short-term success in spreading rapidly but do not last long in the member pool. Others may continue to propagate themselves for thousands of years."[2] Although what we create every day is mercifully called ephemera, it's our secret hope that our work will stand the test of time. Our professional legacy will be measured, not in what design awards we secure, but in the good messages that enter and stay alive in the meme pool as a result of our efforts.

Based on this perspective, performance artist Laurie Anderson is right: "Language is a virus," and designers are fashioners of many languages that endlessly circulate through our society and culture.

So what responsibility do designers have for the message? Do we share in the content with our clients? If we believe we have the training and skill to transmit messages, to make them popular, long lasting, or capable of influencing behavior, do we bear some responsibility for what we transmit? Nancy Denney Essex, of SX2 in Chicago, believes that the designer's role is specific. "The way I see it, if we decide a client is holding a wasteful or socially irresponsible position on a project, we must bring a solution to the problem. We must do everything we can to rectify the situation. I disagree with those designers who would say it's none of our business. The great thing about being a designer is that everything is our business. Besides, as human beings, we're involved whether we choose to recognize it or not."

Once we've chosen to act in accordance with our personal beliefs, in what ways can we outline our professional responsibility? Melanie Doherty, of Melanie Doherty Design in San Francisco, has chosen to focus on issues of visual clarity. "It's our responsibility to help make information accessible and to approach our craft with sincerity. One of our clients is a medical center. For example, projects that involve health-education issues should not include stylistic self-indulgence. It just doesn't have a place here. I believe we must use the design of information to help make people responsible for themselves."

Can we fulfill our obligation by creating compelling posters and pretty logos? Can we automatically prescribe the best modes of transmission for every social need? Probably not. Michael Beirut, of Pentagram New York, cites a passage from the novel *Clockers* by Richard Prince: "The walls of the waiting room were hung with black-and-white cautionary posters, encircling Strike [the protagonist] with admonitions, the subjects ranging from AIDS to pregnancy to crack to alcohol, each one a little masterpiece of dread. Strike hated posters. If you were poor, posters followed you everywhere—health clinics, probation offices, housing offices, day-care centers, welfare offices—and they were always blasting away at you with warnings to do this, don't do that, be like this, don't be like that, smarten up, control this, stop that." Clearly, designers should choose the most effective media to transmit their messages, and the process of choosing the best media requires care and sensitivity.

Many designers compartmentalize social responsibility by occasionally doing pro bono work. Bill Drenttel, of Drenttel Doyle Partners in New York, offers the definitive guideline for doing pro bono work. "Social responsibility is something you do every day with the same attitude you have in maintaining your business. In advertising, pro bono work is structured through an ad council or in other ways—the work is done to win awards in competitions, and that's fundamentally corrupt. There is a basic rhetorical question that needs to be asked: '*What would you do if you couldn't sign your name to the work?*' Would you be willing to do the work without the credit?"

It is relatively easy to recycle, to privately support worthwhile causes, and to conduct ourselves in socially and politically correct ways. Our families, friends, colleagues, employers, and employees support and encourage us every step of the way. Even the direction that product marketing is taking these days reflects how social responsibility is increasingly becoming a part of our daily lives.

What is difficult is living up to the challenge that we provide for ourselves in believing we have the talents and abilities to work for what will make the world in some way better—by taking social responsibility to conduct ourselves *professionally* as we do personally.

Do we have a responsibility to gain a thorough awareness of our clients' activities and policies? Do we have the courage to withhold our services from clients who willfully pollute our environment or maintain sexist or racist policies? Do we have the tenacity to convince our clients or our employers of their social responsibility? Do we have the will to design with strength and precision the messages that are worthy of our effort and vital to our society and culture? And are we willing to share in the responsibility for the messages we so skillfully help to transmit?

The mission statement of the American Institute of Graphic Arts anticipated Dawkins's theory; it refers to graphic design as a *cultural force*. If it can be defined that way, it is a force that can clutter our lives, waste our resources, and spread confusion. However, if we accept responsibility, it is a force that can help bring clarity to a complex future.

Notes

1. Richard Dawkins, *The Selfish Gene*, (New York: Oxford University Press, 1976).

2. Ibid.

First published in *Communication Arts*, Advertising Annual 1992.

Mirror, Mirror . . .

Peter Laundy

Designers use prototypes to help clients see things they
could make. Why not also use them to help companies see what they could become?

A constant theme of business bestsellers is that incremental improvement is not enough. Tom Peters, Peter Senge, Peter Drucker, and many other experts who aren't lucky enough to have "Peter" somewhere in their names, are telling businesses that they'd better transform themselves fast or die.

A frequent complaint heard from consultants trying to help companies make big changes is that their clients' actions don't follow their words. Phrases like "don't just talk the talk, walk the talk" and "your actions are so loud I can't hear what you are saying" have therefore entered the lecture circuit lexicon. James Champy, one of the two consultants who brought us *Reengineering the Corporation* has just written a sequel in which he expresses the frustration up front. He declares that "Reengineering is in trouble" and laments that "some managers, misled by wishful thinking, believe that merely repeating the key words in *Reengineering the Corporation* is enough to bring about a transformation, like the newsboy in the comic strip who yelled 'Shazaam!' and became powerful Captain Marvel. Managers have been saying 'Fundamental!,' 'Dramatic!,' 'Radical!,' and 'Processes!'—and, lo, that which they proclaim to be so is so . . . they hope."[1]

So on one hand we've got fast transformation seen as a survival issue. And on the other, we've got company after company that can, at best, s-l-o-w-l-y evolve. May I suggest another arrow in the quiver of those helping companies to transform themselves?

If your client reads your bullet presentations, listens to your examples of how other companies have transformed themselves, enthusiastically embraces your suggestions, and then blithely goes off and continues to act in ways contrary to them, do not think that your client is insincere, lily-livered, or dumb. Realize that it is hard to see a sea change—to see what is inconsistent in current behavior or see what it would be like to behave in a way that supports fresh thinking. Also, realize that you can help them to see by showing them prototypes of a wide range of the things they would make were they to incorporate their new intentions into everyday actions.

Transformation Sequence

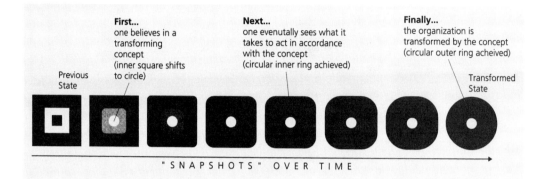

First...
one believes in a transforming concept
(inner square shifts to circle)

Next...
one evenutally sees what it takes to act in accordance with the concept
(circular inner ring achieved)

Finally...
the organization is transformed by the concept
(circular outer ring acheived)

Previous State

Transformed State

"SNAPSHOTS" OVER TIME

My first experience with the power of prototyping to help companies understand the implications of transformative ideas came in the late eighties. A consultant gave his client, whose margins had suddenly come under pressure by competitors who had learned the client's tricks, a recommendation: Shift from being "the low-cost supplier" to being "the supplier that helps its customers buy smart." The company had pioneered warehousing and distribution techniques that had previously provided it cost and speed advantages, but it had not paid attention to such things as developing better items, bundling them in ways that added value, or surrounding those items with more useful information. By adding proprietary intelligence to products, services, and communications, rather than just offering the same products as everybody else at a low price, the consultant suggested the company could reverse the margin erosion. We were asked to review some projects in progress and make prototypes of products and marketing communications that would illustrate the consultant's suggestion.

We put together a notebook of very rough prototypes of "afters" to contrast with the company's existing "befores." One was a sketch of a catalog spread showing a redesigned presentation of surgical masks. It helped the customer buy smart by offering only the alternatives that provided performance differences, and it made them understandable through written descriptions and a chart of features mapped against each mask type. Previously, the catalog contained a redundant laundry list of options with little explanation. A second prototype incorporated ergonomic thinking into the design of thermal plastic dinnerware as an example of providing a better product rather than just better prices in their current line of undifferentiated products. Other prototypes of packaging and a computer-generated report suggested software that could be developed to help the sales force—who had little confidence in aesthetic decision-making—generate pleasing hospital-room fabric and finish combinations to present to hospital administrators. Another showed catalogs reconfigured to target vertical markets within and outside the hospital, so that each could access information appropriate to it.

Together, these prototypes (and many others) illustrated a pattern of behavior consistent with "helping the customer buy smart" so that the company could see itself as it might become. Before seeing the prototypes, the "help the customer buy smart" idea had sounded interesting, but the client simply couldn't see what it would mean in practice.

Based on our learning on this project, and subsequent ones, I've come to understand the following:

Walkie-Talkie

The talk-walking problem is not just a problem of wishful thinking or just of resistance to change. People often really want to see; they take pride in being among those that "get it." It's hard to connect the details of behavior to transforming ideas. So much of a company's current behavior has become invisible as part of the everyday routine and few (if any) employees had ever experienced the behavior that flows from the new understanding (see diagram 1).

Stuff Controls Us

Old ways are not only embedded in organizational structure and processes but also in the tangible stuff made by an organization. These things—products, facilities, and communications—are such a part of habit that their underlying assumptions have become invisible. What Winston Churchill noted about buildings extends to all the things we make—we first shape them, then they shape us.[2] They are manifestations of past ideas, and they help the past ideas quietly endure. Office-interior layout schemes and whole furniture systems result from, then prolong the life of, old ideas about hierarchy. Company identification badges that note seniority (purple for zero to five years experience, orange for five to ten, etc.) support the idea that seniority is important and makes the length of one's tenure visible, abetting the tendency of insiders to dismiss the opinion of "fresh blood" (this in a company that for some time has seen a more adaptive culture as essential). Architectural photographic conventions—make it look beautiful and shoot it before occupants can mess it up—hinder architects from employing photography to study the use of their buildings over time, which could help them understand how people really use their buildings and show prospects that their aspirations include liveability.[3]

Our ancestors, who provided us with a document called the Bill of Rights but no countervailing thing called a Bill of Responsibilities[4], shaped a set of documents that continue to shape our country. They also shaped names that contain old ideas from whose hold we haven't yet escaped. For example, they gave us the name Criminal Justice System for our country's system to reduce crime, with its built-in bias toward actions that involve the processing of criminals. An alternate name, like Crime Reduction System, would help us take a broader more systemic view, incorporating preventative as well as punitive and corrective approaches.

Home is Where the Heart Is

As a general rule, examples from home seem to hit home better, and examples of how "they" in other businesses have acted often don't transfer. As cognitive scientists have found, it is surprisingly hard to transfer ideas from one context to another. For example, many college students who have mastered ideas new to them in school—like Newton's laws of physics—will revert to intuitive explanations that violate Newton's laws when asked to apply them to everyday occurrences in their lives.[5] Ideas that go against invisible assumptions (which are precisely those ideas with the power to transform) or that are illustrated in contexts that are very different from one's own, are especially impervious to transfer.

While benchmarking (the process of comparing your company's practices to competitors and recognized leaders within a pertinent domain) may seem to be evidence that new ideas do transfer, we suspect that benchmarking works best with ideas that offer incremental improvement rather than a transforming change in pattern. And benchmarking does have a downside: It can lead a company to see things more like its competitors, leading to diminished differentiation.

Shaping the Future

Prototyping the things "we" make—a company's products, facilities, communications, and names—puts the "Churchill" effect in the service of transforming ideas. Once made, sketches we shape of things as they could become can turn around and shape us, releasing our imaginations from invisible old patterns of thinking. People can more quickly and deeply see how current behavior is inconsistent with transforming ideas and what they need to do to transform themselves and their organizations.

Early in the Game

Prototyping works best early in a process—before big decisions get made—helping executives get beyond abstractions and understand the tangible implications of the changes they are contemplating.

Biotech Sales

A company selling products to biotech researchers in universities over the years grew more distant from them, no longer seeing researchers as colleagues but rather as mere customers. The shift was gradual, helped by traditional ideas about sales and marketing and by increasing numbers of senior personnel without roots in the scientific-research community.

Within the marketing department, a desire recently emerged to change course and get closer to its research customers. In looking at its communications, we could see that its modus operandi contained a number of things at odds with the emerging intentions. Many communications to their research customers were hype, intent on

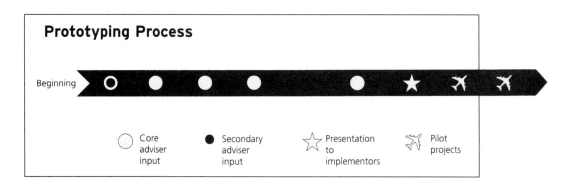

selling, rather than on helping their scientific colleagues make good decisions. Prototypes recast advertisements as "advernouncements" that focused on providing useful information rather than clever promotion. They shifted focus to making useful diagrams, away from making scientific-looking illustrations that were devoid of information.

The company also did not see how emerging information technology could help it get closer to its customers with information systems that provided customers with tailored information and gathered information about them that could be used to help our client better understand their individual customers. We developed a prototype system that would simultaneously cut down the time it would take our client's sales force to restock their customers' supply shelves, help their customers allocate their own costs for supplies among their departments, and help our client get beyond their customers' purchasing agents and gather information about end users.

These and other prototypes helped the company see what it could become. This vision was embraced in the research products division by key marketing people in the United States, in large part because they could see the implications of the prototypes.

Furnishing with an Edge

A contract-furnishings leader saw its industry being marginalized by the greater productivity-enhancing potential of the computer industry as well as by new business theories that resulted in diminished expressions of hierarchical status through office size and furnishings opulence.

A consultant suggested that the company could build a much more persuasive case for the ability of furnishings to impact white-collar productivity. To show the client the transforming potential of a focus on performance enhancement, a team prototyped a variety of examples showcasing trendy cutting-edge furniture, showroom, and communication designers, which contrasted with the company's current practices of following their competitors in appealing to designer specifiers.

Our team prototyped a system designed to support team practices and to perform well through the full product cycle, from furniture specification through refurbishment. At the same time, the prototype built in cost and performance advantages unavailable on the market, as well as an executive furnishing system that focused on performance features rather than just expensive materials. We prototyped showrooms designed not as trendy design statements to appeal to interior designers but rather as stages to make visible performance features. We designed brochures targeted to vertical markets like law and insurance, containing furnishing tips to help readers in the targeted industry achieve a competitive advantage, and of course to see that furnishing could give them their edge and that our contract-furnishings client understood this better than its competitors. We even prototyped a separate parent company and demonstrated its focus on research about work performance.

Together, the sketches helped the company see how it could improve its research efforts to understand performance issues, how it would think about products and communications that supported the performance focus, and how much of its current behavior was in the service of status display and aesthetic refinement simply to appeal to designers' tastes.

Solutions, not Products

A life-insurance sales force was encouraged by its company to provide solutions rather than sell products. However, the old approach was deeply embedded in the marketing materials and process. Products with snazzy names and glossy brochures continued to be provided to the field and encouraged salespeople to show customers products even as they "talked" solutions. The salespeople who understood solution-selling had no use for the materials provided to them and were making do with what they could make for themselves. Less forward-thinking salespeople, however, had simply purged the word "product" from their vocabulary and replaced it with "solution."

To help the company see how to provide solutions, we sketched an array of materials that supported a different process. They included software that allowed salespeople using notebook computers to build a customer insurance-need profile, take it back to the office and build a proposal with the help of an automated computer system, and then print a document tailored to the precise needs of the client and title it something like "An insurance plan for John and Mary Swift." As a result, the sales force and those at the central office that provided them with sales aids had a better understanding of what it took to really make the transformation to providing solutions.

In every example, the company had trouble connecting new ideas to the tangible results of those ideas, and therefore had trouble either evaluating the power of the ideas or in convincingly implementing them. The prototypes helped them see the ideas and see what they had to do to pull them off.

The Prototyping Process and Team

Projects, if at all possible, should occur outside immediate deadline pressures and constraints so that the prototypes can demonstrate a more complete adoption of the new ideas. The process should be designed to involve key development people, build understanding and enthusiasm, neutralize opposition, and make the product as good as it can be. Participants within the client company are generally engaged in the prototyping process in one of four ways (see diagram 2):

Project Leader

This person or people are the outside consultant's eyes and ears, making sure the right people are involved and political obstacles avoided. The consultant is greatly hindered without a trusting relationship with a good person inside the client company who is respected and a believer in the new ideas and who wants the company to achieve the transformation.

Core Advisers

This larger group of people is kept informed on progress through reviewing drafts of a presentation to get feedback. These reviews have a number of objectives: to build enthusiasm or diffuse opposition among reviewers for the presentations, to build interest at the highest possible levels if the project doesn't begin at the top, to debug the presentation, and to prospect for new sketch candidates that would provide value. Bend over backwards to include as many of these ideas as possible in the final version so reviewers can see their recommendations incorporated and involve the most influential people possible within the company.

Secondary Advisers

There is usually a larger group of people than the project team who feel they should be part of the process. Such people should be interviewed at project initiation for their input and then shown a late draft. Every effort should be made to demonstrate the late draft has not been cast in stone. To aid understanding, the ideas that inform the prototypes should be presented in words and diagrams, and the prototypes should be captioned to note their performance features.

Implementors

Those people that are not part of the approval process, but rather will be part of the implementation process, are shown the presentation as part of receiving their marching orders. However, the presentation should still be presented as "in progress" and feedback sought.

Pilot Projects

Small companies may not have the budgets to undertake projects without immediate payoffs, and large companies will want to quickly begin the process of embedding new ideas into their deliverables. Projects that pilot transforming ideas should advance the company's ability to deliver consistent with the ideas and help key internal and external audiences understand them. The projects should be selected to provide opportunities for small, quick wins, and leaders should provide a zone within the company in which old-view rules can be broken. Vigilance is required, because the "white blood cells" of the organization built around the old ideas will come out and try to destroy a threatening new idea.

Beware of defining pilot projects too tightly up front. A key aspect of a pilot project is that it is prototype-driven rather than spec-driven. Specifications bring past learning to bear on current projects and therefore obstruct change because they define both problems and solutions in accordance with old ideas. Instead, progress in project definition and solution comes as generations of prototypes are revised. The project team uses quick sketches to simultaneously learn what it thinks and to record its progress.

Designers and Prototyping Transforming Ideas

Designers, who have the ability to prototype things that flow from other people's points of view, are natural candidates for members of teams to help companies see transforming ideas. Designers from outside a culture are particularly useful because they can see what is invisible to those inside the culture and are therefore able to break old patterns more easily. However, to be effective, we designers must adopt some transforming ideas ourselves. We must:

- Tolerate initial ambiguity and expect to aid project definition as well as project solution.

- Learn to think of artifacts like an anthropologist would—as manifestations of the maker's behavior and culture, rather than just as we normally do—as a combination of delivered functionality and aesthetic composition.
- See ourselves as group facilitators rather than design deliverers.
- Encourage client participation and try to help them do it themselves with their traditional resources. If they can do it themselves, the transformation is successful.
- Be satisfied without a tangible delivered artifact, because prototypes in this context are means to a changed understanding, rather than an end product.
- Learn the difference between "good enough to show the idea" and "a really good design" and don't waste time going after the latter in situations that only require the former.
- Learn patience, because, from a designer's perspective, an organization's understanding changes slowly.
- Realize that seeing is only part of the answer. Once clients start to understand they will be asking you how they should go about changing their organization.

The relationship between the project team and the company, come to think of it, is more like one between a psychiatrist and patient than between designer and client. The subject is the emerging self-understanding of the patient and the objective is a transformed company, not a specific new product or communication. The process takes time and requires a lot of careful listening, trust, and candor. It allows the designer to earn a good wage because the effort at transformation is critical. But projects are always in danger of rejection by forces fighting for the status quo.

If you succeed in helping the company transform itself, you, like a psychiatrist, will be dimly, if fondly, remembered, as your client confidently marches into the future proud of its ability to succeed on its own.

Notes

1. James Champy, *Reengineering Management: The Mandate for New Leadership* (New York: HarperBusiness, 1995), 35.

2. Stewart Brand, *How Buildings Learn* (New York: Viking, 1994), 3.

3. *Ibid.*, 55.

4. Scott Russell Sanders, *Utne Reader* (March-April 1995): 30 (originally published in *Georgia Review*).

5. Lewis J. Perelman., *School's Out* (New York: Avon Books, 131.

First published in *Communication Arts*, Photography Annual 1995.

Read Viemeister was the quintessential twentieth-century
designer. He was born during the roaring twenties and graduated from Pratt in 1943.
He began his career as director of styling for Gordon Lippincott where it launched
Industrial Design magazine and the Tucker car. With Budd Steinhilber, he founded
Vie Design Studios in 1946, and he helped organize the Industrial Design Society of
America in the sixties. He designed automobiles, buildings, products, packages,
logos, and exhibits. He was successful, a widely respected professional, and he loved
his work. He was also my father.

After he died last August, I went home to Yellow Springs, Ohio, to sort through
his papers. I found much more than I expected to find. There were architectural
drawings of his future "office" that he'd done as a kid, photographs of him as a
teenager at the 1939 World's Fair, brochures from his early days with Lippincott, as
well as sketches and project proposals from throughout his career.

His papers showed that nearly fifty years ago he did business just like I do now.
His proposals looked a lot like mine, his projects were divided into the same kinds
of phases, and, after adjusting for inflation, his hourly rate was almost identical to
mine. He also grappled with the same design ignorance from clients and the public
that I grapple with today.

At first, I thought it was really great that we had so much in common. But then
I started thinking about all the things that have changed in those fifty years. And I
began to wonder why the design profession hasn't changed. Even when *Business
Week* predicted three years ago that *design* would become the buzzword of the
nineties, nothing happened. Instead the buzzword today is *quality*—the very essence
of good design. But why aren't people talking about how designers can improve
quality? I think it's because the profession is stalled, and I think it's stalled because it
doesn't have a good idea of where it's going. It has not only lost sight of its future;
it's lost sight of the future.

I used to think that all the real advances in technology had happened during my
grandparents' lives—electric light bulbs, automobiles, airplanes, telephones, the

Bomb, the Pill, computers, television, etc.—and that technology has simply been evolving from those blockbuster inventions of yesteryear. But the change from their biplane to our 747 is more than evolutionary. The changes that we're seeing today are fundamental and revolutionary, changes so dramatic and radical that the next century won't be anything like this one. In the future, designers will not only create logos, toasters, computer interfaces, and virtual realities, they will also define the complex interplay of living organisms.

As Margret Morgan-Hubbard wrote in *Environmental Action*, "We are among the first generations in human history to journey toward responsible management of the global ecosystem." And neuropsychiatrist Richard Restak thinks that with new drugs "we will be able to design our own brain." These responsibilities should cause the design business to explode.

To survive, we must reengineer our design profession and our businesses. We have to break the frame, recognize our potential, and live up to it. We must find better and faster ways to deliver high-quality work to our clients. We must find ways to fully integrate the design process into the business process. We must also improve the quality of designers so we will be smart enough and strong enough to do, undo, and not do. We must improve the quality of our work because our work can improve the quality of people's lives.

That Vision Thing

The optimistic designers and architects of the modern movement believed their work was going to substantially improve the world, and they inspired my dad to launch his design career. Kandinsky and his pals gave the Communist revolution a graphic vocabulary that defined the Soviet Union. For the 1939 World's Fair, Norman Bel Geddes created "Futurama" and Henry Dreyfuss built "Democracity" as testaments to their vision of the future. Designers transformed new technologies into things people wanted: streamlined cars, modern highways, turbocharged appliances, inspiring buildings, and visionary graphics. Walt Disney built Disneyland and dreamed of building a genuine Experimental Prototype City of Tomorrow (EPCOT). Guys like Paul Rand, Massimo Vignelli, and Milton Glaser designed the international identity systems that propelled corporations around the world. Those were the years when designers created models for how things could be, and their dreams of utopia drove our economy through World War II and into the seventies.

But then, shifting from artists and visionaries to "problem solvers" and "communication managers," the design profession continuously de-evolved to meet the increasingly narrow requirements of business and industry. Of course, it's difficult today to have a vision of a beautiful future when we are confronted with the world's big problems like population, pollution, and AIDS. But who would have thought that just when science and technology are delivering us to the threshold of a more realistic utopia, we would be stuck with too many pessimistic and shortsighted designers?

In this same column in 1993 (March/April), William Drenttel, president of Drenttel Doyle, pointed to the "dumb-designer syndrome" or designers' desire "to hide behind the right side of the brain." He believes, "This [syndrome], in some cases, flows directly from the historically inferior position designers hold in many worlds.

Magazine art directors seldom have the power of editors . . . and corporate art directors are usually in staff positions without line responsibility." Industrial designers suffer from a variation of the same disease, denying their intuition and talent and trying to legitimize their genius with ergonomics and statistics.

For a profession that bills itself as innovative and visionary, this is a disaster.

"Open the Pod Bay Door, Hal."

By the year 2001, we may be able to talk our computers through the design of a new brochure. By then, we may also have figured out exactly how computer technology fits into our profession.

Computers have been a real dilemma for designers. On one hand, they're powerful tools that have created lots of new opportunities. On the other hand, they've empowered our clients to mimic "designer" results and question the value of hiring a real professional. At the Cooper-Hewitt's "Edge of the Millennium" conference in 1992, Lorraine Wild said, "The relationship of designer to client, already tenuous, could be on the verge of obliteration since the production-related reasons for any client to hire a graphic-design consultant are decreasing steadily. Obviously job security is driving graphic designers crazy."

While computers erode the traditional crafts that form the foundation of our profession, they are also opening up entire new frontiers. Big thinker Neil Postman points out in his book *Technopoly*, "Every technology is both a burden and a blessing." In an era when kids don't learn anything in school and TV has nothing to add, there certainly is a need for professional designers to translate raw data into information that people can use. (So what if 98 percent of American adults don't know what design is? According to a four-year study by the U.S. Department of Education, only 50 percent of them can read.)

Definitions of literacy are changing, and designers are well-positioned to have a strong and positive influence on the new ways that people consume information. Text will remain an essential component, but it is not the only way to store and share ideas. The Information Age may have caused us to reach information overload, filling our minds' landfills with all that extra verbiage. However, a new visual language could help us manage our massive piles of data. Designers can use this opportunity to define the structure of these new languages. In the process, we can redefine design, maybe even position the profession as the gatekeeper to this new communications industry. There are unlimited possibilities for the designer or, as science fiction writer Bruce Sterling points out, "virtual reality is capable of absorbing infinite amounts of human ingenuity."

Power Shifts

In order to prosper in the next decade, corporations are looking very critically at their business processes. They are down-sizing, resizing, and right-sizing. They are paying more attention to core competencies and leveraging their strengths into new business opportunities. They recognize that the world is changing, and they are shifting their paradigms to meet the challenge.

Designers must take a critical look at their own businesses. For instance, if we sell our work based on hourly fees and position our "product" as a "service," our design work will be viewed as a generic commodity equally available from the lowest-priced supplier. However, if we are contracted on a royalty basis or a long-term retainer, we are immediately elevated to the role of a partner in the enterprise. We are consulted on a range of issues far beyond the normal design discussions, and we assume an integral role in the client's business.

We must think long and hard about the value we bring to our clients. We must stop thinking about designers as gods and we must not allow clients—or design organizations—to treat us as slaves. We must shift our own paradigms and redefine our relationship with the new paradigms of industry. We must stop being codependent and start being change agents.

Global culture is going through its own paradigm shift. Not only is the control of wealth, knowledge, and power in flux, the very nature of wealth, knowledge, and power is up for grabs. I hope we find a democratic solution because that's the only fair way for the world to distribute all its stuff. And besides, if democracy is the rule, then design is the tool.

So, What's a Designer?

According to Japanese samurai designer/performance artist, Katsuhiko Hibino, "We can't wait for our clients to tell us what to do. We have to show them."

In today's world, design is an invisible profession. So if we're going to show our clients just how much we can do for them, we're going to have to start speaking up. We're going to have to start educating not only our clients but also the media and the general public about the value of design. At a recent meeting of "Design and Cultural Industries" sponsored by the Vorm'geving Instituut (Dutch for the "Form Giving Institute," based in Amsterdam and directed by John Thakara), Smart Design's strategist, David Hales, worried that most design professionals only speak the language of design, effectively limiting their ability to broadly communicate their story.

Our incestuousness has finally caught up with us. For example, design awards seldom recognize work that means anything special to the general public. Lots of meaningful work is not done by the designers whom the profession labels its "best." In fact, the "best" pros are sometimes responsible for the worst work.

The general public has such little awareness of our profession that they wouldn't miss us if we all packed our bags and went to Rome. Most people see design as style or decoration, not as better "function" or "communication." They think that a lot of "designer" stuff is stupid and expensive. They like the stuff that Robert Venturi and Denise Scott Brown called "ugly and ordinary" in *Learning from Las Vegas*. They really want something that architect Constantin Boym calls "Searsy."

When we get on our soapboxes and start preaching the need for even more design, they must think we're absolutely mad. We keep yelling louder and louder about how important our work is, and they can't imagine how more stupid designer junk is going to improve their lives. We have to stop talking about more design until people have a good understanding of what design is doing and has already done for them. Designers have to move from an invisible profession to one that is generally perceived as instrumental in making good things happen.

Let's take a page from marketing's handbook and start speaking in the languages that reach the people we want to reach. Design really is for everybody—ours is not a profession of and for elites. Our power comes from our ability to reach the masses.

How about Utopia?

In the Stone Age, there were no special designers. (Everyone made their own spears.) In the Middle Ages and beyond, craftsmen designed and made their own wares. It wasn't until the Industrial Revolution that design became separated from both the user and the manufacturer. That enormous shift interrupted the natural integration of design in peoples' lives.

Now as we move into the postindustrial era, new technology is again making it possible for everyone to become their own designer—and I don't mean everyone should open their own studio and join AIGA. Everyone won't need to make their own TV or car, but they will make design an important part of their lives. We should be encouraging people to acquire the skills, pursue their talents, and stop conceding authority to presidents, police, rock stars, actors, and even designers. Design will be one way that people will "act locally," and when that happens, design will become so integrated into the workings of society that it will be transparent. (Wouldn't it be cool to go from an invisible profession to a transparent one?)

In the preface to his new book, *The Ecology of Commerce*, Paul Hawken writes, "We must design a system where the natural everyday acts of work and life accumulate into a better world as a matter of course, not a matter of conscious altruism . . . Good design can release human-kind from its neurotic relationship to absurd acts of destruction . . . The urge to create beauty is an untapped power . . . Imagine yourself a designer."

The Last Straw

The current slump in the world economy is no ordinary recession. It's a gigantic, multifaceted paradigm revolution. Everything about the world economy is changing. Old jobs aren't being replaced with similar new ones because the basic concepts of work and wealth are changing. George Bush was only a little early when he said, "I want to make sure that everyone who has a job wants one."

Design has an important role as the world realigns itself. Our first goal should be to improve the quality of people's lives by empowering them with our designs. However, we must be much more inclusive and expansive as we go about our work. Back in 1968, Richard Farson, chairman of the Western Behavioral Sciences Institute, spoke at the national conference for the Industrial Design Society of America organized by my dad and Pierre Crease. Farson said, "The professional is having to redefine his role as manager of resources that exist in the population he is trying to serve, rather than regarding himself as the resource . . . Our task is one of designing systems in which the components become the designers in self-determining self-renewing activities."

Today, the design profession is a prosthetic device. We prop up our culture, we make it look good, but we keep it crippled. Technology, ecology, and society are demanding a new breed of designer—holistic, eclectic, emotional, and empowering.

These new designers will go into the future, not only as scouts and pioneers, but as leaders who understand contradiction and diversity. Let's skip the world domination. Let's move toward a new utopia where everyone is capable of designing their own future. Let's create a world where individuals are free to explore their potential and pursue their dreams, just like Read Viemeister did throughout his career.

First published in *Communication Arts*, May/June 1994.

More than a quarter century ago, the painter Ad Reinhardt declared that his new black-on-black canvases were the "last pictures which anyone can make." The critics raved, and many agreed with the "Black Monk" that his masterpieces would be history's "ultimate" paintings. Unfortunately, other artists refused to hand in their brushes, so art continued.

But ever since, modern art has resembled a doomsday cult on the day after the deadline for the end of the world. The true believers awakened one day to find that the sun had risen, the mad prophet had disappeared, and they all had to find something to do with the rest of their lives. They dissolved into factions with rival theories about what happened, what it meant, and what they were going to do next.

This predicament is what they now call Postmodernism. And if you're confused about it, it's probably because you're beginning to understand it. Art critics to the contrary, Postmodernism is actually easy to explain, so I thought I'd take a crack at defining a few of its basic terms.

Modern art: It's best to get this out of the way first. In the future, modern art won't mean what it does now. It will mean "the kind of art they did in the twentieth century." Like saying "Baroque" or "Romanesque," to call something "Modern" will be to date something.

Contemporary art: A handful of people who grew up before TV still think that all artists either paint like Picasso or like Norman Rockwell. That was true eighty years ago, but these days all artists want to be popular. If they were starting their careers today, Rockwell and Picasso would probably both be painting on black velvet.

Art history: In the Stone Age, artists expressed themselves with bold pictures on the walls of their caves. Then there was a period of transition that lasted roughly 10,000 years. Then came modern art. Now we can express ourselves again. If you want to know the details, you can go to art school and spend thousands of dollars, but this is basically what they'll teach you. I've boiled it down.

Cubism: This was a movement started by Picasso and Braque to distinguish their work from what Cézanne had already done but failed to give a name to. In modern art, naming your art movement is a must. Cubism is still the most important art movement for the same reason that John D. is still the most important Rockefeller. All the other art movements are like downtown Rockefellers, and you can forget about them unless you expect to encounter an art category on Jeopardy.

Surrealism: An archaic term. Formerly an art movement. No longer distinguishable from everyday life.

Futurism: This was a movement of intellectuals who wanted to replace tradition with the modern world of machinery, speed, violence, and public relations. It proves that we should be careful what intellectuals wish for, because we might get it.

Dada: Dada artists were ironists. Duchamp was their star, and his masterpiece was a urinal. He ended his life playing chess. He claimed he was making an art statement. My grandfather was a prankster, too. And he ended his life playing chess. But since he did it to keep from being bored, no one thought it proved anything. This suggests that Dada artists are exempt from the general rule that ironists are the biggest victims of their own irony.

Abstract expressionism: After World War II, the United States emerged as the world's superpower. American companies like Cities Service and Esso, which had once been regional businesses, became international corporations. They adopted abstract names like "Citgo" and "Exxon" to give themselves world-class status. Since multinational giants couldn't have little pictures of red barns or weeping clowns in the lobbies of their Bauhaus buildings, abstract expressionism emerged as the world's most overrated form of interior decoration.

Minimalism: During the era of the Bugaloo and the Frug, abstract expressionism expanded into a large ball of hot gas, then suddenly collapsed into a black hole, where it still sits, spinning and refusing to give off light. This event was called minimalism. A lot of people believed it was the final stage in the evolution of art, but it turned out to be just another space-time warp in the gravitational field of Western culture.

Pop art: In aristocratic societies, rich people used to commission exquisite paintings for their walls. Years later, cheap imitations would filter down to calendars in gas stations. In our democratic society, this works backwards. Here, art begins as the kind of picture you'd find on a matchbook cover. Then expensive imitations of it wind up on the office walls of plastic surgeons and Hollywood agents.

Op art: I can never keep my mind on op art. It always reminds me of The Continental Op, Dashiell Hammett's detective. That reminds me of The Maltese Falcon, which reminds me of Humphrey Bogart, which reminds me of Play It Again, Sam. That reminds me of Woody Allen, and the next thing I know, I'm thinking about Diane Keaton. I don't know if anyone else has a similar experience with op art.

New art: New art follows old art. Comes before new improved art.

New-wave art: Modern art as it would have been done by The Big Bopper, The Del Vikings, or Sam the Sham and The Pharaohs. New-wave art was the rage of the eighties. Now it's exhibited in Oldies but Goodies Museums, usually in black and pink frames.

Graffiti art: Many people decorate their homes with designer graffiti, even though most of them would probably have real graffiti scoured off the outside of their buildings. Personally, I think that graffiti artists should go to the homes of their patrons with spray cans and make their living rooms look like subway cars. This would separate serious lovers of graffiti from uptowners spelunking for art thrills.

Realism: Currently, realistic paintings are valued for their craftsmanship. In the next century, when art will be packaged as virtual-reality software, realistic paintings will sell the way Shaker furniture does now. Shaker furniture will sell the way Van Gogh paintings do. Teddy bears owned by Elvis will come to auction only occasionally.

Commercial art: Anything done by an artist with a cash register by the door. Commercial art is traditionally delivered to a client in a brown paper bag with an invoice stapled to the outside.

Fine art versus commercial art: In commercial art, you find out how much they're going to pay you. Then you do the work. In fine art, it's the other way around.

"That's not art, that's illustration": Almost everybody is an artist these days. Rock 'n' Roll singers are artists. So are movie directors, performance artists, makeup artists, tattoo artists, con artists, and rap artists. Movie stars are artists. Madonna is an artist because she explores her own sexuality. Snoop Doggy Dogg is an artist because he explores other people's sexuality. Victims who express their pain are artists. So are guys in prison who express themselves on shirt cardboard. Even consumers are artists when they express themselves in their selection of commodities. The only people left in America who seem not to be artists are illustrators.

"Love me, love my art": Norman Rockwell used to say if a picture was going badly, put a dog in it. If it was going really badly, put a bandage on the dog's paw. This is the basic principle behind victim art.

Tattoo art: Personally I've never liked tattoos, although I think they improve some people—especially the kind of people who hang around tattoo parlors.

Kitsch: In my lifetime, kitsch has progressed from the cynical sentimentality of Maxfield Parrish calendars to the sentimental cynicism of Batman movies.

Star, superstar, black hole: A modern Renaissance man is unlikely to become a celebrity. But any celebrity can be a Renaissance man. The great number of entertainers-turned-painters testifies to this. Look at Tony Curtis, Tony Bennett, Anthony Quinn, Billy Dee Williams, Red Skelton, the artist formerly known as Prince, Ron

Wood, and Frank Sinatra. They all have galleries for their paintings and, as far as I know, there are books about their work. I read an interview with Sylvester Stallone in which he talked about his graffiti paintings. He said that drawing and color aren't important, as long as you get your feelings "out there." I confess that after years of struggling with drawing and color, that was a load off my mind.

Style: Style is the most valuable asset of the modern artist. That's probably why so many styles are reported lost or stolen each year.

Art school: One of the frequent casualties of higher education is common sense. Art education is a good example of this. In high school, most kids draw little more than unicorns and super heroes. Then suddenly, in four years of art school, they're supposed to develop an original style. That's something even Rembrandt couldn't have done. So a lot of students wisely spend their four years cultivating gimmicks they can call a style, and mastering Artspeak. This means that, as professionals, they can say things like "I do purloined images on Naugahyde." Or, "These mutilated Barbie dolls represent feminist praxis in action."

Tradition: There are still some traditionalists, mostly employed by art schools, who continue to paint like the Ashcan School. For years, it's pleased the avant-garde to keep these Amish around to portray the art establishment. But for generations, the real art establishment has been made up of earth sculptors, body piercers, and topless cello players. It's been a long time since a painter of the Ashcan School has even had a prayer.

Cutting-edge art: One percent inspiration, 99 percent attitude.

"Sometimes you gotta break the rules": One of the things not enough people appreciate about modern art is that its philosophy can be summed up as a Burger King commercial.

The avant-garde: Over a hundred years ago, some French bohemians decreed that the purpose of art was to shock the middle classes. It may have been a great idea back then. But these days, the middle classes aren't paying attention. They're all on Jerry Springer or Ricki Lake talking about their cross-dressing experiences or sex with the baby-sitter. It's the cutting-edge artists who have to watch in silence and eat their hearts out, complaining about the state of American culture and demanding more grant money for even more cutting-edge art. In the future, this spectacle of the middle classes shocking the avant-garde will probably become the textbook definition of post-modernism.

The left brain doesn't know what the right brain is doing: Cutting-edge artists who attack tradition must secretly believe that tradition will survive to enshrine them as the wild and crazy geniuses who destroyed it.

Craftsmanship: In traditional art, craftsmen worked within certain conventions. Occasionally those conventions would be redefined by acts of genius. In modern art, everybody has to redefine art all the time. This might have made our era another Renaissance, if only there had been a sudden explosion of geniuses in the world. But since ego is more common than genius, Postmodern art is destined to be more narcissistic than heroic.

Art Theory: The typical modern artist produces a small body of work wrapped in a theory. Some even dispense with the work itself and exhibit only their theories on typed sheets. To me, this seems a sensible economy of style. If the purpose of art is to redefine art, then words should do the trick. There's no use cluttering up the world with redundant examples.

Self-expression: The crowbar used by artists to pry open the Pandora's Box of self-indulgence for everybody else in society. Fifty years ago, it was the dream of every bohemian artist to be seen getting out of a limousine wearing blue jeans and sneakers. Today, it's the dream of probably half the people in the country.

The miracle of authenticity: The faith that if we're all authentic and express ourselves, society will benefit. A charming ideal, but it overlooks the obvious. There are a lot of authentic jerks and idiots in the world. Encouraging them to express themselves will never do anybody much good, much less society.

Emotion: Modern artists paint their feelings for the same reasons Fra Angelico painted Virgins. Retailing your emotions is the holy sacrament of psychotherapy, which is the twentieth century's version of revealed religion.

"Raw energy": The heroic artist tried to master his craft. But for the self-expressionist, mastery is a form of denial: Self-expression is only authentic when it's raw. This means that a self-expressionist is at his peak when he's least handicapped by experience. Indeed, self-expressionists who learn how to draw usually become mediocre.

Instinct: Back in the prehistoric jungle, all the animals who trusted other animals got eaten. The only ones who survived to reproduce were the ones who instinctively feared everybody and bit their heads off. This explains why so many people—like artists—who trust their instincts behave like crocodiles.

Romanticism: Romantic artists start with the belief that human imperfection is caused by imperfect societies. Unfortunately, this often leads them to believe they can improve people by smuggling improvements into society through the Trojan Horse of art.

Poets are the unacknowledged legislators of the world: It's every artist's fantasy to run things. I know personally, I'd be happiest as dictator of a small island. The problem is that romantic artists are usually too disorganized to run their own lives, let alone their societies. And most societies are too sensible to let them try it.

Consciousness-raising art: An all-purpose excuse for the artist to cast himself as a pearl before the swine of democracy. Whenever I know that an artist is trying to raise my consciousness, I have flashbacks of Jane Fonda, Sissy Spacek, and Jessica Lange lecturing Congress about the realities of farm life.

Issue movies: When society ignores a Romantic artist, he fortifies himself with delusions of grandeur and persecution. Modern issue movies are a perfect example of this: The films in which alienated heroes invariably struggle against greedy corporations and corrupt government could only have been made by frustrated artists working on the assembly lines of Hollywood.

Media studies: If you're a college student, you can now take courses on Elvis, the Beatles, or Rush Limbaugh. You can write a Ph.D. thesis on the meaning of "Rosebud" in Citizen Kane. I thought that the whole point of pop culture was to have something you didn't have to study in school.

The medium is the message: This is an overall rule of thumb for baby boomers. Boomers also confuse emotions for thoughts, sentimentality for sensitivity, and public relations for public policy.

"Art Event": Postmodern artists believe their work can change reality if it gets sufficient media attention. So the twentieth century, which began with Ezra Pound advising artists to "make it new," ends with artists trying to "make it news."

Political Art: Political art expresses the clichés you agree with, unlike propaganda, which expresses the clichés you don't.

Painter/Activist: I distrust anyone with a slash in his or her job description. I've met too many actor/waiters and rock musician/electricians.

Auteur: A white-collar artist who tells blue-collar craftsmen what to do, then takes the credit. It might help craftsmen everywhere to remember that the same logic that makes Steven Spielberg the auteur of *Schindler's List* makes Pope Julius the auteur of the Sistine Chapel ceiling. Roll over, Michelangelo, and tell Bramante the news.

Mixed-up media: In Modernism, reality used to validate media. In Postmodernism, the media validate reality. If you don't believe this, just think how many times you've described some real event as being "just like a movie."

Deconstructionism: A philosophy that defines the artist as a cork bobbing on the tides of history. The artist can never understand what he's doing, but a deconstructionist can. Naturally this makes the deconstructionist the artist's superior.

Poststructural analysis: Many people have observed that truth is stranger than fiction. This has led deconstructionists to conclude that it's stranger than nonfiction as well.

Forever Jung: Postmodernists believe that truth is myth, and myth, truth. This equation has its roots in pop psychology where people also believe that emotions are a form of reality. There used to be another name for this state of mind. It was called psychosis.

Life imitates art: Not true. Art imitates life. Life imitates high school.

The Counterculture: When I was a kid, I was part of the hippie press. Like a lot of us back then, I believed that everything personal was political. In one way, the counterculture succeeded. We married art to politics. At first, this was good. It brought the compassion and ambiguity of art to public debate. But increasingly, as artists exploit political themes to demand attention for their work, I've concluded that we misjudged the long-term risks. Namely, that we might produce a community of artists with no more integrity than politicians.

Multiculturalism: Multiculturalists believe that an individual's self-worth is a function of his ethnic identity—a philosophy of self-esteem arrived at through the logic of racism.

Conspicuous sensitivity: I've never understood why multiculturalists, who so often condescend to the clichés of their own culture, are so eager to embrace the clichés of cultures they know nothing about.

Art and Democracy: In a democracy, the ideal is compromise. In art, it isn't. Many of the contradictions in postmodern art come from the fact that we're trying to be artists in a democratic society.

A herd of independent minds: A lot of artists say they'd be happy in a classless society. But artists are often the first to deceive themselves. Put them in the kind of utopia they sentimentalize, and in no time at all they would be binding their feet, lengthening their necks, or flattening their heads, just to be different. Artists will never be satisfied, and anyone who tries to satisfy them is a fool.

Elitism: Democracy reduces the large distinctions between individuals. This magnifies the status of petty distinctions and causes some to see even variations between individuals as a form of inequality. But the desire for recognition is relentless. People will always find some way to stand out. Some will paint masterpieces. Some will master the art of blowing out candles through their ears. If all the people in the world were worms, some would still be glowworms and the rest would want to be.

Art and Technology: In the nineteenth century, the camera made a realist of the man on the street. Now the computer can make anybody a desktop cubist. Technology may or may not be destiny, but I doubt that machines will replace art any more than wheels have replaced feet.

Information superhighway: Where ideas of the future will go to sit in the traffic of facts.

Waiting for Van Gogh: In the world most of us have grown up in, popular art has inherited and exploded all the forms of art that came before it. Everything from the primitive art of tribal societies to the fine art of aristocratic ones has been thrown into the cement mixer of modern culture, along with its juxtapositions of celebrity and anonymity, poverty, and sudden wealth, and the continuous swooning of the popular media over trends and fads. The truth about Postmodernism is, we haven't really figured out yet how artists are going to thrive in modern mass societies. We're all experiments.

© 1996 Brad Holland

Brad Holland originally wrote this essay for *Illustration: America,* a book on the work of twenty-five illustrators published by Rockport Publishers. The essay has developed a life of its own, for even before the book came out, *Atlantic Monthly* convinced Holland to let them print excerpts in their July issue just as we had determined to run this newly edited longer version.

DK Holland is a communications strategist, senior art director, and writer, and, as
such, serves as consultant for various advocacy groups. A graduate of the Parsons
School of Design and the New School for
Social Research, she began the Design
Issues column in *Communication Arts*
magazine in 1990 and has been its editor
ever since.

Prior to forming DK Holland LLC
(*www.dkholland.com*) in 2001, Holland was a principal of the Pushpin
Group, where she directed the design of the international licensing programs for Dr. Seuss, Mattel's Barbie, and Marc Brown's Arthur. Prior to
joining Pushpin in 1995, she was part of the team that repositioned
King's Supermarket and Cooper's Coffee, both high-end retail chains in
the New York metropolitan area.

Holland is author and art director of several books on packaging
and marketing, including *Great Package Design* and *Marketing by
Design*. She produced *Graphic Design: New York*; *Graphic Design:
America*; *Signs and Spaces*; and *Design in Depth*. She has been listed
in *Who's Who of American Women* since 1978 and *Who's Who in the
West* since 1980.

In 1990 Holland produced the Ethics and Business Practice panel
discussion, several videos, and the ethics game "Where Do You Draw the
Line?" for the AIGA. She has conducted seminars for both IBM and
Hallmark, instructing their design managers in such topics as working
successfully with designers and understanding ethics in business practice. She was named the Hallmark professor of design at the University of
Kansas and the head of the Hallmark Design Symposium at KU in 1995.

In 1998 Holland wrote the much-lauded two-part article "Keeping Promises: The Impact of Brand Images on Society" for *Communication Arts* magazine, and in the same year was a presenter at the AIGA Brandesign Conference in New York. In 1999 she was presented with the prestigious Walter Hortens Award for Outstanding Achievement in Professional Practice from the Graphic Artists Guild.

Holland works in Manhattan near Union Square. She lives in a nineteenth-century tanner's shop in historic Fort Greene, Brooklyn, with her cocker spaniel, Walt Whitman, and tiger cats, Frida Kahlo and Frank Lloyd Wright.

Carolyn McCarron is a communications strategist for watersdesign.com, where her responsibilities encompass strategic design planning, writing, and graphic design. She previously worked as a senior designer for Houghton Mifflin Company. She has a B.F.A. in graphic design from the Rhode Island School of Design, and an M.A. in advertising and communications design from Syracuse University. She has written articles for *Communication Arts*, *Adobe* magazine, and the *AIGA Journal*.

Véronique Vienne is the author of *The Art of Doing Nothing* and *The Art of Imperfection*, as well as *Something to be Desired*, a collection of essays on design. She is currently a contributing editor to *House and Garden* magazine, with a monthly column, *Past Perfect*. She also serves on the board of the Society of Publication Designers (SPD) and teaches a course called "The Integrated Studio" for the Masters Program at the School of Visual Arts.

Ellen Lupton, who received a B.F.A. from the Cooper Union in 1985, is a writer, curator, and graphic designer. She is chair of the graphic design program at Maryland Institute College of Art in Baltimore is curator of contemporary design at the Cooper-Hewitt National Design. She has curated numerous exhibitions, including *Mixing Messages: Graphic Design in Contemporary Culture* (1996); *Design Culture Now: National Design Triennial* (2000); and *Graphic Design in the Mechanical Age* (1998).

Hugh Dubberly is a prinicpal in Dubberly Design Office, a firm focusing on interaction design and information design. At Apple Computer in the eighties and nineties, Hugh managed cross-functional design teams, creative services, and corporate identity for the entire company. While at Apple, he served at Art Center College of Design in Pasadena as the first and founding chairman of the computer graphics department. He later moved to Netscape and became Vice President of Design. Hugh teaches in the Graphic Design Department at San Jose State University and the Institute of Design at IIT.

Philip Marshall Durbrow is one of the world's leading authorities on corpo-
rate identity. Formerly vice chairman of Landor and currently chairman of
Frankfurt Balkind, Philip has personally led over two hundred corporate
identity programs for such companies as GE, Caterpillar, Cotton
Incorporated, Walt Disney, 20th Century Fox, the World Wildlife Fund, the
Tech Museum, San Francisco Ballet and the Nobel Prize Committee.

William Drenttel is a designer and publisher who works in partnership
with Jessica Helfand in Falls Village, Connecticut. Their studio, Winter
House, is a historic 1931 modernist structure, which they restored in 2000.
Drenttel and Helfand focus on editorial, education and new media projects,
as well as writing, designing and packaging books and publications. Bill is
President Emeritus of the American Institute of Graphic Arts and a board
member of the Cooper-Hewitt National Design Museum. He is a graduate
of Princeton University.

Tucker Viemeister, a graduate of the Pratt Institute, cofounded Smart
Design (famous for creating OXO Good Grips) and opened Frogdesign's
New York office. He works in a partnership with the young Dutch industrial
design group, Springtime, and has organized national conferences for the
ACD and IDSA. He has taught at Yale and the School of Visual Arts, among
other schools of design, and edited the book *Product Design 6.*

Peter Good is a graphic designer and illustrator of posters, books, graphic
identities, collateral, exhibits, and U.S. postage stamps. His work can be
found in the collections of the Cooper-Hewitt and Library of Congress museums as well as internationally. In 1992, he was honored by the Connecticut
Commission on the Arts for lifetime achievement and generosity to the arts
community. A principal of Cummings & Good, he lives and works in
Chester, Connecticut, with his wife and collaborator, Janet Cummings.

Justin Vood Good is an artist and writer. His works are primarily in the
media of charcoal, ink and gouache, and reflect affinities with the traditions
of minimalism and conceptualism. He is currently a graduate student of
philosophy at Boston University, where he is working on a Ph.D. disserta-
tion on visual perception. He lives in Somerville, Massachusetts.

J. Phillips Williams is a principal and creative director in the firm Design:
MW specializing in establishing the images of clients through collateral,
packaging, Web sites and interactive CDs, and advertising. Recent projects
include print collateral, visual direction for advertising, and an interactive
sales kiosk for the new cosmetics line *Isabella Rossellini's Manifesto.* A
professor at the University of the Arts in Philadelphia, he holds a B.F.A.
from the Rhode Island School of Design and an MA from Yale University.

Cecelia Holland was born in 1943 in Nevada, grew up in New Jersey and
Connecticut, and graduated from Connecticut College in 1965. A Guggen–
heim Fellow and winner of the Stone Award, she has written more than

twenty books and numerous articles in a variety of genres, including historical fiction, nonfiction, science fiction, and criticism. She lives in northern California.

David Sterling completed his M.F.A. in 1978 at Cranbrook Academy of Art. After serving as Art Director of *ID* magazine for three years, he, along with Jane Kosstrin, established the New York design firm Doublespace in 1979. He founded World Studio in 1992 and World Studio Foundation a year later. He continues to serve as a lecturer and a professor at the School of Visual Arts. In 1997, he was presented with the prestigious Bronze Apple Award from the Industrial Designers Society of America.

Maggie Macnab is a visual communicator who specializes in logo design and corporate identity development with work published in *Communication Arts*, *Graphis*, *Step by Step*, *Print*, and others. She is past president of Communication Arts of New Mexico and an instructor of logo design at UNM. Her current project is *"eyeku: the soul of symbol"*, an educational design resource that includes Web site, traveling exhibit, workshop and book.

Michael Bierut is a partner in the New York office of the international design firm Pentagram and President Emeritus of the American Institute of Graphic Arts. He is a coeditor and designer of *Tibor Kalman: Perverse Optimist*, and of the *Looking Closer* anthologies of design criticism. A graduate of the University if Cincinnati's College of Design, Architecture, Art and Planning, he is currently a Senior Visiting Critic at the Yale University School of Art.

Sean Kernan is coauthor, with Jorge Luis Borges, of *The Secret Books*. His photography has been published in the *New York Times* magazine, *Communication Arts*, *Graphis*, and *American Photography*. He has shown at the Museo de la Ciudad de Queretaro and Kunsthaus Santa Fe, as well as at the Photosynkiria, the Friends of Photography, the Whitney Museum, and the Sarah Morthland Gallery. He studied English at the University of Pennsylvania, then worked in theater for several years before starting to photograph.

John Bielenberg founded Bielenberg Design, recently merged with a new company called C2, in San Francisco in 1990. A teacher at the California College of Arts and Crafts, he continues to produce highly conceptual, deceptively minimal work for commercial clients. He regularly challenges the design community with privately published projects under the name Virtual Telemetrix, Inc., addressing topical issues in design. He lives in Maine.

David Lance Goines, artist and writer, was born May 29, 1945 in Grants Pass, Oregon. In 1968 he founded Saint Hieronymus Press in the same Berkeley printshop where he had learned his trade. There he has remained, designing and printing his work, which includes many well-known posters, using both letterpress and photo-offset lithography. He is the author of five books and has collaborated on three, and his work has been the subject of four others.

Mark Fox, "a master at the specialized task of designing logos," has had his work recognized and published by, among others, *Affiche, Graphis*, and *Communication Arts*. His posters have been collected by the Library of Congress and the San Francisco Museum of Modern Art, which featured a one-man exhibition of his work in 1999. He currently teaches design at the California College of Arts and Crafts, and has served as president of the San Francisco chapter of the American Institute of Graphic Arts.

Larry Keeley is a strategic planner who has specialized in creating systems of innovation for over twenty years. President and cofounder of Doblin Group, an innovation strategy firm, Keeley has worked with a wide variety of companies, among them Apple, Hallmark, McDonald's, Motorola, and Xerox. He teaches graduate innovation strategy classes at the Institute of Design in Chicago, the only design school in the country with a Ph.D. program. He is presently completing a book on innovation leadership.

Michael Cronan has contributed to the collections of the Library of Congress, the Smithsonian Institute, the SFMoMA, and was featured in an exhibit at the Museo Fortuny in Venice, Italy. Founder of the Cronangroup and creative director of Cronan Artefact, his Walking Man line of apparel won International Design Magazine's Product Gold Award. He has served as product development director of the SFMoMA Museum Store and as president of the San Francisco chapter of the AIGA.

Peter Laundy, a graduate of Princeton University and the Yale School of Art, is a senior business strategist at the innovation strategy firm the Doblin Group and is a professor with the graduate Design Planning program at the Illinois Institute of Technology's Institute of Design. He has particular expertise in applying business strategy across multiple innovation categories, involving both research and practical application. Maintaining that "business strategy and brand strategy are two sides of the same coin," Laundy uses cutting-edge development techniques to create unique and distinctive business design.

Brad Holland, "an undisputed star of American Illustration," began writing and drawing professionally at the age of seventeen. One of the founding artists of the *New York Times* Op-Ed page, he has completed covers for the *New Yorker, Time, Newsweek*, and *Graphis*. His work has been the feature of museum exhibitions worldwide and is represented in the permanent collections of MoMA and the Library of Congress. He has been awarded 27 gold medals from various design societies, and was elected unanimously to the international design organization, Alliance Graphique International.

Index

BOOKS FROM ALLWORTH PRESS

AIGA Professional Practices in Graphic Design edited by Tad Crawford (paperback, 6 3/4 x 9 7/8, 320 pages, $24.95)

The Advertising Law Guide by Lee Wilson (paperback, 6 1/4 x 9 1/4, 272 pages, $19.95)

Emotional Branding by Marc Gobé (hardcover, 6 x 9, 352 pages, $24.95)

Design Literacy by Steven Heller and Karen Pomeroy (paperback, 6 3/4 x 9 7/8, 288 pages, $19.95)

Design Literacy (continued) by Steven Heller (paperback, 6 3/4 x 9 7/8, 288 pages, $19.95)

Design Culture edited by Steven Heller (paperback, 6 3/4 x 10, 320 pages, $19.95)

Education of a Graphic Designer edited by Steven Heller (paperback, 6 3/4 x 9 7/8, 288 pages, $18.95)

Texts on Type: Critical Writings on Typography edited by Steven Heller and Philip B. Meggs (paperback, 6 3/4 x 9 7/8, 288 pages, $19.95)

Graphic Design Timeline: A Century of Design Milestones by Steven Heller and Elinor Pettit (paperback, 6 3/4 x 9 7/8, 272 pages, $19.95)

Design Dialogues by Steven Heller and Elinor Pettit (paperback, 6 3/4 x 9 7/8, 272 pages, $18.95)

Looking Closer 3: Classic Writings on Graphic Design edited by Michael Bierut, Jessica Helfand, Steven Heller, and Rick Poynor (paperback, 6 3/4 x 9 7/8, 304 pages, $18.95)

Looking Closer 2: Critical Writings on Graphic Design edited by Michael Bierut, William Drenttel, Steven Heller, and DK Holland (paperback, 6 3/4 x 9 7/8, 288 pages, $18.95)

Looking Closer: Critical Writings on Graphic Design edited by Michael Bierut, William Drenttel, Steven Heller, and DK Holland (paperback, 6 3/4 x 10, 256 pages, $18.95)

Please write to request our free catalog. To order by credit card, call 1-800-491-2808 or send a check or money order to Allworth Press, 10 East 23rd Street, Suite 510, New York, NY 10010. Include $5 for shipping and handling for the first book ordered and $1 for each additional book. Ten dollars plus $1 for each additional book if ordering from Canada. New York State residents must add sales tax.

To see our complete catalog on the World Wide Web, or to order online, you can find us at *www.allworth.com*.